RECOMMENDATIONS

Par For The Soul is not simply a book about golf - it is a thoughtful reflection on the deeper lessons the game quietly teaches those willing to pay attention. It reflects on the deeper lessons golf teaches beyond the scorecard. It captures the mental discipline, resilience, and self-awareness required not to just play the game well, but to grow through all the struggles of trying to get better. This book is clear, insightful, and relatable even to a former professional golfer that has played for over fifty years. Golf has a mindset, character, and focus that enables continuous improvement both on and off the golf course. Therefore, I highly recommend *Par For The Soul* as a joyful addition to your golf reading and contemplation.

Most Sincerely,

Chip Beck

4-Time PGA Tour Champion and 3-Time Ryder Cup Participant

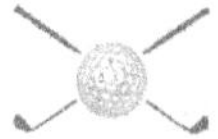

"I highly recommend *Par for the Soul* as an outstanding journey connecting golf and life in a meaningful, practical way. If you're open to learning life's most important lessons through the rhythm of practice, play, setbacks, and comebacks, I strongly recommend adding *Par for the Soul* to your reading list. It's a book you won't just read — you'll carry its lessons with you long after the final putt drops."

Jim Ott, *Three-Time NCAA DIII National Coach of the Year and Head Men's Golf Coach at Illinois Wesleyan University*

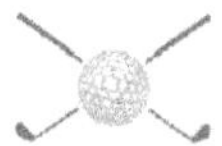

"I enjoyed reading *Par for the Soul* and found it insightful, thoughtful, introspective, and intrinsically motivating. The ties between the game of golf and life are indeed amazing and whether golfers or not, I believe readers will resonate with the messaging and enjoy the personal reflections Par provides."

Jackie Slaats, *member of the Athletic Hall of Fame, former Athletic Director and current Vice President for Career Advancement and Community Engagement at Lake Forest College.*

PAR
FOR THE
SOUL

Finding Meaning and Powerful Life Lessons
Through the Game of Golf

SCOTT DOTSON

Published by Thomas Augustine Publishing

ISBN (Paperback): 979-8-9956756-0-0

ISBN (EBook): 979-8-9956756-1-7

Library of Congress Control Number (LCCN): 2026909444

Copy Editor: Sarah Everest-Jindrich

Proof Editor: Matteo Pichietti

Cover design: GetCovers.com

Interior design: YD La Mar

This book is a work of original nonfiction. Some names and identifying details have been changed to protect privacy.

For permissions, inquiries, or additional resources, contact: scott.dotson@sbcglobal.net

Printed in the United States of America. First edition.

CONTENTS

Dedication

To my son Joel: Always know that you are deeply loved. This book is inspired by you and the joy we have shared on and off the course. May these words bring you a sense of all that I wish a father could lovingly share with his son.

For my "beta readers": thanks to each of you for your support and encouragement along the way. Your feedback was more than valuable – Mark Dotson, Steve Stufflebam, Ron Nahser, Consider Ross, Fr. Kevin Feeney, Norton O'Meara, John Favale, Matteo Picchetti, Doug Cassidy, Frank Arvia, Jack and Jeanne Burke, Cole Benson and Scott Weston.

For Steve and Deb Carr: this project would not be moving forward without you. Success leaves trails. Thanks for sharing your path and allowing me to follow in your footprints!

FOREWARD
by Ron Nahser

What has the soul got to do with golf?

Can golf, rather than just being a game of enjoyment, frustration, camaraderie, competition, and ups and downs, also be a living laboratory for character formation of moral virtue to build a better world? And, if so, how? And why is the message of *Par for the Soul* desperately needed today?

If you are like many of us, you share the instinctive feeling that there is more to Golf than the simple act of swinging the club. Yes, there is a physical, mechanical level of golf but Scott Dotson's "deceptively simple" appearing book tells a different golf story, following Arnie Palmer's quote which opens the Preface:

> "Golf is deceptively simple and endlessly complicated; it satisfies the soul and frustrates the intellect."

And that is a promise of this remarkable and unique book: to examine more closely the movement of Spirit in golf to satisfy the soul which then teaches the intellect. Scott covers a lot of ground as we meet him first in his Preface and Introduction, then through his imaginative 18-hole round – even with a 19th hole - and finally he gives a virtual poem in his final chapter on what it all means.

For starters, it isn't often you find a book where the references move first to Napoleon Hill's 1937 best seller *Think and Grow Rich,* and then move to David Foster Wallace's Kenyon Graduation Address, Buddha, the Bible, M. Scott Peck, and Tiger Woods and Aristotle. And that's just in the first chapter. (St. Augustine – half of Scott's late-in-life two Confirmation names - plays a key role later). You get the idea of the range of Scott's research, not to mention the extensive references to songs, movies, and books. These concepts of connection and relatedness are richly displayed throughout *Par*.

Whatever your work in the world, the questions, descriptions, and stories in this challenging book may give you insights into your work and path as well. And let's be clear, Scott's story is not addressing a new question of moral formation. It is part of moral history going back to Aristotle and St. Augustine, a star witness in *Par's* final chapter about meaning and the spiritual forces in golf.

How are they all connected? That is the thrilling story of this book which also tells the development of Scott's mind and soul, an evolution we all need to go through. Scott told me one day that he was writing a sort of memoir, loosely inspired by Harvey Penick's famous *Little Red Book.* He thought such a reflection on the merits of golf and lessons he has learned might be of interest to family and a few friends.

Over time, however, he realized, and many of us agree, that this is a much bigger story of golf, not just as a pastime, but as a deep reflection on moral education and a teacher of the practice of character formation that we all can learn from and is much needed today. I certainly have, and you may as well, as you read his life-defining book.

Scott tells us the real meaning of golf is to teach the fundamental importance of virtues and values which create our visions and world-views and then drive our behavior. That is a perfect summary of American Pragmatism which originated the blazingly simple Pragmatic Maxim: The meaning of a belief, concept, and virtue is known by the evidence. The biblical "By your fruits you know them." Or as Scott says, the ball flight is the evidence – the ball will tell you what you're doing if you listen.

In Scott's telling, we can even think of the golf course as sacred ground, a "sanctuary". There is substantial historical evidence for this bold claim. In fact, that's where golf officially began at St. Andrews course in Scotland.

The story begins in the 5th century when a Greek monk, St. Regulus was driven by a vision to carry the bones of St. Andrew, the first disciple of Yeshua (Gr. Jesus, John 1:40) to the far ends of land in the west. He landed on the shores of a peninsula in Fife (shipwrecked, the legend says) and established a Celtic ecclesiastical community dedicated to St. Andrew. The land became known as St. Andrews and over time came to be the center of religion with the largest church in Scotland. St. Andrew became the patron saint of Scotland, and his cross became the Scottish flag. And 1,000 years after St. Regulus arrived, Scotland's first university, University of St. Andrews was founded, and the world's first golf course followed 300 years later.

And the remarkable story of this sacred land is a part of the larger Scottish story, which gives further historical evidence for Scott's emphasis on values and the soul, and the course as a sanctuary. The connections between golf and spirit are undeniable.

THE SCOTTISH ENLIGHTENMENT: THE CREATION OF GOLF'S HISTORICAL CONTEXT

Yes, golf emerged on sacred ground when on the common-use fields of the burg of St. Andrews, a group of townspeople requested permission to dig holes and hit balls with rudimentary equipment. At the time, large portions of land—including the St Andrews links—were under the control of the Church and the Crown.

The pivotal event came in 1552, when Archbishop John Hamilton, the highest church authority in Scotland at the time, issued a charter that granted legal permission for the townspeople to play golf on the links, which functioned as an official ecclesiastical authorization. This act is the closest historical equivalent to a church "blessing" of the course.

For 200 years they "played the holes" (gowfe), talked, and improved the land until it was officially recognized as the Society of St. Andrews Golfers in 1754. These early Scottish golfers (noblemen, professors of philosophy from University of St. Andrews – a 10-minute walk from the course – and landholders) codified the rules and etiquette along the lines of "moral sentiments or purpose" and saw the links as a testing ground for the very virtues—patience, respect, and honesty—that Scott explores in this book.

Every town of any size in Scotland at that time had their societies of local leaders, like the nearby Edinburgh Society where figures such as David Hume and Adam Smith discussed and debated ideas "to promote the good of the country". They all had this focus because they were living at the time of the world-changing thinking driving the Scottish Enlightenment - founded on insight that the practice of these "moral purposes and sense/sentiments" is the key to happiness and flourishing. And this philosophy of the virtues had far-reaching consequences.

St. Andrews was not just intellectually and historically, but also geographically, connected with the movement. In 1755, 84 miles to the north of St. Andrews, in Aberdeen, the fellows of Marischal College were completely overhauling their curriculum to include in the 3rd semester the emerging sciences for the first time in education – anywhere - and reinstituted scholastic philosophy to include Natural Philosophy and the study of the movement of the Spirit (Pneumatology) in the fourth semester.

And in 1759, 72 miles to the southwest, Adam Smith, chair of Moral Philosophy at the University of Glasgow, was publishing his 1st edition of *The Theory of Moral Sentiments*. (He followed with An Inquiry into the *Nature and Causes of the Wealth of Nations* in 1776, a momentous year for us all.) Many of the faculty and graduates of the 5 Scottish Universities (at the time, England, with 4 times the population, had 2 universities) traveled to join the emerging American universities, teaching many of our Founding Fathers.

With this background, think of where Thomas Jefferson, Benjamin Franklin, and John Adams got the inspiration to write the immortal sentence: "We hold these truths... unalienable rights...Life, Liberty and the pursuit of Happiness". As they did in their day inventing democracy, we need to re-ignite "moral sentiments" to re-invent modern democracy. The moral lessons learned from the Scottish Enlightenment and its disciples, including those members of the Society of St. Andrews Golfers, might be the people to study. Later day students of the game, like Bobby Jones, did.

GOLF AT ST. ANDREWS FOR MORAL DEVELOPMENT: THE BOBBY JONES CASE

It is a famous "coming of age" moral development story of 19-year-old extremely talented Bobby Jones at the 1921 British Open. After a bad first two days and a worse first nine on the 3rd day, he teed off at 11th Par 3 "Short" into the notorious "Strath bunker". 4 shots later out of the bunker but still not on the green, Jones picked up his ball, tore up his scorecard and walked off the course, the ultimate sign of disrespect.

The Scottish press was ruthless. After reflection, humbled and remorseful, Jones came to see the course's irregularities and perceived imperfections as opportunities to listen for what the game can teach. Don't try to dominate the course, be patient, leading to his simple, but life-changing insight: "Golf is the closest game to the game we call life…you have to play the ball where it lies."

With this wisdom, in 1927 he returned to the course he once detested and won the Open by six shots while setting a new scoring record.

In 1930, Jones won again at St. Andrews, claiming victory in the British Amateur Championship. He would go on to win the Open Championship, the U. S. Open and the U. S. Amateur Championship as well in 1930, becoming the only golfer to ever win all four major championships in the same year.

Later in life, in 1958, ailing and barely able to stand, Jones returned to St. Andrews to receive their Freedom of the Burg of St Andrews award (he was the second American – Benjamin Franklin was the first in 1759) and gave his moving "Freedom of the City" address in Graduation Hall at the university. Jones was greeted with what the New York Times described as a "soul-stirring ovation."

After thanking the officials and townsfolks, he said: "I could take out everything from my life but my experiences here at St. Andrews and I would still have a rich, full life." In the next sentence, essential for our purposes of moral philosophy, he says: "The game of golf is not just a collection of strokes, but a test of character."

Jones's life tells the story of the development of his character, like the arc of his career, as he brought together his head and heart and fell in love with the game because of the lessons he learned at St. Andrews. Remember this story as you read about St. Augustine in Scott's inspirational final chapter on Finding Meaning in *Par for the Soul*.

This is why I think Scott's book, viewed as part of the long history of golf and the land it is played on, is so important and timely now. We see the need for moral education, reflection, decisions and action daily (pragmatic inquiry) to meet the challenges of war, income inequality, and degrading ecosystems. And golf is a unique, popular, and accessible way to practice moral reflection. Think if leaders in organizations of all kinds, especially those who purportedly "love" the game, read *Par for the Soul*, reflected, and then took its messages of values and vision and decided to put the lessons into action. Think of how the world would be better, just, and compassionate…"the pursuit of happiness."

Finally, the practice of golf, in Scott's engaging thought development story, aims to prepare us to see the course as a "sanctuary" – updating the long history of moral development - and listen to what the Spirit has to tell us: to seek not total self-reliance and dominance over or fight with the game, but be in relationship – friendship, trust, love – with the game, with others, nature, and Creation.

So, as the book's introduction concludes; "Class is in session. And the course is ready to teach." Read the book and get ready to listen, learn…and play.

Ron Nahser, PhD.
DePaul University, Chicago, IL
Director, Urban Sustainable Management Programs - Emeritus
Sr. Fellow, Institute for Nature and Culture

University of Redlands, San Anselmo, CA
Presidio Center for Sustainable Solutions
Provost – Emeritus

BTW, here is how my learning from Scott began.

After a career in advertising, I graduated at 55 with a PhD to become a late-in-life academic and practicing doctor of Moral Philosophy - American Pragmatism. I also am a late returner to golf, now a 35.2-handicap golfer.

Several years ago, Scott joined our Thursday foursome after one of our members retired. Scott volunteered to help Fr. Kevin Feeney - Dean of Formation - ret, Mundelein Seminary/University of Saint Mary of the Lake, and me to one day break 100. (Our 4th member and foursome Captain Sid Ross, a retired banker with a steady 19 handicap, doesn't need Scott's guidance.)

More important than golf instruction, Scott has helped me to see clearly and appreciate golf as a lab, a "classroom" as he calls the course in this book. We play, we practice, we struggle and we laugh. Fr. Kevin broke the 100-barrier last year. I am still working on getting there. I won't give up, and I know Scott won't give up on me either. Class is in session every Thursday and having immersed myself in *Par for the Soul* over the winter, I am inspired and eager to put its lessons to good use. My soul is good and my spirit is strong. I feel as though I have already broken 100! May you find yourself feeling inspired as well in your reading of *Par*.

PREFACE

I love the game of golf. I love to play it, practice it, watch it, read about it, talk about it, and think about it. I love the beauty of the course, the smell of fresh air, cool morning rounds, footprints in the dew, the warmth of the sun. I love the silence, the pace of walking and playing, the trees, the birds, and the lack of stress. I love the connection and joy of playing with friends, the laughter, the needling, the support, and the encouragement. I love the quiet competition with myself and with others, the challenge, the imagination, and the creativity. I love the feeling of a well-struck shot, the rare moment when the body and mind are in sync, and I love the opportunity for redemption after a horrible shot.

You see, golf has always been more than a pastime for me—it has been a teacher, a companion, a sanctuary, and at times, a mirror. The game has a way of revealing truths that are often hidden in the rush of everyday life. It slows us down, asks us to be present, and challenges us to confront not just the terrain before us, but the terrain within us.

Arnold Palmer, one of the best golfers of all time, and one of the finest human beings to ever live, once said, "Golf is deceptively simple and endlessly complicated; it satisfies the soul and frustrates the intellect. It is at the same time rewarding and maddening—and it is without a doubt the greatest game mankind has ever invented."

To me, Arnold was describing not only golf, but life itself. In fact, I believe "**<u>Life</u>** is deceptively simple and endlessly complicated; it satisfies the soul and frustrates the intellect. It is at the same time rewarding and maddening—and it is without a doubt the greatest thing God ever created."

As a "Seeker," my passion for golf was born from years spent walking fairways and pathways, not just in pursuit of lower scores, but in pursuit of life's deeper understanding. The lessons I've learned on the course have echoed through my experiences in leadership, business ownership, family life, fatherhood, friendship, and personal growth. This book is my attempt to capture those echoes and offer them to others who may find themselves searching for meaning in the midst of challenge, change, or quiet contemplation.

This book is not just about how to play better golf. It is about how golf can help us live better lives. Here sport, spirituality, and practicality intersect in reinforcing ways that have helped me to learn, grow, and continue searching for better ways to navigate life itself. Each chapter explores a principle—passion, trust, humility, courage—that shows up both in the game and in life.

These are not abstract ideas; they are lived experiences, shaped by moments of triumph and failure, clarity and confusion, solitude and connection. They are lessons learned in the dirt, on the grass, in relationships, in church, in books, in movies and in song lyrics—reinforced daily, one experience at a time.

I wrote this book for anyone who has ever stood over a ball and felt the weight of more than just the shot, for anyone who has ever looked in the mirror and wondered what their life is all about. This book is for those who have wrestled with doubt, celebrated small victories, chased improvement, and sought grace in the face of imperfection. Whether you are a golfer or not, I believe the metaphors and messages within these pages can speak to our universal human journey.

The structure of this book follows a rhythm, like the 18 holes of a golf course—beginning with the inner game, moving through values and actions, and ending with reflection and renewal. Like a round of golf, it invites you to start with intention, navigate challenges, and finish with perspective.

I am grateful for a lifetime full of mentors, friends, and family who have helped shape my thinking, encouraged me on the journey, and touched my heart one moment at a time. Your wisdom and encouragement are woven throughout these pages.

In his 2022 Grammy Awards acceptance speech for Album of the Year with *We Are,* Jon Batiste said, "I believe this to my core: There is no best musician, best artist, best dancer, best actor. The arts are subjective. The great thing about art, the great thing about music, is that it finds people when they need it most." That expresses deeply my belief about books as well. May *Par for the Soul* find you when you need it most.

I hope you will find your own stories reflected here, and may you be inspired to take dead aim at your truth, your growth, and your soul. It is my hope, my belief, and my prayer that you will find something of value in these pages, something that blesses you and carries your spirit to new heights.

Welcome to *Par for the Soul.* May it meet you where you are and walk with you toward where you're meant to be.

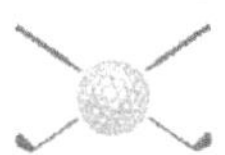

Author's Note: You will find "Swing Thoughts" sprinkled throughout the book. They are offered as an easy takeaway. I always find that I play best when I carry a single Swing Thought with me throughout the round. As an example, here is a Swing Thought for this Preface:

<u>Take Away:</u> Success leaves trails—do what successful people do and you will be successful too.

<u>Contact:</u> I like to share what works for me, hoping it will help others as well.

Follow Through: As you read *Par for the Soul*, I encourage you to follow a piece of helpful advice I found in the book *Tribe of Mentors*, written by Tim Ferriss: "Have a radically open mind, but make your own decisions!" Enjoy.

ACKNOWLEDGEMENTS

I have been blessed way more than I deserve in this life, and golf has been a big part of those blessings. I want to thank and acknowledge all the people who have given me their love, time, and presence on the course over the years, including:

Childhood: Thanks to my parents, Paul R. Dotson and Frances Ellen Stufflebam Dotson, for introducing me to the game and making sure I had opportunities to play.

High School: Thanks for playing and supporting my passion – Uncle Bob Stufflebam, Coach Gary Luallen, Rod Koppenhoefer, John Hauptman, John Hagen, Dave Sunderland, Joe Beatty, Kevin Schwulst, Tom Bley, Brad Grogg, Dave Wuethrich, Keith Komnick and Scott Munro.

Early Career: Thanks for making work and golf such a joy – Dave Stanicek, Ray Norvell, Rod Hoff, Jim Ritchie, Dave Schulthes, Keith Anderson, Rod & Laura Koppenhoefer, Glenn & Janice Reed, Wes Tanac and Ted Ferg.

Mid-Life: Thanks for all the great times – Joel Dotson, Paula Reed, Steve Virant, Sid Hodges, Eric Peacock, Jim Knight, Larry Yuhasz, Roger Gillie, Paul Gunderson, Brian Mayday, Tyler Driskell, Brian Hayes, Kevin Fountain, Tom Beverly, Tyler Hodges, Justin Luft, Josh Tropea, Chris Pope, Rob Love, Scott Sobbry, Pat Budd, Jay Jahnke, Skip Riley, Bill Giroux and Trevor Ballard.

Hot Springs Village: Thanks for the awesome times and

memories – Mark Dotson, Steve Stufflebam, Paul Dotson, Jody Meyer Dotson, Jack Harness, Regan Heitz, Matt Lacy, Steve Stolz, Jay Miller, Eddy Daves, Sid Hodges, Eric Peacock and Beck Hembree.

Class Reunions: Go orange, go black! Cindy Lankford Pennington, Dave Wuethrich, Greg Ring, Kevin Schwulst, Tom Bley, Dave Zerfas, Greg Janese, Dave Reynolds, Lowell Simmons, Scott Munro, Mike Yowell, John Knobloch and Blaine Brown.

Recent Years: Thanks for including me: Fr. Kevin Feeney, Ron Nahser, Consider Ross, Norton O'Meara, Phil Mozell, John Favale, Fr. Mike Nacius, Steve & Kathy Mahon, Logan Dejanovich, Ryan Peavey, Wade Gurych, Cole Benson and Scott Weston.

In addition to those from the golf course, I am blessed to have had the following significant people and groups comprise the river of my life (my apologies to anyone inadvertently omitted):

My sister Paula, Barbara Jane Dotson, Grandpa and Grandma Stufflebam, Aunt Mary Stufflebam, the Stufflebam cousins, the Hembree Family, the Hanlin Court crew, Joe McCauley, Steve Nash, Gary La Duke, Barney Guethle, Kevin Hadley, Jenny Streeter, Maggie Gosnell, Jim Aaberg, Dave Ananias, Bill Bryan, Mike Moritz, Stan Wing, Kevin Kelly, Arnold & Betty Herring, Gary Ewen, Terry Brown, Tim Hallem, the Hague Family, Neil Brown & family, Bill & Joanne Stevens, Erik & Gary Milliren, Kraig Komnick, Scott Meece, Harry Beemer, Fred Walk, Mary Ryder, Dan Kuglich, Mike Pence, Jim Weygandt, Rich Bugge, Becky Duke, Kathy Keck, Fred Gore, Loren Karge, Randy Birky, Ed Allen, Barb Gillis, Jeff Rich, Leo Kepner, Lori Miller, Dave & Bev Brenner, the Pub II softball team, Bud Lawyer, Keith Anderson, Denny Marquardt, Diane

Marquardt, Rod White, Ron Bays, Gordie Glover, Tom Meyers, Jack Schroeder, Neil Goodsell, Diane Lovekamp, Alan McKimmy, Jimmy Rigsby, Suzie Letterle, Vince Beggs, Kristy Tiegs, Pam Lund, Chris Grunska, the Investment Accounting crew, Sandy Goodman, Larry Walner, Jim Irving, Ron Hammond, the Auditing Dept. crew, Lori Beeson, The Satyrs softball team, Mark Langenfeld, Rich Irby, Jim & Susan Kessler and Family, Rob Baake, the Sperm Whales softball team, the Daves family, The Bruise Brothers softball team, Irene Alarcon, Pam Dady, Texas Accounting crew, Tim McCoy, Bernie Taflan, Ladene Sanderson, Sharon Parish, Tim Harden, Jan Miyahara, the Oregon Accounting Crew, Wings, Jerry Pocopanni, Payne Stewart, Huey Lewis, Mel Brown, Ron Pennington, Joyce Soebbing, Don Taylor, Michigan Accounting crew, Tim Cartwright & family, Harry Ahrens, Tom Early, Sharon Eisfelder, Pat Koschik, Clem Gill, Tom Duve, Chris Birk, George Pomey, Bill Dufek, Ron Hubbard, Ron Bodine, Joe Gill, Phil Gill, John Cosner & Family, Dale Wanty & Family, Cleon & Lorena Seaver, Terry & Joanne Smart, Frank & Pat Fulcher, Mike Williams and Family, Dale & Mary Karr and Family, Kurt & Molly Jeppesen, Marble United Methodist Church Family, Irma Ward, Milan Big Reds football, basketball and baseball teams 2012 – 2018, Dave Kaiser & Family, Adam Gilles, Randy Smith, Tommy Lindeman and Family, the Milan 2014 Boys Basketball State Championship Team, Mac Davis & Family, Nate Oats, Jim & Jennifer Harless, Connie Dotson & Family, Brenda O'Neill, Tammy & Tim Bolog, Trevor Bolog, Alan Hale, Don Harkness, Isabelle & Duane Schultz & Family, Millard & Marie Phillips, the Greater Milan Area Community Foundation, Lucy Ann Lance, all the policyholders who trusted me with their business, Stonebridge Golf Club Staff, Barton Hills CC staff and members, Mike Tirico, St. Joseph Parish – Libertyville, IL., Dave Retseck, Maria & Bob

Maglio, the RCIA crew, Sean Walker, Deacon Dan & Martha Welter, Bob & Char Shaw, St. Mary's Parish – Lake Forest, IL., Doug & Kathleen Cassidy, Bob Kaeding, Frank & Lenore Arvia, Dean and Marlene DeBritto, Jim & Deb Patyrak, Mark & Renee Kalbus, Roger & Roberta Sona, Tom & Sally Coyle, Steve & Deb Carr, Irene Potts, Pat Burns & Family, Gail Burns, Crystal Point Bld 5 crew, John & Faith Favale, Knollwood Country Club members and staff, Mark & Arianna Miller, Ken Leitch, John & Laura Coleman, the Budzius Family, Al Olson, Matteo Picchetti, the Printing Services crew, Coach Tam Tills, Makayla Campbell & Family, Jamie Springstead & Family, Lake Forest College Women's Basketball Team 2025, Jackie Slaats, Lake Forest College ITS Team, Library crew and OCM crew, Scott & Ellen McCollom, Brian and Barbara McCaskey, Sandeep Pilli & Sharmistha Singh, Fr. John Kartje, Dr. Charise Russo and Chip Beck.

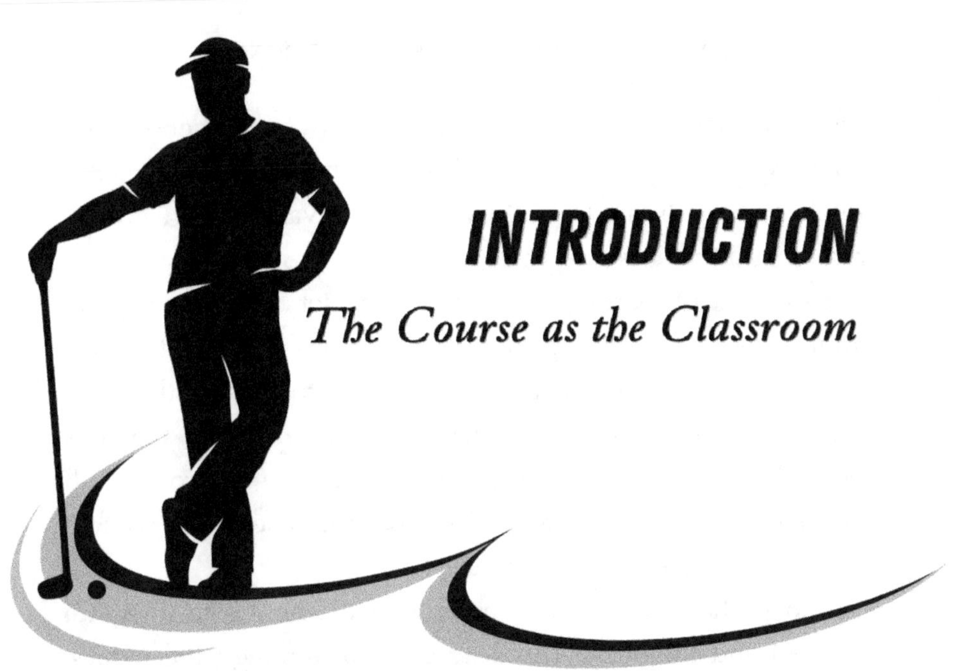

INTRODUCTION

The Course as the Classroom

Every round of golf begins the same way: you step onto the first tee with a plan, a hope, and a sense of possibility. But somewhere between the opening drive and the final putt, something else happens—something quieter, deeper, and far more important than the scorecard will ever show.

You learn.

The golf course, at its core, is a classroom. The fairways are the hallways. The greens are the tests. The hazards are the lessons you didn't expect but needed anyway. And every shot—good, bad, or bewildering—is a teacher.

But unlike the classrooms of our youth, this one has no graduation date. Golf invites us into the posture of a lifelong learner—someone who stays curious, open, humble, and willing to grow. The game rewards those who keep asking questions, keep experimenting, and keep showing up with a willingness to learn something new about the course, the swing, and themselves.

On the course, you are both the experimenter and the experiment. You test ideas, approaches, attitudes, and adjustments.

And at the same time, the game tests you—your patience, your resilience, your honesty, your ability to reset after a mistake. Golf becomes a living laboratory where the variables are always shifting and the data is always personal.

This kind of learning requires a mindset that goes beyond simple answers. Golf teaches us the power of "both/and" thinking in a world that often pushes us toward "either/or." You can be confident and nervous. Disciplined and creative. Focused and relaxed. Grateful and hungry to improve. Golf refuses to fit into tidy boxes, and so does life. The course teaches us to hold complexity with grace.

And perhaps most importantly, golf teaches us to integrate the head and the heart. The head gives us strategy, mechanics, and reason. The heart gives us courage, presence, and meaning. A great round requires both—just as a great life does. When the head becomes too loud, the swing tightens. When the heart becomes overwhelmed, the mind loses clarity. But when they work together, something beautiful happens: you play with wisdom, intention, and freedom.

Golf is also a place where science and art meet in perfect tension. The science is undeniable—angles, force, momentum, geometry, biomechanics, physics. But the art is just as essential—feel, rhythm, imagination, creativity, intuition. A swing can be measured in numbers, but it is expressed in motion. A shot can be calculated, but it must also be created. Golf teaches us that mastery lives at the intersection of precision and poetry.

In this way, the game becomes a bridge between the Humanities and moral philosophy. It asks the same questions philosophers have asked for centuries: Who am I becoming? How do I respond to adversity? What does integrity look like when no one is watching? How do I live with purpose, humility, and grace?

Golf becomes a canvas for character, a stage for virtue, and a mirror for the soul.

Golf's curriculum is vast. It teaches the mental lessons of focus, discipline, and emotional regulation. It teaches the physical lessons of balance, tempo, rhythm, and awareness. It teaches the philosophical lessons of paradox, acceptance, impermanence, and perspective. It teaches the spiritual lessons of presence, gratitude, humility, and surrender. It teaches the practical lessons of preparation, decision-making, and problem-solving. It teaches the moral lessons of honesty, integrity, respect, and responsibility. It teaches the inspirational lessons of resilience, imagination, and the joy of possibility. And it teaches the cultural lessons of connection, community, tradition, and shared experience.

And golf does something even more remarkable: it reveals the connective tissue between all of these disciplines. It shows us that the mental and the physical are inseparable, that the philosophical and the practical inform one another, that the spiritual and the moral shape how we show up, that inspiration and culture give meaning to our effort. Golf doesn't just teach these lessons in isolation—it weaves them together into a single, coherent way of being. If we are willing to learn, golf becomes a guide for living a better, fuller, more intentional life.

Most of us don't realize we're being taught. We think we're just playing a game. But the course has a way of revealing what we need to see: our habits, our reactions, our fears, our resilience, our capacity for patience, humility, courage, and trust. It teaches without lecturing. It instructs without judgment. It invites us to pay attention.

The beauty of this classroom is that the lessons are never abstract. They show up in the body, in the breath, in the moment you stand over the ball and feel the tug-of-war between confidence and doubt. They show up in the walk between shots, when you have time to reflect, reset, and choose who you want to be on the next swing. They show up in the relationships forged on the course—moments of encouragement, honesty, frustration, laughter, and grace.

This book is built on a simple belief: If we're willing to learn, golf will teach us everything we need to know about living a better and more meaningful life.

Not because the game is perfect, but because it mirrors the imperfect, beautiful, complicated nature of being human. The same principles that shape a round—focus, discipline, acceptance, imagination, resilience—shape our relationships, our work, our leadership, our faith, and our inner world.

In these pages, we'll walk the course together. Each chapter explores a principle that shows up both in the game and in life. You'll see how the course becomes a teacher, how the swing becomes a metaphor, and how the journey from the first tee to the eighteenth green becomes a map for navigating the terrain within.

This is not a book about playing better golf, though you may find your game improving. It's a book about learning—learning from the game, learning from and about yourself, and learning to live with more intention, clarity, grace and peace.

So take a breath. Step onto the tee. Class is in session. And the course is ready to teach.

LIFE LESSONS
FROM GOLF

1 HOLE #1: THE IMPORTANCE OF MINDSET

395-YARD PAR 4

This hole, called "Mindset," is a tough opening par 4 at 395 yards, the last half of which is significantly uphill. The kidney-shaped green slopes steeply from back left to front right, with protective traps located on both the left and right sides fronting the green.

THE FIRST TEE

Golf, like life, is won first in the mind. Before the swing, before the scorecard, there is the inner game. This chapter explores the mental dimension of success, drawing from philosophy, scripture, and the fairways of experience.

While standing on the first tee, I take a few moments to take in my surroundings and consider how lucky I am to be playing. I'm about to start a 4+ hour adventure with good friends, or if I'm really lucky, I'm playing with my son Joel, my brother Mark, my cousin Steve Stufflebam. I bask in the sunlight and admire the beauty of the tee box, the fairway, and the trees (which I'm likely to visit up close after my drive).

I close my eyes and listen to the wind rustling through the leaves; I might be fortunate enough to see and hear some songbirds. It is peaceful. Tranquil. And I remind myself to enjoy the moment and enjoy the day. I usually remind my playing partners, "Let's have fun today. Golf is meant to be fun. If we're not having fun, we're not doing it right."

I wasn't always this way. I'm now 66 years old, and this moment of connection with God's creation has been a few years in the making. In fact, I can tell you the very moment it began. On March 6, 1983, I found myself at Brokaw Hospital in Bloomington, Illinois, just after 7 a.m. I was in a room with my father, Paul R., my older sister, Paula (35), and my older brother, Mark (29). As the baby of the family, I was 23 years old on that day.

A doctor came into our room and said, "It's almost time." We followed him across the hall where my mother, Frances Ellen (Stufflebam) Dotson, was dying of ovarian cancer. We circled her bed, and the silence was broken only by her breathing—the "death rattle" of lungs filled by pneumonia. She was comatose, and cancer had changed her so much I could barely recognize her.

After a few minutes, the rattle stopped. She was gone. The rest of the family quietly retreated to the other room. I didn't follow. Mom's eyes were still open, so I closed them just like they do in the movies. I slowly walked over to the hospital room window and looked out to see the sun rising.

As I looked toward the sun, two very distinct thoughts popped into my head. First, there must be more to life than the shell of my mother left in that bed. And second, I could either be sad my mother was gone, or I could be happy to have had almost 24 years with her.

These comforting thoughts would launch a lifetime of seeking the meaning of life while fueling a fascination with the power of the mind. The strange thing was, for the first time in my life, I became acutely aware that I had the power to choose my thoughts. I had the power to control how I would react to events beyond my control.

I was almost 24 years old, a college graduate, two years into a career, engaged to be married, and I was just learning one of the most powerful lessons I would learn in my entire lifetime. Maybe I was incredibly naïve until then. Maybe most people learn this early in life. But I hadn't realized I had the power to choose my thoughts—that I could control my reactions to events, instead of events controlling me. I discovered I could think, choose, and respond and not just react to whatever happened.

No matter the situation, I have—we all have—agency!

I didn't master that lesson then. But I understood it. Or at least its potential. Truth is, I'm still integrating that lesson to this day. I can choose my thoughts and consciously choose my reactions.

How long have you known that lesson? How long have you been working on mastering your thought process? When did you realize you have such a great power—to be the master of your own ship? Do you control your mind, or does your mind control you? It is never too late to start!

THE POWER OF THOUGHT

Napoleon Hill once wrote, "Whatever the mind can conceive and believe, it can achieve." Hill was a great proponent of planning and visualizing. He understood that everything starts in the mind. You think it, you picture it, then you take the steps necessary to create it.

Napoleon Hill's book *Think and Grow Rich*, first published in 1937, is one of the most influential personal development and success books of all time. It's not just about financial wealth, it's about achieving success in any area of life through the power of thought, action, and persistence. It is about thinking, choosing, and then creating.

When you study golf and life, you realize everything starts in the mind. Whether you jump when you are startled, or when you calmly grab your golf club, or you pour your morning coffee, or you are talking or texting with a friend, it all starts in your mind. It starts with your thoughts. Your mind thinks it and then it communicates to your body how to execute every action.

The same is true for decisions. Whether you are deciding how hard to hit your putt, choosing to play a risky or a safe shot, when you are deciding what to eat for dinner or what to say to your frightened child, it all starts in your mind.

The point is: your thoughts are powerful. They are the forerunner of words, actions, and decisions. Everything you do, say, value, and believe flows from your thoughts. So, choose your thoughts wisely, because you can!

How do you do that? How do you choose your thoughts? Intentionally. Choose thoughts that serve you and the people you love. And delete thoughts that don't serve you and your loved ones. Step back from your thoughts. Let them flow before you as an observer and then choose the ones that serve you best.

Choosing your thoughts takes great effort and focus. It takes great commitment. Why? Because not all of your thoughts are good ones.

Studies show that each of us has between 60,000 and 80,000

thoughts per day. No wonder I'm so tired at the end of each day. Wow.

The key is to filter those 70,000 or so thoughts and use the best of them to your advantage. Think of it like a buffet dinner. Pick and choose what you like, what serves you, and ignore the rest.

You can find a wonderful presentation on this topic on YouTube (and in book form) in David Foster Wallace's famous 2005 commencement speech at Kenyon College, titled *This Is Water*. One of Wallace's main themes is that he was born with a pre-disposition, that he is "hard-wired," to see things as though he is the center of existence. This makes it easy for him to get annoyed, frustrated, and irritated with the boring tasks (and people) that come into everyday life.

The antidote for Wallace, and for all of us, is to consider and choose better ways to think. To find alternate perspectives and look at every event with conscious intentionality of thought. Listen to *This is Water*. Learn how to think. It is 20 minutes well spent.

So, how does this all play out in golf? How does this play out in life? Start by being aware of your thoughts. Be conscious of what is happening in your mind and what is going through your thoughts. Claim your power and take the wheel over unconscious and mindless action. Don't live in a zombie-like state. Don't be a slave to reaction.

Question your thoughts and use only those that answer the question: Does this thought serve me? Be intentional. Be conscious. Fuel yourself with positive thoughts. Understand that your thoughts are powerful. Embrace powerful thoughts that lead toward your target. This is how you take positive action and build good character.

In golf, this is evident in the way players visualize their shots before execution. The mental rehearsal becomes a blueprint for success. Golfers consciously choose the shot they want and need to play, factoring in yardage, wind, elevation, shot shape, and trajectory. Good golfers are intentional about how to play the shot and they commit to their process, including choosing thoughts to relax and trust their ability.

We are called to do the same thing and use the same process in what we do off the course as well. We cook meals and follow recipes. We plan trips and vacations. We play roles as spouses, parents, siblings, and friends. We spend lots of our lives working for a living. And we do all of these things having 70,000 or so thoughts a day that direct words, actions, and form decisions. Thoughts are powerful. Choose them wisely!

For the spiritual reader, consider this from scripture: "Do not conform to the pattern of this world, but be transformed by the renewing of your mind." – Romans 12:2

And consider the Zen: "The mind is everything. What you think, you become." – Buddha

While professional golf has an abundance of stories that exemplify "Winning in the Mind First" and "The Power of Thought," I believe there is none better than Tiger Woods's incredible victory in the 2008 U.S. Open, which is widely regarded as one of the most dramatic and courageous performances in golf history.

Woods played the entire tournament with a torn ACL in his left knee and two stress fractures in his left leg. He had undergone knee surgery two months earlier and was visibly in pain throughout the event. Despite this, Woods chose to compete, knowing it would likely be his last event of the season.

When his doctor advised him to skip the tournament due to the torn ACL and two stress fractures, Tiger replied: "You can do what you want with my leg at the end of June, Doc. But I'm playing the U.S. Open. I'm going to win."

Throughout the tournament, Tiger winced and limped and fought through pain with nearly every shot. His 12-foot birdie putt on the 72nd hole to force a playoff is one of the most iconic moments in golf history—followed by his signature fist-pump celebration.

The following day, Woods claimed the championship, his 14th major title, defeating Rocco Mediate in a 19-hole playoff. Woods underwent reconstructive knee surgery shortly after and missed the rest of the 2008 season.

PARADOXES AND BALANCE

Golf teaches us to live in paradox: confidence with humility, aggression with patience, hit down to make the ball go up, swing easy to hit it far. In his wonderful book *Golf and the Spirit*, M. Scott Peck talks about the paradox of "try but not try." I suspect every golfer has experienced the struggle of trying too hard. You grip the club tighter; swing harder and faster; tension fills your body, and the result is enough to make you want to explode.

Not trying is ineffective as well. In Tai Chi, the focus is to achieve the state of "push, no push." There is a balance point where the effort of trying is relaxed and just right.

Aristotle spoke on this topic in his discussion of virtue as the mean between extremes. The golfer must find the balance between deficiency and excess. Don't try enough (deficiency) and your play is poor. Try too hard (excess) and your play is poor. The sweet spot is in the middle, "try, not try." Balance is important, not only physically in the golf swing, but also mentally as you approach the game. Embrace the balance of "try but not try."

Aristotle detailed the virtue of courage as a balance between the deficiency of cowardice and the excess of recklessness. Consider areas where balance is important in your life.

We have all felt the tension between the demands of work and those of family, the challenge of healthy eating versus enjoying a few treats, and the need to balance caring for others and caring for ourselves. We know the peace and fulfillment that lie in the balance.

Aristotle emphasized the importance of this balance in discussing the concept of Eudaimonia (pronounced *you-day-moh-NEE-uh*), a central concept in ancient Greek philosophy. Eudaimonia is often translated as "happiness," "flourishing," or "living well," but its meaning goes much deeper than just feeling good.

Aristotle believed that true eudaimonia comes from living a life of virtue—developing good character traits like courage, wisdom, justice, and temperance. He noted that humans are rational beings, and eudaimonia involves using reason well—making thoughtful decisions, pursuing knowledge, and engaging in meaningful reflection.

He cited eudaimonia as a lifelong process. Eudaimonia is not a fleeting emotion or moment of pleasure. It's about the overall quality of a life—how well someone lives over time. Lastly, Aristotle noted the importance of self-realization. This is closely tied to the idea of fulfilling one's potential—becoming the best version of yourself.

Lao Tzu, the founder of Taoism and the author of *Tao Te Ching* (The Way and Its Power) speaks to the importance of balance in saying, "When you realize nothing is lacking, the whole world belongs to you." More recently, in the movie *The*

Karate Kid, Mr. Miyagi proclaimed, "Balance good, life good. Whole life must have balance."

CERTAINTY VS UNCERTAINTY

Golf is a game where you must embrace uncertainty. Wind, terrain, and nerves all play a role. Yet the champion embraces uncertainty with a calm mind. The tension between certainty and uncertainty is where growth happens, where opportunity unfolds, and perspectives are expanded.

Part of the joy in golf is found in the uncertainty. Before every shot, there is a bit of wonder—how will it turn out? There are seemingly countless variables that may affect the result. You plan your shot, choose your club, start the backswing and then the downswing, and you make contact and follow through. And the ball can go anywhere. You may even miss the ball altogether. Even the professionals will whiff, and the best of them will miss one of every four fairways from the tee and one of every four greens in regulation.

SUMMARY

Winning in the mind first means cultivating clarity, balance, and trust. It is the foundation upon which all success is built—on the course and in life. Like a muscle, your mind is trainable. Train your mind to be your servant. David Foster Wallace often referenced an old cliché in saying, "The mind is an excellent servant but a terrible master."

HOLE RESULT: 395-YARD PAR 4

A solid drive finds the left rough with overhanging trees blocking the second shot to the pin. A low draw 6 iron ends up 5 yards short left of the green. We use a 54-degree sand wedge to chip to 5 feet. "C'mon Scott, you've got this. You've made a hundred putts like this before." The uphill right to left 5-footer slides into the side of the cup. Par.

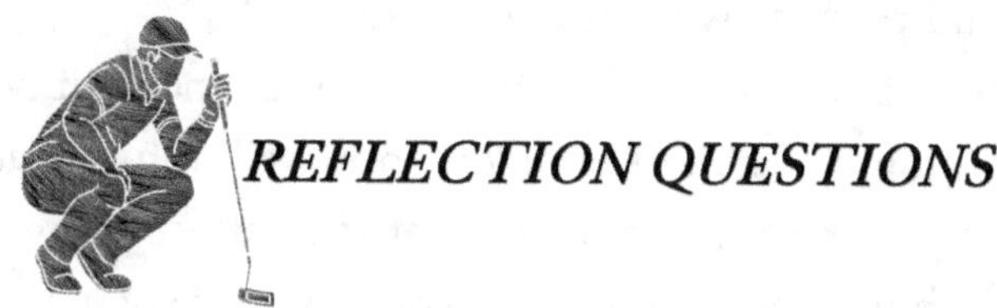

REFLECTION QUESTIONS

1. What thoughts dominate your mind before you face a challenge?
2. Do you control your thinking and actions, or do they control you?
3. How do you maintain balance in your daily life?
4. How do you deal with uncertainty and imperfection in your life?

BOOK RECOMMENDATION: *THE MENTAL GAME* BY DARRIN DONNELLY

In *The Mental Game*, Donnelly tells the story of a struggling athlete who meets a mysterious mentor and learns timeless lessons about mindset, confidence, and resilience. The book blends storytelling with practical wisdom, emphasizing how mental strength—not talent alone—determines success. It teaches readers how to overcome fear, silence self-doubt, and stay focused under pressure.

This chapter of Par for the Soul explores how golf—and life—is won first in the mind. Donnelly's book reinforces this idea by showing how belief, visualization, and emotional control shape outcomes. Both works highlight the importance of inner clarity, balance, and trust in the face of uncertainty.

MOVIE RECOMMENDATION: A BEAUTIFUL MIND (2001)

A Beautiful Mind portrays John Nash's triumph over schizophrenia by mastering his own thoughts. His journey shows that winning begins within by choosing clarity over illusion, discipline over chaos, and resilience over fear. True victory is mental: learning to live above the noise and trust reason.

SONG LYRIC TO CONSIDER:

"So often times it happens that we live our lives in chains, and we never even know we have the key." From the song *"Already Gone"* by The Eagles

2 HOLE #2: PASSION AND FOCUS

521-YARD PAR 5

The second hole, called Passion and Focus, is a challenging par 5 with trees left and both trees and out of bounds right. The downhill tee shot leaves an uphill second shot toward a narrowing fairway. The third shot must be played from the center of the fairway as the elongated green is protected by traps and overhanging trees on both sides. Par is a good score here as the hole gets more demanding the closer you get to the green.

Passion fuels purpose, while focus directs it. In golf, as in life, clarity of vision and intensity of heart are essential. This chapter explores the power of passion, awareness, the discipline to resist distractions, and the wisdom of "taking dead aim."

PASSION

Passion can be defined as a powerful and compelling emotion or feeling. Passion drives a person toward something they deeply care about. It can manifest in many forms—love, creativity, ambition, purpose, or even obsession. At its core, passion is the fuel that energizes action, often making challenges feel worthwhile and making goals meaningful.

When I say I love golf, that I love everything about it, I'm saying I'm passionate about the game. I'm passionate about playing, practicing, watching, reading about, talking about, and thinking about golf. I have a special excitement for and appreciation of all these aspects within the game.

Where do you literally see and hear the greatest passion in golf? Without question, it is at the Ryder Cup. I believe Ryder Cup matches are the most passionate—even the greatest event in all of sport. More so than the Super Bowl, the Stanley Cup, soccer's World Cup, or the Olympics. Each of those events is a blockbuster, but the Ryder Cup tops them all when it comes to passion from players and fans alike.

The Ryder Cup is a biennial men's golf competition between teams from Europe and the United States, with hosting duties alternating between venues in Europe and the United States every two years. This event offers 28 games of hole-by-hole match play over three days, pitting the 12 best men from Europe against the 12 best from the United States.

Every one of the 24 participants will tell you that these matches provide the most pressure they will feel in their entire professional careers. This team vs. team event is intense. I will admit, I'm a patriot, and I fully support the Americans. I'm all in for the USA. And, if possible, I will watch every shot of every hole of the matches, even when the Euros host the event and coverage starts at 5 a.m. Central time on each of the three days of play.

I'll dress in red, white, and blue. And I will rise and fall with every hole (all 504 of them) and every match (all 28 of them) won or lost. It is an emotional roller coaster, an intense experience of joy, of agony, of "the thrill of victory and the agony of defeat," as Curt Gowdy used to say on the *Wide World of Sports.*

Players and fans alike—roughly 50,000 in person and nearly 200 million with video views across roughly 50 countries—experience emotions at a level unique to golf and most sporting events.

Believing he let team USA down, Scottie Scheffler, the number one golfer in the world, cried openly during the 2023 Ryder Cup after suffering a historic and emotionally crushing defeat in the Saturday morning foursomes. The tears weren't about self-pity. They came from embarrassment, frustration, and a deep sense of responsibility.

To be sure, Scheffler was not the first, and he won't be the last, to shed tears after a devastating defeat. Ryder Cup history is also filled with tears of joy streaming down the faces of the victorious players too. Intense indeed.

That's the thing about passion—it involves a unique intensity that fuels action. Passion carries intense emotions.

It was passion that fueled Kent Broussard as he joined the Louisiana State University marching band in the fall of 2025 at the age of 66. Broussard first fell in love with the LSU Tiger Marching Band as a 9-year-old attending a football game in 1968. The sound, the energy, and the pageantry of the band left a lasting impression. He dreamed of one day being part of it, but life took him elsewhere. He became an accountant, raised a family, and built a successful career in government and the beverage industry.

As he approached retirement, Broussard asked himself what he truly wanted to do. The answer was clear: join the LSU band. To do that, he had to enroll at LSU as a student, relearn the tuba after 45 years, train physically, run 25 miles a week, and practice music daily. Then, he had to audition competitively, with no special treatment from the band director.

Broussard made the final band roster, making him the oldest member of the LSU Tiger Band by 41 years. His acceptance was met with cheers from fellow students, and his story quickly went viral. On September 6, 2025, Broussard marched onto the field in full uniform, tuba in hand, fulfilling a dream nearly six decades in the making. That is passion directing purpose. That is passion fueling action.

FOCUS

Focus is a close cousin of passion. In fact, passion and focus work together. While passion is the emotional drive for something, focus is the mental discipline and ability to concentrate your attention and effort on the desired result. Passion gives you the why and starts the fire, while focus provides the how and keeps the fire burning. Without passion, focus and effort can feel like a grind. Without focus, passion can fizzle out and scatter.

In golf, it is passion that makes you want to play and practice. It is passion that drives you to improve. However, focus is what dictates how you play and what you experience as you play. Focus dictates what and how you practice—doing the right things right. Focus dictates how you improve and what part of your game you choose to work on improving the most.

By now, you may be wondering, "How good a golfer is this guy, Scott Dotson?" Like all golfers, the answer depends on the day. I play to a 9 handicap from the senior tees, generally scoring between 78 and 84. I have discovered that there are lots of different ways to shoot 82. Decent for a 66-year-old who is now a once-a-week golfer who hits the ball both short and crooked. In my best days, age 50 – 55, my handicap hit a low of 6 from the middle tees. That was a direct result of what I call "The Lesson of Joe Durant."

In 2010, my son, Joel, was a senior playing on his high school golf team in Milan, MI. In early March, Joel's coach asked if I would like to be an assistant coach. More specifically, she asked if I would talk to the team at their kick-off meeting, with emphasis on the importance of the short game—chipping and putting.

I am into research and preparation when doing presentations. So, I turned to the PGA Tour player statistics for 2009 to get some insight and prepare to talk with the team. What I discovered was amazing.

In 2009, Joe Durant led the PGA Tour in the ball striking categories, hitting 74.3% of the fairways from the tee and 73.8% of the greens in regulation. Joe was the number one ball striker in the world. I took two lessons from this. First, even the best in the world miss the target one out of every four times. This tells me I should not get too upset when I miss the target. Bob Rotella said the same thing in his book *Golf Is Not a Game of Perfect*.

The second lesson was a dramatic revelation for me, and I have found it to be the same as I have shared it with golfers of all levels over the last 15 years. As the best ball striker in the world, where do you expect Joe Durant finished on the PGA Tour money list in 2009?

Top 30 (qualified for the Tour Championship)? Top 75 (qualified for most majors)? Top 125 (needed to keep full playing status on tour)? Top 150 (needed to keep conditional status as a player)? How about number 176—not good enough to keep his playing privileges on the PGA Tour. Astonishing, isn't it? I was blown away to learn this. The best ball striker in the world did not score well enough to keep his playing privileges. Wow!

Next, I turned to the 2009 PGA Tour statistics for "Scrambling"—combined chipping and putting. The scrambling leaders, in order, were Tiger Woods, Steve Stricker, and Phil Mickelson. They were the best at getting the ball in the hole from off the green.

I turned to the money list. The top three money earners, in order, in 2009 were Tiger Woods, Steve Stricker, and Phil Mickelson. That's right, the best ball striker in the world was number 176 in earnings while the top three players in chipping and putting were the top three players in money won that year.

This gives credence to the golfing adage "drive for show and putt for dough." Woods, Stricker, and Mickelson show us the importance of passion and focus—not only doing the right things right but doing the most important things right. They chip and putt well because they focus on it. They practice it most.

Another player who is a big proponent of the short game is Raymond Floyd. In Floyd's book, *60 Yards and In*, the four-time major winner details that he hits 60% of his shots from within 60 yards of the green during most rounds. And Floyd claimed, as the amateur player's score goes up, so does the percentage of shots hit within 60 yards of the green. My experience tells me he is right on with those numbers. I have two friends who regularly score over 100, and 75% of their shots come within 40 yards of the pin.

In 2010, armed with the knowledge from Raymond Floyd's book and the lesson of Joe Durant, I totally changed my approach to the game of golf, including my practice routine.

I used to go to the range once a week. I would bang a bucket of balls, mostly with the long clubs, and maybe hit a few putts before going home. That's what you'll see most people doing if they practice at all. My score improved 5 to 7 shots when I made a couple of changes. First, I took my bucket of range balls to the chipping green and hit through it twice. The first bucket would be used for running chips and the second for hitting lofted chips, including a few from the sand. This improved my chipping game considerably.

Then I would putt for 30 minutes, mostly from 5 feet and in. Why? Because the difference between 78 and 84 comes down to how many of the eight or so putts you make in a round from 5 feet and in. Think about it. How many putts in that range do you have in each round? And how many do you make?

I found that I made many more of those 5-footers when I practiced this way. I had confidence on the course, knowing I'd just made a bunch of short putts in practice. I would tell myself, "Nothing to it, Scott, you've made a hundred of these this week." As Anthony Robbins says, "Repetition is the mother of skill." And success breeds success. The last thing I would do with my bucket of balls was to go hit them on the range—mostly at short targets.

My favorite practice range had pins at 75, 95, and 115 yards. I hit 25% of the bucket to each one. My wedge game improved dramatically. I got to where I could hit those distances, seemingly in my sleep. The last 25% of the bucket went to middle irons, the driver, and the three wood. Practice this way, and you'll beat your friends who are focused on the driver at the range! "Chicks dig the long ball," but the scorecard loves the short game.

Scoring Swing Thought: Don't get hurt off the tee, hit decent irons, chip well, and putt like a bandit. Do this, and you will see great improvement in your scores.

AWARENESS – SEEING THE UNSEEN

Golf demands awareness—not just of the terrain, but of self. The best players see beyond the obvious. They read the wind, feel the slope, and sense the moment. Awareness is the gateway to focus and mastery.

Awareness can be defined as the ability to recognize and understand your surroundings, emotions, and the impact of your actions. In golf and life, awareness helps us adapt, improve, and connect.

Awareness helps golfers stay present, reducing distractions and improving performance. When I am fully present on the course, it's as though I'm connected to everything around me. I feel the elements, my mind is quiet, and I'm conscious of every step along the way. I see the fairway, the areas of danger, the unequal terrain on the tee. I see the flag on the green, and I plan the best route to get there from the tee ("Strategery" as George W. Bush would call it). I am conscious of my playing partners, their positions, and needs.

This awareness and heightened state of alertness boosts my play, it enhances relationships on the course, and it helps me avoid mistakes—particularly mental ones.

I don't look at my cell phone or answer calls. No email. No text messages. I don't think about work. I do not allow concerns about my family or finances or future plans or anything else to enter my mind. This is my sanctuary. I focus and stay present. I am fully present right here and in this moment. Being aware involves heightened senses, heightened concentration, and elim-inating distractions. The only things that belong on the course are the things that help you enjoy your game, your round, and your friends. The rest can wait. Their turn will come.

This same approach is helpful away from the course as well.

Distractions are everywhere on the course and in life. Discipline is the art of saying no to what doesn't matter. Awareness is the art of saying yes and being present with what does matter and is most important in the moment. It is giving full attention to the priority of the present.

Let's talk about cell phones. Your cell phone is a valuable tool. It is almost impossible to navigate life without one. But how do you approach this tool? Do you manage your electronics, or do they manage you? I see so many people that act like Pavlov's dogs around a cell phone. A ring, a buzz, or a ping and they drop everything to see what's going on. People interrupt important activities to check their phones constantly. Stop. Focus.

When I am having dinner with my wife, talking with my friends, or golfing with my son or my brother, there is nothing I will let interfere with our time. When I work, I work. When I am with family, I am with family. When I am playing with friends, I am playing with friends. The term BOUNDARY comes to mind. Be disciplined. Keep the main thing the main thing. Nothing else is more important than being present—being focused and aware—right where you are, with the people you are with, doing whatever you are doing.

I try to be aware of the unspoken messages of behavior. After all, behavior is a language. While you're texting someone else, you are telling the person you're with that they are a lower priority. Why do we do that? Be present where you are. Awareness is the key.

Inspirational Quote: You will never reach your destination if you stop and throw stones at every dog that barks. – Winston Churchill

Scripture: Let your eyes look straight ahead; fix your gaze directly before you. – Proverbs 4:25

Zen: When walking, walk. When eating, eat. – This quote reminds us to be fully present in whatever we're doing. Awareness is not about multitasking—it's about immersing ourselves in the moment.

TAKE DEAD AIM

One of the best golf books I have read is *Harvey Penick's Little Red Book*. It is a beloved classic in golf literature, offering timeless wisdom from one of the sport's most respected instructors. Unsurprisingly, Penick has a short game focus, and he advises to spend most practice time on chipping and putting to lower your scores. My favorite lesson, and one of Penick's most iconic and enduring pieces of advice from *The Little Red Book* is called "Take Dead Aim."

Penick taught that before every shot, a golfer should narrow their focus and commit fully to a small, specific target. Instead of vaguely aiming for the fairway or green, he encouraged players to pick a precise spot—like a tree branch or a patch of grass—and aim directly at it.

Penick explained that taking dead aim sharpens performance and focus. By visualizing a clear target, golfers reduce mental clutter and indecision. This allows you to block out the distractions of sand, water, and other dangers that create doubt. In addition, committing to a target helps build confidence and leads to more accurate shots. Taking dead aim also helps your mindset and process to control your physical execution. This is akin to the lesson from the movie, *Seven Days in Utopia*, which calls us to "See it, Feel it, and Trust It (SFT)."

Penick first shared this advice with Betsy Rawls, an eight-time major winner, and it became a guiding principle for many top players, including Ben Crenshaw. Today, "Take Dead Aim" is considered a mantra for golfers seeking simplicity, precision, and presence on the course.

Harvey Penick's advice to "Take Dead Aim" is more than a golf tip—it is a life philosophy. It means choosing your target with intention and committing fully. It means eliminating distractions and zeroing in on your desired result with focus and belief.

No matter where you are or what you are doing, the advice to "Take Dead Aim" can help you succeed. Take dead aim as you plan time with your family. Take dead aim as you plan your diet or your exercise program. Take dead aim with your personal and professional goals. Take dead aim in your relationships. Focus on the target. Eliminate the distractions. Take Dead Aim.

Inspirational Quote: The successful warrior is the average man, with laser-like focus. – Bruce Lee

Scripture: Set your mind on things above, not on earthly things. – Colossians 3:2

Zen: When you focus on problems, you get more problems. When you focus on possibilities, you have more opportunities. - Buddha

Golf Anecdote: Jordan Spieth often speaks of picking a precise target and trusting his swing to get there. Spieth often attributes his success to "picking small targets." Take dead aim.

SUMMARY

Passion gives us energy, while focus gives us direction. Awareness, discipline, and intentionality help us to take dead aim as we navigate both golf and life with purpose.

HOLE RESULT: 521-YARD PAR 5

Good drive down the left side of the fairway, avoiding the OB and trees right, followed by a solid three wood to 90 yards out. We take dead aim and hit a 54-degree wedge to 8 feet. Another putt breaking right to left goes in center cut. Birdie (with a smile and a slight fist pump). Score: 1 under after 2 holes.

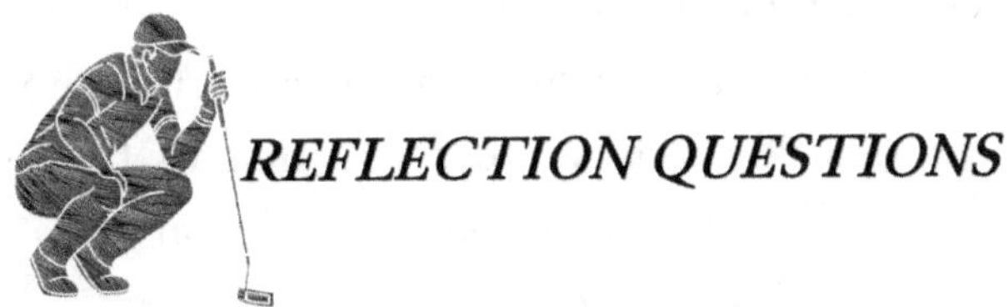

REFLECTION QUESTIONS

1. What ignites your passion, and how do you stay connected to it?
2. What do you focus on?
3. What distractions do you need to eliminate to stay focused?
4. Would people describe you as Aware and Present in the Moment? Are you a slave to your cell phone?
5. What does "Take Dead Aim" mean in your personal or professional life?

BOOK RECOMMENDATION: *WHY THE BEST ARE THE BEST* BY KEVIN EASTMAN

In *Why the Best Are the Best* by Kevin Eastman, the concepts of passion and focus are central to understanding what separates elite performers from the rest. Eastman defines passion as "The pull inside of me that comes from the love I have for something; the emotion that pushes me past the impossible." Passion is not just enthusiasm. It is a driving force that fuels persistence even in the face of failure.

While the book doesn't isolate "focus" as one of the 25 power words, it is deeply embedded in Eastman's philosophy. He stresses the importance of intentionality, which is about acting with purpose and keeping goals front of mind. This kind of focus is what enables champions to consistently execute the fundamentals, maintain discipline, and stay committed to their routines—even when motivation wanes.

Together, passion and focus form a powerful duo: passion provides the emotional fuel, and focus ensures that energy is directed toward meaningful, goal-oriented action.

SONG: "LOSE YOURSELF" BY EMINEM

Eminem's "Lose Yourself" is a powerful anthem that deeply explores the themes of passion and focus, making it one of the most motivational tracks in hip-hop history.

The song captures the emotional intensity of someone who is fully committed to their craft. Eminem's character, B-Rabbit, is portrayed as a struggling artist who channels his inner turmoil and ambition into his music. Lines like "You better lose yourself in the music, the moment," emphasize the need to be completely absorbed in one's passion and focus. The urgency and desperation in the lyrics reflect a burning desire to succeed, even when the odds are stacked against him.

YOUTUBE: JIMMY V ESPY SPEECH

With cancer riddling his body, Jim Valvano gives a speech which is passionate, inspiring and focused on the formation of the Jimmy V Foundation which has raised over $400 million in the fight against cancer since its inception in 1993. This is the best 11 minutes you will spend today—watch it!

MOVIE TO WATCH: *RUDY*

The movie *Rudy* is a classic story of passion and focus, centered around Daniel "Rudy" Ruettiger's relentless pursuit of his dream to play football for the University of Notre Dame.

Rudy's passion is the emotional engine of the film. Despite being told he's too small, not smart enough, and lacking athletic ability, Rudy's love for Notre Dame football never fades. His passion and focus drive him to overcome repeated rejection, physical hardship, and personal loss. It's not just about playing football—it's about proving to himself and others that heart and determination matter more than talent or privilege.

3 HOLE #3: CHOICE & INTENTIONALITY
345-YARD SPLIT FAIRWAY PAR 4 (WATER HOLE)

This hole, called "Choice," is a short hole that requires strategic play. Beginning 200 yards from the tee, the fairway splits right and left with a 20-yard-wide pond separating the fairways. You can choose to lay up short of the water and leave a second shot of 150 yards in, or you can play aggressively down either side to shorten your approach shot—but this brings water into play.

Life, like golf, is a series of choices. Each swing, each stance, each club selection reflects our intentions. This chapter explores the freedom to choose, the weight of consequences, and the power of living with purpose.

THE FREEDOM TO CHOOSE

Golf offers endless choices—club, shot shape, strategy. Life is no different. We are free to choose, but we are not free from the consequences of our choices. Every decision shapes our path and our character.

Standing on the tee, we are faced with choices and decisions to make. On this hole, a shortish par 4, we have fairway to the right and fairway to the left with a water hazard in the middle, starting 200 yards out. How do you choose to play the hole? An aggressive tee shot has a good chance to be rewarded with a birdie. But a wayward aggressive shot will likely lead to a double bogey. This is a risk-reward hole. Your choice. What do you choose?

Me? I would hit my 190-yard three wood from the tee to take the water out of play. Then, a solid six iron should give me a birdie putt. In golf, my choices are generally made to avoid the big number. If I can make 3 without risking 6, why take the chance? If I have a good chance at a birdie putt without risking a lost ball, why take the risk?

It becomes a value decision. My choice reflects my values. You may choose differently. And, if you do, I wish you the best, and I hope your choice works well for you. The good news is, we both have the freedom to choose. And in golf, as it is in life, you will experience the consequences of your choices. That is another one of the great things about golf. You make choices, you play, and you experience the consequences of your choices over 18 holes.

If you choose to be aggressive and hit good shots, you may well make birdie as a result of your choice. If you choose to be aggressive and hit a bad shot, you will likely make a big number as a result of your choice. You are free to choose. You are not free from the consequences of your choices.

The same freedom to choose exists in our lives off the course as well. We usually aren't free from the consequences of our choices off the course either. Golf holds us accountable for our choices. Sometimes, we don't hold people accountable, or they don't hold us accountable, for choices made in other facets of life. Golf is not an enabler. People often are. Golf teaches us to make better choices. Enablers do not. Are you an enabler? Do you know an enabler? Do you know anyone who has not been held accountable for their choices and behaviors? I do. And it usually results in a big number in the game of life.

An excellent book on the subject of choice is *Choices* by Shad Helmstetter. In this book, Helmstetter asserts that our brain, particularly our subconscious mind, is much like a computer. Our task is to understand that we have some bad programming installed in our minds from many sources and to delete the bad programming and replace it with better programming.

This takes effort. Making good choices takes awareness and conscious effort. And who is responsible for your thinking and your choices? You. You are responsible and accountable to use your freedom to choose. Think about it. How many choices do you make in a day? Some are small. Some have big implications. Did you know that, according to Psychology Today, the average American makes approximately 35,000 decisions per day?

You make choices about what to eat, what to wear, what to do. You make choices about your education, your effort, your relationships. You choose what goals to pursue, where and how you work, and how to save and spend your money. You make choices about your health, your exercise, and how to pursue your hobbies. You choose your attitude, how to deal with problems, and how to respond to failure. You choose how to treat your family, your friends, and your co-workers.

You make choices around your ego, how to spend your time, and how productive you will be any particular day. You choose whether or not to engage passers-by, what to believe about others, and your level of generosity. You choose the way you talk to others, and you choose the way you talk to yourself. You choose whether to seek change and learn new information and new skills. You choose whether or not to expand your comfort zone.

Right now, you are choosing whether or not to consider the words on this page. At least, you should be making that choice. Consider Helmstetter's words, "It is your programming that has created your choices in the past. It is the choices you make starting today that will create your future programs."

Helmstetter also says, "No one can make your choices for you. Your choices are yours alone. They are as much a part of you as every breath you will take every moment of your life."

You have free will to choose. In fact, you have the responsibility to choose. What you don't have is the freedom to escape the consequences of your choices. Claim your power to choose. Fill your mind with thoughts that serve you. Listen to podcasts. Read books that fuel your thinking and your character growth. Take in information and programming that makes you better. And choose to consciously use those resources with every choice you make.

Inspirational Quote: As Maya Angelou said, "Be the best you can be. And, when you can be better, then choose to be better."

Scripture: If you choose you can keep the commandments, they will save you;

if you trust in God, you too shall live; he has set before you fire and water - to whichever you choose, stretch forth your hand. - Sirac 15: 15 - 16

Zen: The way is not in the sky. The way is in the heart. – Buddha

Golf Anecdote: Phil Mickelson's bold choices on the course often led to spectacular wins—and instructive losses.

INTENTIONAL LIVING

In golf, intentionality means committing to each shot with clarity and purpose. Kevin Eastman's book, *Why the Best are the Best,* reminds us that awareness and intentionality are keys to a meaningful and successful life.

What do you value and want more of in your life? And what do you want no part of in your life? Have you thought about your values recently? In October of 2018, I completed one of the best mental exercises I have ever given time to. I was reading Eastman's book, *Why the Best are the Best*. In his book, Eastman encourages his readers to take a sheet of paper and list what they value. I filled the left column of the page with things like Family, Love, Freedom, Golf, Time, Efficiency, Relationships, and more. I encourage you to do this right now. Take a moment to consciously record what you value.

On the other side of the sheet, Eastman encouraged readers to embrace the "Power of No." What if there was no … Family, Love, Freedom, etc.? I listed things I did not want in my life. No Distractions, Hate, Waste, Mindlessness, etc. I encourage you to do this as well, right now. I found this to be a very powerful experience. Embrace the "Power of No" and eliminate the unwanted.

When you know what you value, and what you do not want in your life, this gives you a powerful roadmap for living intentionally. This tells you what to choose to do. This tells you what to choose to pursue with your time, talents, and resources. BTW, this is not a static document. I review my values list at least once a week, and I amend and add to the list as life unfolds, changing my perspectives and values as I learn and grow. Knowing your values is a very grounding place from which to live. Knowing your values makes it easier to be true to yourself and to live intentionally. Knowing your values makes it easier to make choices that serve you and lead you where you want to go—and it helps keep you from making choices that do not serve you well.

One of the biggest dangers and drains in life is "drift." One day we know ourselves, our desires, and our direction, and a few years later we wake up in a strange life in a strange place, and we don't even know how we got there. When we are not intentional, we are often then unintentional, or, even worse, numb. We find ourselves drifting, and our path meanders in ways we are not even aware of. Knowing your values and living intentionally will help keep you from getting lost.

Have you ever sat down with a fresh bag of chips to watch a show? It is easy to get lost in the trance of entertainment and suddenly most of your chips are gone. The bag is nearly empty. You have eaten almost a whole bag of chips without even realizing it. Surely, I'm not the only person who has done that. That is living unintentionally.

It is so easy to get lost in television, streaming, social media, work, and other distractions. It is easy to live "numb from the neck up." We have so many ways to escape our daily lives and get lost in distractions and activities that eat our time and energy but add little to no value to our being. We disconnect in lots of ways—from our family, from our friends, from ourselves. And, when we do this, we drift. We lose connection with ourselves and the people around us. And we slowly get lost without ever realizing we are gone.

If you want to live intentionally, a good question to carry with you is: "Why am I doing this and is this serving me?" That is essentially the thought behind dieting. Be aware and make intentional choices. Choose what serves you. Anything else, let it go.

If you want to live intentionally, I encourage you to consider another excellent resource – Harry Kraemer's book, *Your 168 – Finding Purpose and Satisfaction in a Values-Based Life*.

In his book, Kraemer points out that we all—every one of us—have the same 168 hours in a week to use as we choose. Kraemer encourages us to use these 168 hours wisely, and he encourages us to use our time, effort, and attention in a manner that is true to what we value most. His book is about living and choosing to live intentionally according to your values. You have 168 hours coming this week, how will you choose to live them?

How do you use your 168? Pay attention to your week. How much time do you spend on the various things that fill your calendar? Does your use of time reflect your values? To live in alignment with your values, what do you need to choose to do differently with your 168?

Inspirational Quote: The privilege of a lifetime is to become who you truly are. – Carl Jung

Scripture: Be very careful, then, how you live—not as unwise but as wise, making the most of every opportunity. – Ephesians 5:15-16

Zen: When you walk, just walk. When you sit, just sit. But whatever you do, don't wobble. – Yunmen

Golf Anecdote: Rory McIlroy speaks often about playing with intention, knowing his game plan and sticking to it. Make a plan, then work your plan.

CONSEQUENCES AND GROWTH

Every choice carries a consequence. In golf, a risky shot may lead to glory—or disaster. In life, our decisions shape our character, one act of will at a time. Growth comes from owning our choices and learning from them.

One of the great things about golf is that you get instant feedback and instant results from your choices and execution. Only one person plans the shot, chooses the club, and makes the swing—you, the golfer. There is no one to blame for the result but you. There is also no one else to credit for the good results. Golf is built on accountability. Your results in golf are a clear reflection of your execution and your choices.

Let's be real about choices. They are not all easy, and they are not all inconsequential. Whether I eat cereal, eggs, or yogurt for breakfast is not a major choice. Which route I choose to drive to work is unimportant in the long run. What shirt I pull from the closet is no big deal. These kinds of choices are relatively simple. They require minimal brain power, and the consequences are really unimportant. I won't remember any of those decisions a year from now, or likely even a week from now.

Some choices are very challenging and have extremely important consequences. Choosing whether or not to stay in a turbulent relationship is a hard choice. Deciding what to do with your teenager who won't listen and won't behave involves critical choices with lifelong consequences. Dealing with a loved one battling addiction is incredibly challenging. Deciding how to move forward after a cancer diagnosis calls for extremely difficult choices. And deciding whether or not to look for a new job presents you with several hard decisions around what to do and when to make the change.

The truth is that making hard choices is hard. But not making necessary choices is a poor decision. You see, claiming your ability and your responsibility to make choices is one of the most powerful things you can do. Making hard choices is a powerful step in dealing with uncertainty. Choosing provides clarity and certainty in the face of uncertain times.

Claiming your power to choose allows you a bit of control in a seemingly uncontrollable situation. And having a solid grip on your values is a great asset that will help you immensely when facing hard choices. Making choices is powerful. Claim your power.

I was fortunate to grow up with a father who encouraged decisiveness and action. He not only allowed me, but he encouraged me to make my own choices from an early age. Paul R. would tell me, "Choose something son—even if you are wrong, you'll learn something." I don't recall my father ever second guessing my choices, even when they were made by a very naïve young man. And he always supported me when my choices ended badly. He would ask, "What can you learn from this, son?" I did a lot of learning the hard way.

My dad would also tell me, "Son, good judgment comes from experience, and experience usually comes from bad judgment." The best way to learn to make good choices is by making choices. And no one bats one thousand with their choices.

Paul R. also understood that life is always in motion, and very few decisions and choices are permanent. If a choice caused problems, I could always make a choice to fix what went awry. That is true with most choices we make. The consequences of our choices are rarely fixed in stone. There are a few choices you cannot undue, but those are few and far between. Embrace your power to choose, and when necessary, choose again.

In golf, we can have "Mulligans" and do-overs. We also can

have do-overs in other aspects of our lives. Sometimes we must apologize, repair some damage, and put forth a genuinely sincere effort in order to do so. But with learning and ownership of our choices, we can grow and become better. That is life.

When we choose to say things that are hurtful, we can own that choice and apologize and repair the damage. Bad choices provide the opportunity to change and do better. Repairing builds trust—trust in ourselves and trust with those we hurt.

One of the greatest choices we can make is to embrace life-long learning and growth. Choose to learn and grow continuously. Choose improvement. Every event and every person we meet offers lessons if we look for them. Choose to expand your knowledge and your skills. Why? Because you don't know what you don't know. Plus, you don't know what you are capable of. Dedicate your life to learning, growing, and improving. It is a choice you will never regret!

Another powerful choice is the decision to constantly build strength of character. No matter what happens to you, you can find ways to grow stronger. Unfortunately, character is often built through struggles and bad choices. Perhaps that is the origin of the saying, "Whatever doesn't kill you makes you stronger." Build mental muscle with every struggle. Build character with every bad choice. Choose to constantly build your character.

It is also important to realize you don't have to fail in order to build character. You can build character from success, and you can choose to learn from others in building your character as well. Remember, success leaves footprints for you to follow.

Here is an interesting point. If you make the choice to learn, grow, and build your character, you can do those things regardless of results. I can tell you from experience, though, that life is much easier and better when you focus on making good choices.

The key is to make the powerful choice to use every experience to learn and grow no matter what. Improving our character never stops—we are all a continual work in process.

Inspirational Quote: We are our choices. – Jean-Paul Sartre

Scripture: Whether you turn to the right or to the left, your ears will hear a voice behind you, saying, "This is the way; walk in it." – Isaiah 30:21

Zen: No snowflake ever falls in the wrong place. – Zen Proverb

Golf Anecdote: Payne Stewart's choice to lay up from the rough on the 18th hole of the 1999 U.S. Open at Pinehurst No. 2 was a pivotal moment in one of golf's most dramatic finishes. When his drive landed in the thick and wet rough, Stewart, needing a par to win, chose to lay-up short of the green with his second shot on the Par 4. Stewart hit his third shot from 78 yards out, leaving it 15 feet below the pin. In a tense and electric setting, Stewart drained the par putt, securing the championship by one stroke over Phil Mickelson.

SUMMARY

Choice is a powerful gift and responsibility. Intentionality transforms routine into ritual. By choosing wisely and living purposefully, we build character and shape a life of meaning both on and off the course.

HOLE RESULT: 345-YARD SPLIT FAIRWAY PAR 4 (WATER HOLE)

Good drive with a solid three wood laying up short of the water. Then a solid six iron to the right front of the green. The uphill left to right breaking putt from 33 feet is hit to two feet short left. Tap in for a no stress par. Score: 1 under after 3 holes.

1. How fully have you embraced your power to make choices in all circumstances?
2. What values do you rely on when making important choices?
3. How can you live more intentionally in your 168?
4. What key lessons have you learned from the consequences of past decisions?
5. How dedicated are you to learning and personal growth?

BOOK RECOMMENDATION: *CHOICES* BY SHAD HELMSTETTER

Choices by Shad Helmstetter is a book that explores how the choices and decisions we make shape our lives, and how we can take control of those decisions to create lasting, positive change.

Helmstetter emphasizes that every aspect of our lives—relationships, careers, health, happiness—is influenced by the choices we make. He identifies 100 of the most important life choices and shows how managing these can lead to a more fulfilling life.

SONG: "THINK" BY ARETHA FRANKLIN

Aretha Franklin's "Think" is a powerful anthem that directly addresses the power of choice, especially in the context of personal freedom, relationships, and societal expectations.

TED TALK: "THE ART OF CHOOSING" BY SHEENA IYENGAR

Iyengar affirms that choice is central to human identity. Choice allows people to express preferences, assert autonomy, and shape their lives. She describes choice as a tool of empowerment, especially in cultures that value individualism. As Iyengar states, "We all make choices, and in doing so, we define ourselves." This TED talk is well worth the 19 minute run time.

MOVIE TO WATCH: *GROUNDHOG DAY*

The movie Groundhog Day (1993), starring Bill Murray as Phil Connors, powerfully illustrates the transformative power of making choices—especially when those choices are made with intention, growth, and compassion.

The repetitive time loop acts as a metaphor for life's routines. Phil is forced to confront the consequences of his choices—again and again—until he chooses to live with intention and integrity. The film suggests that true freedom comes not from escaping repetition, but from choosing how to live within it.

QUOTE FROM TIM FERRIS IN HIS FIVE BULLET FRIDAY EMAIL ON OCTOBER 10, 2025:

"Montaigne, the great French philosopher, adopted these seventeen words as the motto of his life: "A man is not hurt so much by what happens, as by his opinion of what happens." And our opinion of what happens is entirely up to us."

— <u>How to Stop Worrying and Start Living</u> by <u>Dale Carnegie</u>

4 HOLE# 4: LOVE AND COMPASSION
DOWNHILL 158-YARD PAR 3

This hole is a stunningly beautiful par 3. The tee is elevated 60 feet above the circular green below, which is protected by sand traps on the left and right. This hole is also carved between rising hills on both sides. In addition, ahead on the horizon is an awe-inspiring tree covered mountain range—the purple mountain's majesty. It is beautiful enough to describe it as breathtaking. This hole is pictured on the front cover of *Par for the Soul*.

Golf may seem like a solitary sport, but its deepest lessons are about connection. Love and compassion are the forces that bind us, both on the course and in life. This chapter explores the power of creation, the importance of focusing outward, and the transformative nature of willing the good of the other.

You may recall that I professed my love for golf in the preface:

I love the game of golf. I love to play it, practice it, watch it, read about it, talk about it, and think about it. I love the beauty of the course, the smell of fresh air, cool morning rounds, footprints in the dew, the warmth of the sun. I love the silence, the pace of walking and playing, the trees, the birds, and the lack of stress. I love the connection and joy of playing with friends, the laughter, the needling, the support, and the encouragement. I love the quiet competition with myself and with others, the challenge, the imagination, the creativity. I love the feeling of a well-struck shot, the rare moment when the body and mind are in sync, and I love the opportunity for redemption after a horrible shot. I love it.

As I stand on this tee, the past is connected to this moment. You see, this is an actual hole I have played many times before. This is the 17th hole, the signature hole, at the Cortez Golf Course in Hot Springs Village, Arkansas. I am fortunate enough to have played this hole over 100 times between 1985 and today, most recently in May of 2025.

I still remember my first breathtaking view on this tee. It was in September of 1985. My father had just retired from a career at State Farm Insurance. He re-married almost a year after my mother's death, and he and "Wicked Stepmother Jody" had a home on the edge of the course. BTW, you know Jody was a real blessing to our family, particularly for my diabetic father, when we could call her "Wicked Stepmother Jody" to her face and we could all laugh at that, including her.

I was fortunate enough to stand on that same tee with my father over 25 times before he died in May of 2000. Visiting Dad became an annual event in 1985, and starting in 1995, we enjoyed that view twice a year over the last five years of his life. Two others joined us there, my brother Mark and my cousin Steve Stufflebam.

Every time we played that hole, I experienced wonder, awe, and a profound feeling of loving and being loved. And occasionally, I hit a good tee shot and had a chance to birdie that amazing hole. Par was a good score. I love that hole so much. I made my brother promise to sprinkle some of my ashes on the green after I die—I always want to see and hit that green one more time.

The trips to see Dad and Jody, including Brother Mark and Cousin Steve, were always so very special. We would enjoy 4 days of what The *Rhythm of Life* author Matthew Kelly calls, "Carefree timelessness." We had fun, laughter, good food, and drinks. We shared stories and the kind of support and encouragement that lets you know you're loved, even when that word isn't mentioned. Dad wasn't the type to verbalize love. "Feel the Love" was the mantra for those four days of golf and revelry.

Why 4 days, you wonder? Dad would jokingly (and somewhat seriously) say, "After 4 days, fish and company begin to smell—even with family." So, we would squeeze a year's worth of fun into those 4 days and then head back to our homes scattered across the U.S.

Those trips were so special that we continued to visit HSV in May and September every year even after Dad died, until we got old enough to have health issues that would occasionally put a pause in our travel plans. Mark or Steve would invite a friend to be our fourth player, and we would play a friendly competition of nine matches over 4 ½ days. For those who like math, yes, that is 162 holes in five days. That's a lot of golf. It is exhausting but wonderful!

We would play partners with matches consisting of a handicap best ball in the morning, followed by a best position (scramble) match after lunch. Essentially, we would wake up, shower, eat breakfast, play 18 holes, eat lunch, play 18 holes, and then cook dinner and have drinks in the evening. This was a golf boot camp, with great friends, great food, and a few drinks mixed in. The fun started at 6:30 a.m. and lasted well into the night, and then we would start all over again the next day. This was always full-contact fun.

In all, we have played 32 little "grudge" matches over the years. Every one of them has been a treasure. They have been hotly contested, enjoyed to the max, and generally very close matches. I have been a partner with and a competitor against almost everyone who has played in our events. I have been a winner and a loser, just like everyone who has ever played. My record? I had to look this up—my record is 15 wins, 13 losses, and 4 ties. Everyone who has played (11 different players in all) is roughly even on wins and losses.

Of course, it is not the wins and losses, or the great shots, or the clutch putts, or the scores that are most remembered. The cherished memories are the people, the laughs, and the times just being together. There are moments that are timeless and vivid, and some things so funny they still make me laugh out loud years later. We call them "HSV Moments."

For example, Brother Mark earned the name "Fitty Stix" when he accidentally drove his cart over a 150-yard pole in the middle of the fairway. Mark had hit a poor drive and was behind the other three of us. I was his partner, and I took the club I was going to hit next and walked ahead of Mark about 25 yards or so to my ball.

Cousin Steve and his partner, Steve Stolz, were in their cart well ahead of Mark and me. We all watched Mark hit his second shot, and then I stood over my ball and was preparing to play my shot to the green.

Suddenly, we heard a "kaboom!" We all looked back, and Mark was in his cart with the front wheels off the ground, and the 150 pole (made of PVC) was pointing at the green at a 45-degree angle. Mark backed the cart off the pole, saying, "Don't mind me." He stood the pole back up as best he could and tried to rub the DNA evidence off the front of the cart. We all doubled over in laughter as he pulled up in the cart and said, "I was just so anxious to catch up to you guys that I didn't see the post. It was only 3 feet high." We laughed for 3 more holes, and I still laugh about that today almost every time I play and see a 150 post in the fairway.

Another example is what we call "The HSV Scavenger Hunt." Dad liked to make "fufu" Manhattans—a third of whiskey, a third of sweet vermouth, a third of Seven Up, plus a splash of bitters, a cherry, and some cherry juice. For some reason, we always had trouble getting our thirds right with the supplies. One night, we were out of vermouth way too early in the evening. The liquor store was a long way from Dad's house, but his good friends Jack and Dot Harness lived right across the street. They were wonderful, kind old people, and we figured there was a good chance they had vermouth.

So, Mark, Cousin Steve, and I formed a plan—a scavenger hunt. We headed over to Jack and Dot's and knocked on the door. When Jack came to the door, we explained that we were on a scavenger hunt. "What do you need?" he asked. We said we were looking for a Wisconsin license plate, an aluminum base-ball bat, a tampon, or a fifth of sweet vermouth. Jack exclaimed, "I have the vermouth," and he quickly scurried to his liquor cabinet and eagerly handed us the bottle. "Thanks, Jack," we said in unison, and we held our giggles until we got out the front door. Our supply problem was solved.

Nowadays, in honor of Dad, we start every trip with a "fufu" Manhattan toast before we head to the course for the first match. And we always think of Jack and Dot when adding the third of sweet vermouth.

What does all this have to do with love? I think it is love. These trips and these stories represent love. It is the way we remember, we honor, and we cherish not only the past but the present as well. It is being together. Playing together. Making time for this trip together. It is years of time spent together because we care for each other deeply. Yes, we play golf, but it goes beyond that. Golf is just the activity in the center. It is all the laughter, support, encouragement, and the stories that matter. It is the appreciation of each other and all the people who have been a part of this tradition.

It is Paul R., and Brother Mark, and Cousin Steve, and Regan Heitz, and Matt Lacey, and Steve Stolz, and Jay Miller, and Eddy Daves, and Sid Hodges, and Eric Peacock. It is Jack and Dot Harness, and all the other people who have been part of these experiences. Some have died. Some are struggling with health issues. Some have been through divorces, and remarriages, and financial challenges, and house fires, and tornadoes. And we have loved each other, beaten each other, teased each other, and supported and encouraged each other for years.

We have rooted for each other, whether partner or opponent, every step along the way. And this "love" extends well beyond the courses and the annual trips. It never stops. And that is why I love golf. I love these people.

How does this apply to life off the course? It is a model for how to live every day. Make time for and give "carefree time-lessness" to those around you. Have fun amidst the transac-tional life of doing what must be done. Enjoy whoever you are with. Don't get caught up in wins and losses. Eat well. Have a "fufu" drink with your spouse, your neighbor, and your co-workers. Support and encourage each other. Win graciously and accept defeat gracefully. Root for each other. Cherish and appre-ciate the time you have together. Laugh often. Go on a scavenger hunt. Remember the best times, and most importantly, remember the people who made them special.

Be there for your family and friends. Care for those going through tough times. Toast the special memories and special people. Keep a journal of the great moments. Give and receive love. There is nothing better than loving and being loved.

Inspirational Quote: The best thing to hold onto in life is each other. – Audrey Hepburn

Scripture: So I commend the enjoyment of life, because there is nothing better for a person under the sun than to eat and drink and be glad – Ecclesiastes 8:15

Zen: Zen? That's nothing more than full attention with no agenda. — Maxime Lagacé

Golf anecdote: At Ace Golf Club, a group of weekend golfers gathered for their usual Saturday round. The game was far from perfect—slices into the rough, missed putts, and balls vanishing into water hazards. But what stood out wasn't the score; it was the laughter.

After the round, they didn't rush off. They lingered, sharing stories, sipping drinks, and reflecting on life. One golfer raised a toast: "Here's to the bad shots that made us laugh, the good ones that made us cheer, and the friends who made it all worthwhile."

CREATION AND OUTWARD FOCUS

True greatness is not found in self-centered ambition but in creating value for others. In golf, this is seen in sportsmanship, mentorship, and camaraderie. Focusing outward allows us to transcend ego and embrace community.

My regular Thursday foursome consists of me, Ron Nahser (age 87), Sid Ross (age 83), and Father Kevin Feeney (age 73). Each of us is old enough to have our own health issues that make the game a challenge. My golf ministry with these men is to help Ron and Fr. Kevin break the 100 barrier. I must admit that their perseverance is impressive.

Ron, in particular, is the focus of my efforts to help. Bless his heart, Ron has just had a hip replacement, and his eyesight is failing. But his spirit and enthusiasm for golf is inspiring. I joke that I am his "Jiminy Cricket."

Ron hits a lot of good shots, but he rarely sees them. He also hits a few nasty shots in each round, and the sand is his kryptonite. But Ron keeps plugging and plays with rare enthusiasm. I really love Ron, and I love golfing with him.

My role in our Thursday rounds is twofold; I play my own ball, and I try to shepherd Ron and Father Kevin on the path to 99. Truth is, I play my ball, and then I caddie for Ron. I help Ron find his ball, choose his clubs, rake his sand traps, and read his putts. I also try to share what I can about strategy and mental aspects of the game. Ron is like my Zen golfing grandfather. And it is a gift to play with Ron every Thursday. No one shoots 115 with more joy and a better attitude than Ron. At the end of every round, Ron makes a point of enthusiastically thanking me for helping him learn and play that day.

The truth is, I am the one who should be thanking Ron. It is a blessing to shepherd him around the course and work with him on the range. We talk and we play and we struggle and we celebrate successes together. Helping Ron with his game helps me stay grounded in my own game. Helping Ron with his thinking and mental approach helps me with my thinking and mental approach. It is a case where the teacher gets more out of the experience than the student.

The lesson here is that the best way to stay out of your head and avoid the fight with your own inner demons on the course is to "out-focus." It is so easy to get frustrated and start fighting the swing and the mental game. Tension and negative thoughts can take hold of you and ruin your round and enjoyment of the game if you're not careful. The antidote for that is to "out-focus," and to search for wonder and awe.

"Out-focusing" is the method and process of taking in the environment outside of and around you. This takes you out of your own head, out of your own thoughts and inner dialogue, and it allows you to focus elsewhere.

Rather than question your swing mechanics and get upset with your score, take in the beautiful creation before you—the beauty of the grass, the trees, the flowers, the Blue Heron in the pond, the hawk overhead. Rather than fight your inner demons, focus on your playing partners and their successes. Don't go inward and get discouraged. Rather, focus outward and experience the wonder in front of you.

An excellent book on this subject is Dacher Keltner's, *Awe – the New Science of Everyday Wonder and How it can Transform Your Life*. Keltner teaches us that "awe allows us to get outside of ourselves, and it integrates us into larger patterns—of community, of nature, of ideas and cultural forms." Further, Keltner calls us to see "how awe arises in encounters with the wonders of life and leads to a vanishing of the self, to wonder, and to saintly tendencies."

Golf calls us to experience awe as we play—awe in the nature of creation and the natural beauty we play in, awe in the creativity of shot making, awe in the rare, perfectly struck drive, or the flushed iron, or the perfect chip, and awe in the great putt as it falls in the cup.

Getting out of your head and seeking wonder and awe is a great practice off the course as well. If you find yourself in your head, your mind racing, thoughts going 100 miles per hour, try out- focusing.

Go to a park, walk in the woods, sit by a pond or a lake, and just take in the beauty and peace of creation. Or sit and people watch on a bench, watch a child play with a bug, take in a concert, or just spend time doing things with and for your family and friends. Make time to talk to people you love. Talk about their interests, their successes, their struggles. Be there for someone. See them. Love them.

There is no better way to feel connected, loved, and at peace than to experience awe and wonder as you lovingly serve someone else. That is how I try to live as a husband, father, brother, friend, and as a stranger—I try to live as a loving servant, and I am in constant awe and wonder with the world and the people around me.

Inspirational Quote: Life's most persistent and urgent question is, what are you doing for others? – Martin Luther King Jr.

Scripture: Love your neighbor as yourself. – Mark 12:31

Zen: When you love, love as if the person is a flower. Water it, give it sunlight, and never try to possess it. Let it grow in its own way. – Thich Nhat Hanh

Golf Anecdote: Arnold Palmer was known not just for his skill, but for his compassion, kindness, and generosity toward fans and fellow players.

WILLING THE GOOD OF THE OTHER

One of life's most interesting questions is "What is love?" That is a complex question with many answers.

Greater Good Magazine says, "Love is at the heart of the human story. It connects us to each other, drives us to nurture and protect, and gives richness and meaning to our lives. Though love can feel like a mystery—a force beyond science—research reveals its deep roots in our biology and its core role in our survival as a species."

While romantic love often steals the spotlight, it's just one piece of the puzzle. Love comes in many forms. What unites them is that all types of love involve:

- A deep, unselfish commitment to nurture another person's well-being—even to put their interests before your own.
- Emotional, cognitive, and behavioral dimensions— they involve our feelings toward others (in a fleeting moment or over long periods of time), our perceptions of them (we really see them), and actions we take to support them or express our care for them.

In that light, love doesn't just give us warm feelings and inspire affection and devotion. It also helps us bridge divides, cooperate, and promote collective well-being. Love is key to leading a flourishing, meaningful life, and it comes in many varieties, including self-love, romantic love, familial love, companionate love, compassionate love, loving across differences, love of strangers and humanity, and love of animals, nature, and the sacred.

Evolutionary scientists see the origins of love as an integral part of our adaptive success as a species. As Anna Machin writes in, *Why We Love*, "Love stems from cooperation, and cooperation is our route to survival." Love didn't just appear as a romantic ideal; it evolved as a powerful motivator, driving early humans to form lasting social bonds, protect one another, and create communities that ensured survival. Those capable of love forged the connections necessary to thrive, pass on their genes, and shape the future of our species.

This perspective suggests that love is not simply a feeling, it's a core biological drive that fundamentally shaped who we are today."

The Catholic in me believes we were made from and by love —created by God who is love. We were made to be in relationships and to live in service and in support of others. We are not the center of the universe. We are called to lovingly share the universe.

Love is not a feeling. Love is a choice to seek and act for the good of another. There is nothing better in this world than loving and being loved. We are made for love, hard-wired for love and connection. To give and receive love is a noble calling, both on and off the golf course. And sharing life with and serving others is at the heart of why we exist.

Inspirational Quote: Compassion is not a relationship between the healer and the wounded. It's a relationship between equals. – Pema Chödrön

Scripture: For God so loved the world that he gave his one and only Son, that whoever believes in him shall not perish but have eternal life. – John 3:16

Another scripture: Love the Lord your God with all your heart and with all your soul and with all your mind. This is the first and greatest commandment. And the second is like it: Love your neighbor as yourself. - Matthew 22:37–39

Zen: When you realize that everything is interconnected, you gain compassion.

Golf Anecdote: During the Ryder Cup, players often support teammates and opponents alike, showing compassion, respect and empathy.

WIN-WIN THINKING

In golf and life, the highest victories are those that uplift everyone. Win-win thinking fosters collaboration, mutual respect, and shared joy. It's not about beating others; it's about bringing out the best in yourself and in each other.

Inspirational Quote: A rising tide lifts all boats. – John F. Kennedy

Scripture: Carry each other's burdens, and in this way you will fulfill the law of Christ. – Galatians 6:2

Zen: The flower does not compete with the flower next to it. It just blooms.

Golf Anecdote: In team formats, like the Presidents Cup, players often sacrifice personal glory for the good of the team.

SUMMARY

Love and compassion are the heart of a meaningful life. By focusing outward, willing the good of others, and embracing win-win thinking, we create fulfillment and a legacy of connection and kindness.

HOLE RESULT: DOWNHILL 158-YARD PAR 3

A solid seven iron finds the left-center of the green. The downhill left-to-right breaking putt from 18 feet rolls just past the cup, leaving an easy tap in par. Score: 1 under after 4 holes.

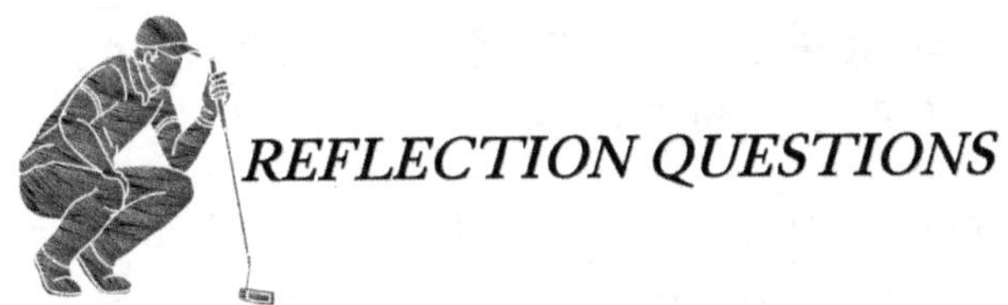 *REFLECTION QUESTIONS*

1. How do you practice love and compassion in competitive environments?
2. How do you "out-focus" to get out of your own head?
3. Where do you experience awe and wonder?
4. What does "willing the good of the other" look like in your relationships?
5. How do you cultivate win-win thinking in your personal and professional life?

BOOK RECOMMENDATION: THE BIBLE

Love is one of the most profound and recurring themes throughout the Bible. Love is portrayed not just as an emotion, but as a divine principle and a way of life. The Bible presents the recurring theme of God's gift of love and grace to man, mankind's sin and betrayal of that love, and God's powerful act of loving forgiveness.

SONG: "THE POWER OF LOVE" BY HUEY LEWIS AND THE NEWS

Released in 1985 and famously featured in *Back to the Future,* Huey Lewis & the News' "Power of Love" is more than just a catchy rock anthem—it's a tribute to the life-changing, uplifting, and universal nature of love—one that can heal, inspire, and connect us all.

ANOTHER SONG: "I JUST CALLED TO SAY I LOVE YOU" BY STEVIE WONDER

Stevie Wonder's "I Just Called to Say I Love You" is a heartfelt expression of love and compassion conveyed through simplicity and sincerity, showing that love can be spontaneous, genuine, and every day—not tied to holidays or dramatic moments.

The song celebrates the idea that emotional connection matters more than material gifts or elaborate declarations, reflecting empathy and care—a desire to make someone feel valued and remembered. And, the song's gentle tone and lyrics convey a sense of emotional warmth, reinforcing the importance of being present for others in quiet, meaningful ways.

MOVIE TO WATCH: *FINDING FORRESTER* (2000)

Finding Forrester (2000), directed by Gus Van Sant, is a poignant fictional drama that explores the unlikely bond between Jamal Wallace, a gifted African American teenager from the Bronx, and William Forrester, a reclusive Pulitzer Prize-winning author.

Finding Forrester reminds us that love and compassion aren't always romantic—they're found in mentorship, friendship, and the courage to believe in someone else's potential. It's a story of how two very different people change each other's lives through empathy, trust, and the power of connection.

ADDITIONAL MOVIES FOR CONSIDERATION

If you want a romantic show, you can always watch *The Notebook*, *Titanic*, or my wife's favorite *The Painted Veil*. Also, you will not find a movie that depicts love more clearly than *The Passion of Christ*.

5 HOLE #5: GRATITUDE
357-YARD PAR 4

This is a simple, straightforward hole called "Gratitude," a short par 4 protected by sand traps short left and right. The green is large and flat, with the tee slightly elevated. You can see all the trouble and the accessible green is in plain view. This hole gives you a bit of a breather and a chance to record a good score. It is a "peaceful, easy feeling" on the tee.

Gratitude is the quiet force that transforms how we experience life. In golf, it brings joy to the game regardless of the score. In life, it shifts our focus from what is missing to what is present. This chapter explores the contrast between being and doing, experiencing and thinking, and how gratitude deepens both.

Gratitude can be beneficial to the soul. According to Webster's Dictionary, gratitude is the state of being grateful. Gratitude is deep thankfulness. I am always deeply thankful to be on the golf course. I always have a deep appreciation for the game, for grass and the breeze, for my playing partners, and the challenges and opportunities that unfold from shot to shot over 18 holes.

I never take for granted the fact that I get to play golf. I never take for granted that I get to walk the course, smell the grass, and swing the club. I never take for granted that I get to play with the people I am playing with. I never take for granted that my sore back and pinched nerve at L5/S1 may lead me to give up this great game someday.

Not to be morbid, but I know we are all just a heartbeat away from not being able to play, from not being able to gather on the course. Things happen. All it takes is one fall, one accident, one health issue that results in a lifestyle change, and the ability to gather and play is erased forever. Life is constantly in motion. And I am conscious of the gift of friendship and the gift of the ability to play and practice golf. To me, that is gratitude—to be conscious of the gift, to be thankful for the gift, to be aware of the transitory nature of the gift.

I carry this same feeling of gratitude with me off the course as well. Whether I am at home, with friends, at work in my part-time job at Lake Forest College, buying groceries, walking through town for exercise, or in a forest preserve photographing birds, I experience a state of gratitude.

I am grateful for family, for friends, for food and drink. I am grateful for oceans, lakes, and ponds that I visit. I am grateful for Sandhill Cranes, Egrets, Bald Eagles, and Great Blue Herons. I am grateful for books, music, and movies. I am grateful for the St. Louis Cardinals, the Kansas City Chiefs, and the Michigan Wolverines. I am richly blessed. I have been given so many wonderful gifts to enjoy. I try to honor the gifts.

Gratitude is a simple thing. It is a mindset. Gratitude is a choice, a passion, a focus, an act of love. Gratitude is a practice. And gratitude is a gift in and of itself. Give yourself the gift of gratitude. Live thankfully. Did you make the time to complete your values list on Hole 3–Choice? Now is a good time to write down what you are grateful for. Make journaling a habit. Take time with every meal to give thought to a few things you are grateful for. With time, you will train yourself to be grateful in the moment, as events unfold and as people join you in those moments.

Modern life often glorifies doing—achieving, producing, performing. But golf teaches us the value of simply being. Standing on the tee box, breathing in the morning air, and feeling the club in your hands-these are moments of presence. Gratitude begins when we slow down enough to notice. Doing is important, but being is more important. Be grateful in and for all things.

Inspirational Quote: We are human beings, not human doings. – Deepak Chopra

Scripture: In everything give thanks: for this is the will of God in Christ Jesus concerning you. – 1 Thessalonians 5:18 (KJV)

Zen: If you realize you have enough, you are truly rich. – Lao Tzu

THE PRACTICE OF GRATITUDE

Gratitude is not a passive feeling; it's an active practice. In golf, it means appreciating the game, the course, the company. In life, it means noticing beauty, expressing thanks, and living with contentment.

I mentioned in hole 1 that my experience on the first tee of every round is to take in the moment and the surroundings and to commit to enjoying the round with my playing partners. I must admit that I don't do this every morning when I wake up and start my day. But I am going to start that practice right now.

How do you think your life would be affected if you woke up every morning and took a few seconds to take in the moment and the opportunity ahead of you? It may seem to be an odd practice, but how would your daily experience change if you woke up and spent time beginning in gratitude?

Immerse yourself in gratitude for life, for breath, for the person you wake up with. Be thankful for running water, for toothpaste, and for coffee. Feel the comfort of your home, your clothes, and what you eat for breakfast.

Consider just how fortunate you are. Not everyone has what you have. Consider and be thankful for the opportunity you have ahead of you each day. No matter what you will be doing, there is opportunity—for learning, for growth, for enjoyment.

You see, gratitude is a practice. Gratitude is a choice. Gratitude is a mindset. It is easy for us to lose sight of this. Life can be hard. Times can be difficult. The gap between the life we want and the life we are living can be immense.

If we practice gratitude in all things, we will learn to look for and see positives and things to be thankful for even in our hardest times. As Madonna once said, "The worst things that happen to you are often the best things that happen to you, because they force you to grow."

Gratitude is a practice that has superpower. The grateful mindset trumps all of our negative thoughts and mind traps—fear, anger, sorrow, and all the things that can lead us down the rabbit hole to negative experiences.

The best golfers in the world (Rory McIlroy, Scottie Sheffler, etc.) use gratitude to overcome the pressure and nerves of performing in the biggest moments. How? They acknowledge the negative thoughts and emotions, and then they focus on how great it is that they have the opportunity to win and play the biggest shots in the biggest events.

Consider the Japanese kanji symbol for crisis:

危機

This is a really interesting combination of two symbols, with the left symbol representing danger, and the right symbol representing opportunity.

Gratitude embraces the opportunity. Yes, we must recognize when there is danger. We are hard wired to detect danger and heed its warnings. But we also are wired to choose gratitude and embrace opportunity. Practice gratitude. Embrace opportunity. Be thankful in all things, including the challenges that make you a better person.

Consider one more thing: the concept of Every. Kevin Eastman wrote about this in his book, *Why the Best are the Best*. Eastman writes that "Every moment of every day matters, and every day matters on the last day. Adding up the impact of each 'insignificant' event reveals a huge impact on the end result." Eastman's writings are a call to use every moment and to be conscious of the compounding effect of small actions.

For me, Eastman's concept of Every is also a call to be conscious of the fact that every person, every opportunity, every ability I have, and every experience that touches my life is a gift. And I try to be conscious of the importance of honoring all of the gifts in my life. This is at the heart of the practice of Gratitude.

Think about it. Think about all that you have. People who love you—family and friends. Good food, good drinks, and a good place to call home. Consider your abilities, freedom of choice, the game of golf, and the ability to read, learn, and grow intellectually and spiritually.

The opportunity to enjoy music, movies, and other forms of entertainment. The sweet taste of a brownie, the smell of bacon frying, the sound of children playing. We have so much to be grateful for.

Practice Gratitude. Embrace opportunity. Embrace the concept of Every. Be thankful in all things—the good and those times when you experience awe, and the hard times that build character and show you where you need to build mental muscle and grow.

Inspirational Quote: Gratitude is not only the greatest of virtues, but the parent of all the others. – Cicero

Scripture: Enter his gates with thanksgiving and his courts with praise; give thanks to him and praise his name. – Psalm 100:4

Zen: A thankful heart is a continual feast.

Golf Anecdote: Paul Azinger wins the 2000 Sony Open.

When 11-time champion Paul Azinger stood on the tee at the 2000 Sony Open, he wasn't just trying to win a tournament. He was carrying the ache of losing his friend Payne Stewart and his agents Robert Fraley and Van Arden in a tragic plane crash only months earlier—a grief that still sat in his chest like a stone.

Azinger hadn't won in 7 years, winning last in 1993. He had already fought his way back from cancer, already rebuilt his swing, already learned how fragile and precious the walk can be. But the death of his close friends changed the air around him. It made every shot feel like a conversation with someone who wasn't there.

And yet, that Sunday, he didn't try to be fearless. Azinger simply played with the kind of presence you find only after life has broken you open. Shot by shot, breath by breath, he honored the moment, the friendship, and the game they all loved. In a victory that moved the spirit, Azinger movingly claimed the last championship of his career.

Azinger's 2000 Sony Open win is one of the clearest modern

golf examples of living with gratitude, not as a sentiment but as a way of being. His own words make that unmistakable.

Azinger openly said that for four of the six years after his cancer diagnosis, he "saw no hope" and believed he might never win again. When he finally did win, he didn't talk about validation or proving people wrong. He talked about appreciation—for life, for the chance to compete, for the people he'd lost, and for the people who stood by him.

He said the events of the previous year "changed the way I perceive life" and made him "appreciate it more". This is gratitude not as positivity, but as clarity: the kind that comes when you've brushed up against the edge of life and returned with new eyes.

After the win, he immediately spoke about the families of Payne Stewart, Robert Fraley, and Van Ardan—the friends and business partners he had recently lost. He said the victory would be "their first happy moment in a long time".

That's gratitude as offering: a win not held tightly for himself but given away as a moment of light for others. He admitted he no longer saw life through "rose-colored glasses," yet he was "still pretty happy."

That's mature gratitude—not denial, not forced optimism, but a grounded appreciation that coexists with grief, fear, and uncertainty. It's where you realize you can't go back to who you were before the loss—but you can keep going with a deeper kind of courage and appreciation. The kind that doesn't roar. The kind that remembers and honors the people we love. The kind of resilient performance that comes out of the blue, driven by quiet determination. The kind that moves witnesses to tears of joy.

SUMMARY

Gratitude invites us to live fully in the present. It bridges the gap between being and doing, thinking and experiencing. On the course and in life, it transforms the ordinary into the sacred. And gratitude sets the course for how we process our experience in all things.

HOLE RESULT: 357-YARD PAR 4

A pull-hook drive ends up in the trees left. There is a small gap for a low hooking 6 iron to get near the green, but clipping a limb leaves the ball in the right trap. A mediocre sand shot lands on the green, leaving a 20-foot putt for par. The first putt is short and right of the cup. A 2-foot tap in makes bogey 5. Score: even after 5 holes.

Here is where the practice of gratitude helps. If someone told me that I would be even par after 5 holes, would I be happy with that? Absolutely. It is a great day, and we are even par after five holes while playing with great friends. I would be happy to be my usual 5 over at this point.

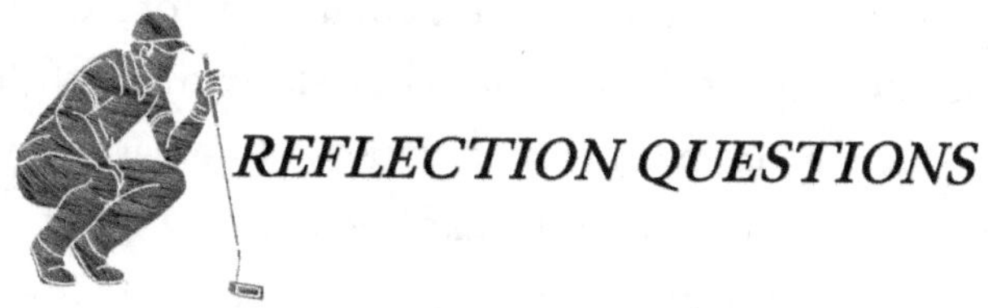

REFLECTION QUESTIONS

1. When was the last time you paused to simply be present?
2. How can you use gratitude to frame your experiences every day?

3. Do you see danger or opportunity as you experience new things?

4. How can the concept of Every help you?

5. What are three things you're grateful for right now?

BOOK RECOMMENDATION: *SIDDHARTHA* BY HERMAN HESSE

Siddhartha by Hermann Hesse is a philosophical novel that explores the spiritual journey of a young Brahmin named Siddhartha as he seeks enlightenment. Siddhartha learns that true wisdom cannot be taught—it must be lived. His journey through asceticism, sensual pleasure, wealth, loss, and father-hood teaches him that every experience, even suffering, contributes to spiritual growth. This realization fosters a deep sense of gratitude for life itself, along with appreciation of the ups and downs in the phases and stages of life.

Gratitude emerges not from comfort, but from the under-standing that every moment—joyful or painful—is a teacher.

SONG: "IN MY LIFE" BY THE BEATLES

The Beatles' song "In My Life" is a deeply reflective piece that beautifully intertwines themes of memory, love, and gratitude. The song's emotional core is steeped in appreciation for the people, places, and moments that have shaped the narrator's life.

Gratitude is expressed with a nostalgic look at the past, acknowledging that some memories remain while others fade. This is a quiet form of gratitude—recognizing the value of expe-riences while honoring both past and present relationships, expressing love and appreciation for everyone who has played a role in the narrator's journey.

The song is a powerful statement of unconditional gratitude for human connection, and it is a poetic meditation on how gratitude lives in memory, in relationships, and in the ability to love more deeply over time. It reminds us that while life changes, our appreciation for its moments and people can grow richer.

MOVIE TO WATCH: *IT'S A WONDERFUL LIFE*

It's a Wonderful Life (1946), directed by Frank Capra, is a timeless film that beautifully illustrates the transformative power of gratitude, especially in the face of despair.

George Bailey, the film's protagonist, feels overwhelmed by financial hardship and personal sacrifice. On the brink of suicide, he believes his life has been meaningless. But when his guardian angel, Clarence, shows him an alternate reality where he never existed, George sees how profoundly he has impacted others—saving lives, helping families, and building community.

Gratitude arises when George realizes the value of his life through the eyes of others. His despair transforms into deep appreciation for the role he's played in the lives of those around him. The film shows that gratitude is reciprocal—when we live generously, others respond with love and support. Gratitude doesn't always come from achieving personal goals; it often grows from recognizing the quiet beauty of a life lived for others.

6 HOLE #6: GIVING
512-YARD PAR 5

This hole, named "Giving," is a shortish dogleg left par 5. The left and right sides of the hole are lined with trees all the way to the green, which is protected by three sand traps. Your first shot is the key shot on this hole. You must hit a 200+ yard drive between the tree lines to set up a second shot, which plays 90 degrees to the left. With a good start, this hole will reward you with a birdie opportunity.

The 5th hole was about gratitude. It was about understanding that everyone, everything, and every moment is a gift which we have been given—a blessed opportunity we have received. This hole puts us on the side of the transaction. Here we are the giver. Now, we are giving to others.

Giving is the heartbeat of joy. In golf, as in life, generosity creates connection, uplifts others, and enriches the giver. This chapter explores how happiness and joy are amplified through acts of giving, both on the course and beyond.

THE JOY OF GENEROSITY

Generosity is not about wealth—it's about spirit. In golf, sharing tips, encouraging others, or simply celebrating someone else's success are acts of giving, as are sharing laughter and helping others look for lost golf balls. Joy flows from this spirit in a generous heart.

Giving can seem to be an esoteric concept in golf. After all, golf is an individual game. You play your own ball, you keep your own score, you repair your own divots, and you choose your own clubs for each shot. Golf also involves a certain amount of competition—with others at times, and always with yourself. But golf is also a game which involves connection with others, often in deep ways that surpass the connection of friendship.

Golf is a game of accountability. Tee times are practically set in stone. Giving starts with showing up. Giving starts with being a companion and an encouraging supporter for the people you are playing with. Our regular group has a standing tee time on Thursdays at 11:06 a.m. I usually arrive around 10:15 a.m. to loosen up, hit a few range balls, and practice chips and putts.

Giving starts upon arrival. I control my attitude. I control my effort and my approach to the people I meet. Golfers are generally very kind and giving by nature. I think the game teaches us to be that way. Giving starts with simply being kind, smiling, and wishing others well as they go out to play.

I'm usually on the range when Ron Nahser and Father Kevin arrive to warm up. I share my bucket of balls with them. After hitting balls, we go to the chipping green and work on the short game, often with some tips on technique and strategy included. After the short game practice, I rake the practice sand trap, and we head to the putting green.

We try to spend 10-15 minutes putting. Again, there are often some words of encouragement and support. Poor Father Kevin, he has a severe case of the yips. His practice strokes are beautiful. But when he goes to putt the ball, it is like he has been hit by a taser. The backstroke is almost non-existent, and distance control is very elusive. He will finish most rounds with 40 putts or more. And he knows it's all in his mind.

I love playing golf with Father Kevin. He is the kindest soul I have ever known. Unfortunately, Father Kevin truly suffers on the course. But he shows up every week. He laughs and makes us laugh. We talk about spiritual and other matters, and he has a gift for making puns. He suffers on and around the greens, but he is as supportive and kind as anyone I have ever met. Father Kevin is a giver. And he is a model of generosity of spirit.

Father Kevin is also, without knowing the term, a great example of living with "mudita." Mudita, according to Wikipedia, is "a concept of joy, particularly an especially sympathetic or vicarious joy—the pleasure that comes from delighting in other people's well-being."

I often see people who are jealous of someone else's success. They are win-lose oriented versus win-win people. And they come from a place of scarcity versus a place of abundance. So many people these days seem to feel that another person's win is a loss for them. I have never seen anything like that from Father Kevin. He is happier for someone else's good shots or birdie than his own. Mudita indeed.

Father Kevin is a servant, a giver, and an encouraging man who truly loves to see others succeed and experience joy. And he does this while suffering through an extremely frustrating case of the yips. The frustration he experiences while putting never interferes with his ability to give support to those of us lucky enough to be in his group.

Speaking of the group, our regular foursome has a tradition of sharing and giving snacks to each other on the 10th tee. It is a highlight of the round. Father Kevin shares Bavarian sausages, Sid Ross gives each of us a Nature Valley bar, Ron Nahser gives us Fig Newtons, and I give each of my friends a Kars Trail Mix bag. I also share Gatorade Zero packets for everyone, so we hydrate and don't cramp up after the round. Sometimes the little gifts bring the most joy. The 10th tee tradition is like Christmas in the summer. Great fun!

So, how does this concept of giving apply off the course? The approach is the same. It all starts with showing up. Give the gift of time and attention. Never underestimate the importance of being present with someone. Be kind. Smile. Hold doors for strangers. Wish everyone a wonderful day.

Only you can control your attitude and your effort. Only you can control what and how much you give. Always aim to give your best. Why wouldn't you?

Take a moment right now and think about it. How are you showing up for others? What are you giving? Do you brighten the day of others or are you draining them with a sour outlook? Be someone who others are glad to see walking toward them. Raise the energy of other people around you. Give your best, even when you don't have your best in you at the time. If you are only feeling 60%, you can still give 100% of what you can.

One of my favorite books is *What You Are Made For* by George Raveling. Yes, that George Raveling—the basketball player and coach, the Nike executive who was pivotal in Michael Jordan signing with Nike, the man who helped coach the U.S. "Dream Team" to Olympic gold.

Raveling's book is all about giving. He points out that each of us is, among many things, made to listen, to dispense love, to serve others, to keep hope alive, and to be a friend. In addition to chapters on these callings, Raveling also asserts that we are made to build our team, to bring people with us, to be a blessing, and to be an answer. We are called to give and serve.

You see, life is not all about you. Life is not all about me. Like David Foster Wallace (*This is Water*), I have learned that I am not the center of the universe. The world does not revolve around me. Life is about connection and relationships. Life is about others. If you have ever played golf alone, then you know that golf is way more fun and a much greater experience when you share a round with others. I enjoy golfing by myself, but the game is far better when shared and played with others.

Relationships are what we are made for. We are made to share, to help, to support, to live in community with others. We are made to receive, and I believe we are made moreso to give.

Inspirational Quote: No one has ever become poor by giving. – Anne Frank

Scripture: It is more blessed to give than to receive. – Acts 20:35

Zen: The fragrance remains on the hand that gives the rose. – Hada Bejar

Golf Anecdote: Tom Watson was known for mentoring younger players, freely offering advice and encouragement.

HAPPINESS AND JOY IN GIVING

Giving is a gateway to happiness. Studies show that acts of kindness boost well-being. In golf, joy is found not just in winning, but in sharing the game.

Golf has many interesting rules and traditions. One of the most interesting traditions is the "gimme" putt. In most official events, golf rules require the player to hit his or her ball all the way into the cup. If you are one inch from the hole, you must still tap it in. Even professionals have missed within six inches of the cup several times over the years.

The "gimme" allows a player to consider their ball holed, while adding a stroke to their score to finish the hole. If your third shot is close to the hole, your playing partners can call a "gimme," which allows you to pick up your ball while finishing the hole with a score of four. In essence, your playing partners are saying, "we believe in you, and you do not need to make that putt. Pick it up. It is good." You are still charged a stroke, but you are not required to make the putt and bend over to get your ball out of the cup.

The "gimme" is more than a time saver—it's an act of love. It expresses confidence and belief in the player receiving the gift. This saves time, and it saves ego and energy. The "gimme" can be an act of mercy.

The "gimme" often comes at the end of a very difficult hole. You struggle off the tee, hit a poor iron or two, and your chip shot is dreadful. You putt once or twice and are still 3 feet from the hole, staring at a 7 on the scorecard. Your playing partners, in an act of mercy, encourage you to "pick it up. That's good." You gather what is left of your battered ego and head to the next hole, feeling appreciative and knowing you are loved by your group. With a deep breath, you gather the confidence and courage to face the next hole. Thanks, guys, for the "gimme." I needed that.

Where do you offer "gimmes" in life? Do you offer a "gimme" to your wife, your children, your mother and father, your brother or sister, your friends and co-workers? I am sure you do. Acts of love and mercy are everywhere—in cups of coffee, filled gas tanks, grocery runs, laundry, paid bills, washed dishes, and meals out at favorite restaurants. I am sure there are countless ways you show up and give of yourself for others. You give hundreds of small acts of service, little hugs, and words of encouragement. You do the little things that make life easier and better for others. And you give your time and energy.

Why do you do these things? Why do you give, often without any acknowledgement or fanfare? Because you love. Because you care. You give because you want to. And, if you are like me, you give because you feel good knowing you are giving your best. Giving is part of being your best self. And, giving makes you happy. There is joy in your acts of generosity and giving.

Here is a question to ponder: Do you get more joy from receiving gifts or giving gifts at Christmas?

Inspirational Quote: Happiness doesn't result from what we get, but from what we give. – Ben Carson

Scripture: A generous person will prosper; whoever refreshes others will be refreshed. – Proverbs 11:25

Zen: Give, even if you only have a little. – Buddha

Golf Anecdote: After winning the 1987 Hertz Bay Hill Classic (now known as the Arnold Palmer Invitational), Payne Stewart made a deeply personal and generous gesture—he donated his entire $108,000 winner's check to a cancer charity, The Golden Circle of Friends program, in memory of his father, William Louis Stewart, who had died of cancer two years earlier.

GIVING AS A WAY OF LIFE

Giving is not a one-time act. Giving is a way of life. In golf, it's seen in respect for the course, kindness to caddies, and encouragement to fellow players. In life, it's a daily choice to uplift and do for others.

One of the interesting things about golf is the nature of charity and generosity that is attached to the game. Most of us who play golf have, at some point, played in a fund-raising event for charity or a special interest. Civic groups, little league teams, churches, and other groups of all kinds host events to raise money for their needs. Every summer and fall, golf courses are filled with 100+ golfers per event, where money is raised through the generosity of the golfers and sponsors who support the fund-raising efforts.

On a grander scale, the PGA TOUR is recognized as one of the most philanthropic organizations in professional sports. It raises money for charity through a well-structured and community-driven model. Here's how it works:

KEY METHODS OF FUNDRAISING

Non-Profit Tournament Model

Most PGA TOUR events are organized by non-profit organizations. The net proceeds from these tournaments —after covering operational costs—are donated to local and national charities.

Corporate Sponsorships

Sponsors fund events, reducing overhead, and increasing the amount that can be donated. Many sponsors also match donations or contribute directly to causes tied to the event.

Pro-Am Tournaments

These events pair amateurs with professionals for a fee,

and the proceeds go to charity. They're a major
fundraising tool and help build community engagement.

Silent Auctions & Raffles

Events often include auctions featuring signed memora-
bilia, golf gear, and luxury experiences. All proceeds
benefit designated charities.

Volunteer Support

Over 100,000 volunteers help run PGA TOUR events each
year. Their unpaid work significantly reduces costs,
allowing more money to go to charity.

Direct Donations

Fans and attendees can donate directly to the charities
associated with each event, either online or on-site.

Charity Partnerships

The TOUR partners with organizations such as First Tee,
St. Jude Children's Research Hospital, TGR Foundation
(founded by Tiger Woods), and Birdies for the Brave (supporting military families).

Impact by the Numbers

- Over $3.6 billion has been donated to charity since 1938.
- Individual events like the Waste Management Phoenix

Open and AT&T Pebble Beach Pro-Am have each raised over $100 million.

In addition to the PGA Tour organization, many professional golfers support countless charitable organizations through the giving of their personal time and money. In fact, most successful pros have established their own foundations in support of their charitable giving. Both Tiger Woods and Rory McIlroy have foundations that have provided charitable funds estimated to be in the hundreds of millions of dollars each. They are great examples of golfers who have been blessed, and in return, they have given back from their blessings.

This is a great example and model for us to live by. We are all blessed. We are in a position to help others. I remember Payne Stewart asking in an interview, "How much is enough? How much do I need? I've been blessed with a good life, good enough to share with others." That inspires me to live with a giving spirit, to live with a generous heart.

I can't say yes to every cause. But I can say yes to many of them. I can say yes to places that have helped shape me—schools, churches, community organizations where I have lived. I can say yes to hospitals, food banks, and organizations like United Way, Red Cross, Wounded Warriors, and Folds of Honor. I can say yes to the homeless in our town, and I can say yes to the Salvation Army and the Veterans Closet.

One of my favorite things to do is to tip workers who rarely get noticed. If you want to make someone's day, give a couple of dollars to the cashier in your McDonald's drive through or the person behind the deli or meat counter at your grocery store. Tip the gas station attendant or the starter at your golf course. It is amazing what a couple dollars and a sincere thank you will do to lift the spirits of the unseen people who take care of you every day. Try it.

Make giving a way of life. You have been given the gifts of time, talent, and treasure. Share them generously. Give without expectation. When you do, you will be richly blessed.

Inspirational Quote: We make a living by what we get, but we make a life by what we give. – Winston Churchill

Scripture: Each of you should give what you have decided in your heart to give, not reluctantly or under compulsion. – 2 Corinthians 9:7

Zen: The more you give, the more comes back to you.

Golf Anecdote: Many professionals, like Ernie Els, Arnold Palmer, and Jack Nicklaus, have founded charitable foundations to give back to communities and causes they care about.

SUMMARY

Giving transforms both the giver and the receiver. It brings joy, builds relationships, and creates a ripple effect of kindness. On the course and in life, generosity is the true measure of greatness, the conquering of selfishness.

HOLE RESULT: 512-YARD PAR 5

A solid drive clears the trees at the left corner of the dog leg. A good three wood leaves 70 yards to the green from the left side of the fairway. The third shot is a chance to "take dead aim." Making a good swing with a 60-degree sand wedge, the ball lands just short of the hole, releases, and hits the stick, stopping a foot from the hole. Father Kevin applauds your shot and picks up your ball, saying, "That is good. Great birdie!" Score: 1 under after 6 holes.

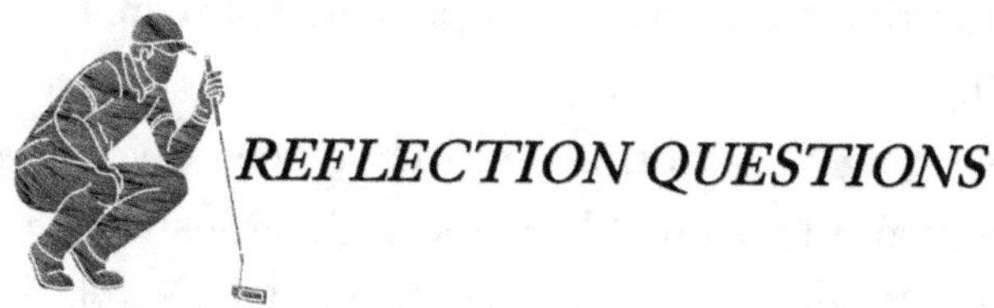

REFLECTION QUESTIONS

1. What does generosity look like in your daily life?
2. How has giving brought you joy in the past?
3. What opportunities do you have to give more freely—time, talent, treasure?

BOOK RECOMMENDATION: *WHAT YOU'RE MADE FOR* BY GEORGE RAVELING

George Raveling's *What You're Made For*, co-authored with Ryan Holiday, is a powerful reflection on purpose, leadership, and legacy—deeply intertwined with the concept of giving, especially in the form of mentorship, service, and impact.

This book challenges readers to ask: "What are you lifting up?" This question reframes success as service to others, urging readers to align their actions with values that benefit their communities. Raveling's life, from standing beside Martin Luther King Jr. to mentoring Michael Jordan, serves as a blueprint for purpose-driven generosity.

SONG: "BRIDGE OVER TROUBLED WATER" BY SIMON AND GARFUNKEL

Simon & Garfunkel's "Bridge Over Troubled Water" is a deeply emotional ballad that beautifully embodies the spirit of giving, especially in the form of selfless support, compassion, and presence during someone's time of need.

The song is a timeless anthem of compassionate giving. It teaches that the most profound gifts are often intangible—presence, empathy, and unwavering support—and being someone's "bridge" can be the most meaningful act of generosity.

MOVIE TO WATCH: *PAY IT FORWARD*

The movie *Pay It Forward* (2000), starring Haley Joel Osment, Helen Hunt, and Kevin Spacey, is a poignant exploration of giving as a transformative force—not just for individuals, but for society as a whole.

At the heart of the film is a young boy's school project: to change the world by doing a good deed for three people, who then each "pay it forward" by helping three more. This creates a chain reaction of kindness, showing how the ripple effect of one act of giving can multiply exponentially with tremendous impact.

Pay It Forward is a cinematic tribute to the power of generosity, empathy, and hope. It teaches that giving isn't just an action; it's a philosophy that can reshape communities, heal wounds, and inspire movements.

7 HOLE #7: LEARNING FROM MISTAKES, FORGIVENESS, AND GRACE

420-YARD PAR 4

This hole, called "To Err is Human," is one of my favorite holes. It is a very difficult and narrow par 4 with water and trees on the left and trees and out of bounds on the right. A small pond stretches in front of the green from 70 to 25 yards in. Standing on the tee, you feel as though you are playing down a bowling alley with hazards on each side. Then your second shot must carry water. This hole is as demanding as it gets. Your drive is the key shot on this hole, and your approach must be well played too. You have to keep it between the tree lines, and you certainly can't go wide left or right as penalty shots can add up quickly here. Par is a great score, and double bogey or worse is always in play.

EMBRACING AND LEARNING FROM MISTAKES

Mistakes are inevitable—in golf and in life. What defines us is not the error, but our response to it. This chapter explores the power of forgiveness, the grace of letting go, and the growth that comes from pain. The mantra, "Next!" reminds us to move forward with wisdom and resilience.

Golf is a game of imperfection. Even the best players hit bad shots. We pull it left, push it right, hook the ball, slice the ball, hit it thin, whiff, and hit it fat. Our chips and putts are short, long, left, right, and just plain awful at times.

It is helpful for every golfer to remember that the best players in the world miss 1 of 4 fairways and greens in regulation. When we are imperfect and make mistakes, the key is to learn, not linger. Mistakes are teachers in disguise, offering lessons in humility and growth.

Golf can be very humbling. It is a game where you try, you fail, and you try again for four plus hours over 18 holes. My typical round will consist of 14 drives (10 of which will be good), 8 fairway woods (6 will be good), 16 irons into the greens (10 will be good), 12 chips (8 will be good), and 28 putts (22 will be good). That is 78 swings, 56 of which will be good, while 22 will not be very good, including 2 shots that will be bad enough to cost me 4 penalty strokes. That is how I get to 82 in most of my rounds.

The truth is, my typical shot breakdown per round is roughly 30% good, 35% acceptable, 30% mediocre at best, and 5% are just dreadful. I always have 3 or 4 shots that are score savers—great chips, made putts from 20 feet, etc.—and I can count on having 3 swings that cost me 4 to 6 shots per round. The difference between 76 and 82 is 3 bad swings.

How do I handle that? How do I deal with that during the round? I find comfort in two concepts that have helped me deal with the bad swings, the mistakes. First, I take comfort in knowing that even the pros, the best in the world, miss 1 out of every 4 shots. Knowing the pros are not perfect gives me permission to not be perfect.

The second great lesson I have learned, and this is a great lesson in golf, is the concept of "Next." You can find this lesson in Kevin Eastman's book, *Why the Best are the Best*. Eastman talks about "The Champion's Compass" (including "Every" on Hole 5), which features the concept of "Next."

THE POWER OF NEXT

"Next" means no matter what happens to us, good or bad, we are called to embrace it, learn from it, let it go, and then focus on the next play, the next shot, the next hole, the next game, etc. Next means the last shot is over. Embrace it, learn from it, let it go, and then focus on the next shot to be played.

Does this mean you don't enjoy a great shot? No. Embrace it. Does this mean you don't get upset with a bad shot? No. Next means you do not let a result linger and interfere with the next opportunity. Next means you squeeze what you need to from one shot, and then you focus entirely on the opportunity existing in your next shot.

Carry the positives and let go of the negatives. Celebrate your victories and learn from your losses and mistakes. I am not good enough to get mad when I hit a bad shot. Plus, getting mad and upset is rarely helpful. In fact, most people find that success breeds success, and frustration usually snowballs into more mistakes and greater frustration. Poker players call the snowballing effect of compounding mistakes as "going on tilt." The concept of "Next" is the antidote for going on tilt.

Golf is a great teacher for the concept of "Next." In fact, golf has helped me actually experience the powerful lessons in the concept of "Next." Golf has helped me understand that the last shot is over and in the past. Learn from it. Let it go. Then the best thing I can do is focus on the opportunity of the next shot and staying present in that opportunity. Hit it, accept it, let it go, and then go focus on making my next shot be my best shot.

"Next" has helped me immensely. Recently, I was playing a short, simple par 4 that should be a birdie hole, and I hit a horrible pull-hook drive into the trees. I tried to hit out from the trees, got greedy, and topped my 6-iron into a sand trap 145 yards from the green. Two dreadful shots in a row, left me in a bad spot for my third. I thought about "Next" and focused on hitting my best shot from the sand trap. My 7-iron flew just as I had pictured it, landing just short of the green and rolling to three feet from the pin. I made the short putt for par.

Ron Nahser asked me how I did that? I told him "Next." I hit two dreadful shots followed by a fantastic shot and made par. "Next" helped me embrace the mistakes (I actually laughed at myself after the second shot into the trap), learn from them (relax and focus), let go of them (no reason to get mad, they are history I cannot undue), and give my best effort on the next opportunity (let's knock this on the green and try to save par).

Here are the 4 Steps in the Concept of Next:

- Own and accept the result
- Learn
- Let go
- Focus on the next opportunity

Each step in the process of "Next" is valuable and worth a deeper look. Start by embracing the result. Own it. Celebrate it. Enjoy it. That is easy to do when the results are good. You should enjoy both the small and the big wins.

But, what about embracing the mistakes? They happen.

None of us is perfect. We are all human. Every golfer hits bad shots. Own them. And remember, failure is just part of the process of becoming successful. There is no reason to be afraid of failure. Mistakes turn into failure only when you give up. Never give up. It takes zero talent and zero character to quit in frustration and defeat. Mistakes happen. Own them. Accept them. That is the only way to move beyond them.

The second step of "Next" is to learn. The only failure is failing to learn and improve and to turn negatives into positives. Some people see the world as static. I prefer the view of Cate Hall, a former Supreme Court attorney, the former number 1 female poker player in the world, and current CEO of the biotech company Astera.

In her TED talk on the importance of personal agency (the capacity to both see and act on all of the degrees of freedom we actually have), Hall says, "Assume everything is learnable—like learning to be more optimistic or curious. Most traits that people think are fixed are actually quite learnable if you believe that they are and put the same kind of effort into learning them that you would everything else." Remember, success leaves trails. Everything is learnable.

My love of learning and my dedication to being a lifelong learner really started when my mother died (Hole 1). This dedication to learning has helped me through many difficult times over the years. One of the most powerful lessons I've learned is that things are always in motion, always in transition. And, like my golf game, life is rarely a straight-line experience. In reality, golf and the game of life are both played from errant shots, including lots of bad lies, with trees, and traps, and hazards in the way.

Golf has taught me to combine the learning element of "Next" with the gratitude element of "Every" (Hole 5). That combination helps me understand that every person, every event, every result (good or bad) is not only a gift, but a gift which offers the opportunity to learn, grow, and improve. Learn from and be grateful for everyone and everything.

Yes, even troubles, mistakes, and challenges are a gift. They help build character. They help you develop resilience. Problems strengthen your mental and physical muscle. Mistakes and challenges show you where you need to grow. And, with the proper mindset, they teach you what you need to learn. The crucible of struggle is a gift.

It can be hard to see struggles as a gift at the time, but think about it, we've all experienced low points that propelled us to our highest levels. Strength is often best built from brokenness. The key is to learn from being broken and to use it as a launching point, as fuel for growth. Don't linger in the aftermath of a mistake. Learn and grow.

Once we have embraced the results and learned from them, the third step in the process of "Next" is to let it go. This may be the hardest part of the process. Sometimes we don't want to let go. Winning is great, and it is fun to be on top of the mountain. But we can't stay there. The only bodies at the top of Mount Everest are the ones that froze to death up there.

Mountain tops are wonderful, but we must come back down. And, as history has proven, the most dangerous part of the Everest experience is the descent. 75% of the deaths on Everest occur after the summit. Coming down can be treacherous. But we must let go of the mountain top, even when we have reasons to resist letting it go. We can't stay there. Life is lived in the valleys.

What about letting go of the negative experiences? Sometimes we want to hang onto those as well. It can be comforting to blame others, to hold grudges, to live in resentment, and to remain in a comfortable place while clinging to fear instead of learning and moving forward. We can hold steady to the past, and we can use the past as proof that the future will be no better than what has happened before. It can be comforting to create distance. And we might prefer safety while weaponizing negative experiences. We can tell ourselves we might be in a bad place, and yet we might choose to stay there so things do not get worse.

The truth is, letting go is hard. It is hard to let go of something or someone we love. It can be even harder when we are hanging onto resentment and anger. But we must develop and nurture the skill of letting go.

There is a beautiful scene in the movie *Top Gun Maverick* where Tom Cruise (Maverick) is visiting Val Kilmer (Ice Man) who is battling terminal cancer. The two are discussing an upcoming difficult mission, and Kilmer is telling Cruise that he must let go of the guilt he has been carrying for years over the death of his former colleague Goose, played by Anthony Edwards. Kilmer tells Cruise, "You have to let him go." Cruise responds, with tear-filled eyes, "I don't know how." Many of us don't know how to let go.

Letting go is a learnable skill. Letting go is a skill that is essential, and yet it is rarely taught. Who taught you how to let go? If you are like me, the answer is no one. I am self-taught. Learning how to let go is another of the many lessons I have learned the hard way. But golf has been instrumental in teaching me this skill.

As you might suspect by now, I do have a couple of great books on the subject, the best of which is *Let Go Now*, by Karen Casey. It is a good read, including many examples of why we should and how we can learn to let go.

Here is a beautiful story about letting go. Two monks, one

senior and one junior, were traveling together. At one point, they came to a river with a strong current. As they approached the river, they saw a young woman struggling to get across. She asked for help.

The monks had taken vows not to touch women, but without hesitation, the older monk picked her up, carried her across the river, and set her down on the other side. The younger monk was shocked but said nothing.

Hours passed as they continued their journey. The younger monk, troubled by what had happened, finally blurted out, "As monks, we are not permitted to touch a woman. How could you carry her?"

The older monk replied, "I set her down on the other side of the river hours ago. Why are you still carrying her?"

This story teaches that sometimes, we hold onto things—judgments, grievances, or past events—long after they are over. True freedom comes from letting go, like the older monk. The younger monk's burden was not the act itself, but his inability to release it from his mind.

One of my favorite quotes about the importance of letting go comes from Mark Twain, who said, "The inability to forget is far more devastating than the inability to remember." We have both a great need and a great power to let go if we choose to do so. Letting go is a choice and a skill that is incredibly freeing.

Drop the burden and bondage of that which weighs on your mind, your heart, and your soul. Put the weight of guilt and shame and disappointment in a bubble and let it float away into the sky. The past is over. The bad shot is over. Let it go. Leave it in the past. Enjoy this moment free of past mistakes.

Can you feel the power of letting go? Can you see the benefit? Is this a skill you want to learn to develop? Consider this powerful question from the author, podcaster, and global influencer Jay Shetty: "What are you holding onto that is getting in the way of your life and your growth today?" Learn to let go. It is an incredibly powerful choice.

The fourth and last step in the concept of "Next" is to focus on the next shot, the next opportunity. The key is to be fully present in the next shot, to begin anew, and to focus your attention and effort on giving your best in the next moment. A great book here is Bob Rotella's *Make Your Next Shot Your Best Shot: The Secret to Playing Great Golf.*

No matter what has happened before, no matter how good or bad the previous shot was, all that matters is the next shot in front of you. The past is over. The future has not arrived. All that matters is this moment, this opportunity right here and now, so enjoy it, and give it your best attitude, your best mental approach, and your best effort. Make your best swing and then go do it again, regardless of the outcome. That is golf. That is life. Next!

Inspirational Quote: Success is stumbling from failure to failure with no loss of enthusiasm. – Winston Churchill

Scripture: Though he fall, he shall not be utterly cast down: for the Lord upholdeth him with his hand. – Psalm 37:24

Zen: Fall down seven times, get up eight.

Golf Anecdote: Payne Stewart missed several make-able putts in the third round of the 1999 U. S. Open. After the round, Stewart's wife, Tracy, told him he was moving his head and looking up early in his putting stroke. Payne practiced keeping his head still before the final round. After clinching the championship with a dramatic 18-foot putt on the 72nd hole, Stewart tearfully embraced his wife, telling her, "I kept my head still all day, Lovey. I did it all day." Stewart understood "Next"— embracing the result of the third round, learning from it, letting it go, and seizing the opportunity to win the championship the next day.

FORGIVENESS AND GRACE

Forgiveness is a gift we give ourselves and others. Grace allows us to release the burden of guilt and move forward. In golf, this means letting go of the last hole and focusing on the next while forgiving ourselves for our poor play. It also means forgiving our playing partners for their failings on the course.

I have hit thousands of really poor shots on the golf course over my lifetime. Similarly, I have made thousands of mistakes off the course during my lifetime. My missteps and errors and misdeeds are beyond my ability to count them. I'm not proud of that fact, but I accept it as part of me. I am human. I am imperfect. The truth is, we are all imperfect. We all make mistakes. We all hit bad shots, and we all hurt others with what we do and what we fail to do. To err is human.

This fact that we are all imperfect means we all need forgiveness. We need to forgive ourselves for our imperfection. And we need to forgive others for their imperfection.

Why forgive? Without forgiveness, the weight of the mistakes, hurt, and damage creates heavy burdens—the burdens of guilt, shame, resentment, and broken trust. That's no way to live.

I am reminded of the saying, "Failing to forgive is like drinking rat poison and then waiting for the rat to die." Learn to forgive yourself. Learn to forgive others. And learn to ask for forgiveness from others.

When we hurt someone or when we are hurt, one of three things can happen, and two of them are problematic. First, we can pretend nothing happened. Ignoring is rarely helpful. Ignoring damage causes contempt and resentment. And the more damage is done and ignored, the greater the buildup of resentment. Relationships rarely last when hurts are ignored. Pretending nothing happened when someone is hurt usually creates a distance that will eventually cause a catastrophic break-up of the relationship.

The second thing that can happen when damage is done and hurt is experienced, is that we can blame the other person for the situation. Again, this will eventually sever the relationship as contempt and resentment becomes insurmountable. You see, ignoring or blaming another person when you hurt them creates disconnection and distance. And distance often results in separation.

The good news is that there is a third alternative, one that is positive and creates connection and stronger bonds. When you own your role in hurtful behavior and offer and seek forgiveness, you build trust and closeness. Forgiveness is the salve that heals hurt. Forgiveness is restorative and repairs broken hearts.

The truth is most people are not good at repairing damage. But we should be. We need to be. Why? Because we do more damage than we care to admit, and the closer we are to someone, the more we will hurt them. We are human. We are imperfect. We all fall short. As St. Paul writes in his letter to the Romans, "I do not understand what I do. For what I want to do, I do not do, but what I hate I do." (Romans 7:15) Paul is writing about life. And his words are just as true for anyone who plays golf.

Since we are imperfect, we should learn the skills of forgiveness and repair. Those skills, like the concept of "Next," are grounded in owning our behavior and learning from that behavior. In addition, a proper repair effort includes a genuine apology for the damage done and a commitment to be certain that the first time is the last time we make that mistake. There is nothing more powerful than a genuine repair effort and genuine forgiveness in response.

What do you do if you are hurt by someone else and they don't try to repair? This is where grace comes in. You give grace. You give forgiveness even when it is not requested. Why? Because forgiveness and grace are both beautiful and profound acts freely given in love and compassion.

This is one of the most important truths in life; we are all loved way more than we deserve. That is grace. Give grace because you are receiving grace in amounts well beyond your awareness of it.

One question about forgiveness—when you forgive, do you forget? That is a deeply personal question, and the answer to that depends on what kind of healing you are seeking. When you forgive, you make a conscious decision to let go of the resentment and contempt that accompany your injuries. Forgetting is a conscious decision to erase memories, and that may not always be healthy. The key is to learn to set appropriate boundaries.

As Rob Dial, author and host of the *Mindset Mentor* podcast, says, "The same boiling water that makes an egg hard is the same boiling water that makes a potato soft. Meaning it's not the events in your life that make you who you are, but the decision on how you use the events in your life to either hold you back or propel you forward to create the life you want. No matter how stuck you are, if you can learn to locate the doors hidden within you, you can unlock inconceivable amounts of freedom."

That is the freedom offered in forgiveness and grace. That is the freedom offered in the concept of "Next." Mistakes are inevitable. To err is human, both on and off the golf course.

Inspirational Quote: To forgive is to set a prisoner free and discover that the prisoner was you. – Lewis B. Smedes

Scripture: Be kind and compassionate to one another, forgiving each other, just as in Christ God forgave you. – Ephesians 4:32

Zen: Let go or be dragged.

Golf Anecdote: Phil Mickelson often speaks of forgiving himself quickly to stay mentally strong during competition. He believes lingering on errors can derail performance, so he practices immediate self-forgiveness as a strategic mindset.

Mickelson has spoken openly about the psychological side of golf, especially the need to recover quickly from setbacks. His philosophy includes:

- Rapid self-forgiveness: He's said that when he hits a bad shot, he immediately forgives himself so he can move on without emotional baggage.
- Staying present: Mickelson stresses the importance of staying in the moment. Dwelling on past shots—good or bad—distracts from the next one.
- Confidence reset: He uses self-talk and visualization to reset his confidence after a mistake, reminding himself of his skills and past successes.

SUMMARY

Mistakes are not the end—they are the beginning of wisdom. Forgiveness and grace free us to grow. Pain, when embraced, becomes a path to healing. The mindset of 'Next!' keeps us moving forward with hope.

HOLE RESULT: 420-YARD PAR 4

A poor drive clears the left trees landing in the pond. After a penalty drop, a hooking 6 iron finds the fairway 110 yards from the green. The fourth shot calls for a full pitching wedge. Trying to hit the ball too hard, this shot is hit thin and finds the pond in front of the green. Another penalty drop—unbelievable. Next! The sixth shot is a sand wedge to 4 feet.

We make the putt for a triple bogey 7. This moves us from 1 under to 2 over par after 7 holes. Next!

REFLECTION QUESTIONS

1. What are the most powerful lessons you have learned through making mistakes?
2. How can the concept of "Next" help you on and off the course?
3. What is your skill level with letting go?
4. How do you practice forgiveness with yourself and with others?
5. Where do you need to repair damaged relationships?

BOOK RECOMMENDATION: *GOLF IS NOT A GAME OF PERFECT* BY BOB ROTELLA

Bob Rotella's *Golf Is Not a Game of Perfect* teaches that mistakes are inevitable, but how you respond to them defines your growth, character, and ultimate success.

Key lessons on learning from mistakes include under-standing that mistakes are part of the process, perfection is an illusion, recovery reveals character, and we are called to move forward rather than dwell on mistakes. Additionally, Rotella teaches that confidence is a choice. We must focus on process over results and our self-image matters.

Rotella's practical takeaways include:

- Let go of perfectionism—it disrupts flow and joy.
- Use mistakes as data, not drama.
- Stay present and trust your preparation.
- Reflect after the event, not during.
- Build a resilient self-image that thrives on learning and growth.

Rotella's wisdom is especially powerful for athletes, performers, and anyone chasing excellence. His message? You don't need to be perfect—you need to be persistent, self-aware, and willing to learn.

SONG: "BRAND NEW DAY" BY STING

Sting's "Brand New Day" is a soulful anthem about embracing renewal, forgiving past mistakes, and choosing hope over regret.

The song reflects on the emotional toll of past failures, espe-cially in love, and the temptation to give up. Sting asks, "How many of you people out there / Been hurt in some kind of love affair?"—a line that sets the tone for a reckoning with pain, disil-lusionment, and the fear of repeating old patterns.

Yet the heart of the song lies in its radical optimism. The recurring phrase "Turn the clock to zero" becomes a metaphor for wiping the slate clean. It's not about denying the past, but about choosing to begin again with wisdom gained from it. Sting sings of selling the stock, spending the money, and starting over—not as escapism, but as a conscious act of transformation.

MOVIE TO WATCH: *7 DAYS IN UTOPIA* (2011)

7 Days in Utopia explores how personal failure can become a gateway to deeper self-discovery, emphasizing that learning from mistakes requires humility, reflection, and a shift in perspective.

The film follows Luke Chisholm, a talented young golfer who suffers a humiliating meltdown during a professional tournament. Overwhelmed by pressure, especially from his overbearing father, Luke flees and crashes his car in the small town of Utopia, Texas. This literal crash mirrors his emotional collapse and sets the stage for transformation.

Luke's public failure isn't just a plot device—it's the crucible that forces him to confront his identity beyond golf. His mistake opens the door to mentorship under Johnny Crawford, a wise rancher and former golfer who teaches Luke that success isn't just about performance but about character and clarity. If you're reflecting on your own journey, especially through golf or creative work, this film offers a compelling reminder: mistakes aren't detours, they are invitations to grow.

8 HOLE #8: ACCEPTANCE

345-YARD PAR 4

This hole, called "Acceptance," is another one of my favorite holes. It is a straightforward 90-degree dogleg right par 4 with trees down the right. The tee shot requires 215 yards to reach the dogleg. If you miss right, the trees are thick, and a possible birdie can easily become a double bogey. With a good drive, a short second shot gives you a chance to attack an open green with traps left and right. This hole is a chance to get a shot back. The key here is to play the hole as it is designed—if you get greedy, you will pay the price.

ACCEPTANCE

Acceptance is not resignation; it is clarity. In golf and in life, we often strive to control outcomes, yet true peace comes from surrendering to what is. This chapter explores the balance between control and surrender, the release of judgment, and the quiet strength of patience.

Golf, in its purest sense, is about acceptance. One of the

prominent rules of golf is "play the ball where it lies." And the ball often lies in very difficult places. A well-struck shot may end up in a divot, or it may take a sideways bounce and finish under the lip of a sand trap. I often find my ball under a bush or near a tree root, and it is common to be in or near rocks, thick rough, tall grass, or wispy heather.

A poorly struck shot can end up in the water, out of bounds, plugged deep in the sand, or in the forest. I've hit many shots with the ball almost waist-high on a hill. And I'm quite experienced at hitting balls in a sand trap with my feet on the grass well above the ball in the sand. I've learned to hit the ball on my knees, and I've become quite skilled as a right-handed golfer hitting the ball from the left side using the back of my club.

I never plan to have my ball end up in these challenging places. My plan is always to play from a good lie in the best strategic spot. I want my drives to be on the proper side of the fairway. I want my irons to find the green in a place where I will have an easy putt. But my plans rarely play out as desired. As stated in the previous chapter on learning from mistakes, "I don't do what I want to do, and I do what I do not want to do."

I play with good strategy, but my execution is often spotty. Sometimes, I hit such dreadfully bad shots that I'm embarrassed and frustrated to no end. When that happens, I usually laugh. Why? Well, what else can I do? It does no good to get angry, to throw a club, or to act like a child. Golf has taught me to be better than that. Golf has taught me to accept the results of my efforts, even when the results are bad.

Acceptance is one of golf's great lessons. You learn to play the ball where it lies. Accept it. As my brother often says, "it is what it is." Golf teaches you to accept the results of your swing, the distances you hit your clubs, and the scores you make on each hole and for the round. Golf reveals your abilities and your failings, the strengths and weaknesses of your game. And on a deeper level, golf reveals your character and your ability to manage and control your emotions, particularly when frustrated.

One of my real struggles during the last few years has been my acceptance of losing distance with age. I am not the same golfer I was ten years ago. I am older, less flexible, and I feel constant pain and fatigue in my lower back and hips. These facts influence my swing, my swing speed, and the distances I hit all of my clubs. The driver that was once 250 yards is now 225 yards. Each of my club distances is 10% shorter than just a few years ago.

It is hard to admit that I now need an 8-iron when I used to hit a pitching wedge. What was a 6-iron is now a 4-iron yardage. Anything over 175 yards now requires five or even three wood. Man, this getting old is hard. But I must accept it. It is what it is. This is not what I would prefer or want. But what can I do? Accept it old man! Accept it and keep having fun!

So, how can this life lesson from golf be useful off the course? Where can you apply the concept of acceptance in your life? The simple answer is just about everywhere. Acceptance is a concept that is useful in every role you play—as a spouse, parent, child, brother or sister, co-worker, neighbor, and even with yourself.

Anywhere or any place you feel frustration, disappointment, anger, or disillusionment, the answer is to embrace acceptance. Most of these negative emotions come from unmet expectations, usually expectations we have of other people. For me, these issues fully arise when I do what I call "seeing the gap."

The gap I am referring to is the gap between what is (reality) and what I see that could or should be (desire). I can easily get frustrated and upset when it seems as though you could build a Walmart between what is and what should be. And the greater the gap, the greater the frustration, particularly if little to no progress has been made with an ongoing issue.

How do you deal with "the gap?" Golf tells me to embrace acceptance. Accept the gap. Accept that you are doing the best you can. Accept that others are doing their best as well. Accept that, yes, things could be better. But there is good right where things stand. Accept the good.

I am not advocating that you ignore desires or needs or what could and should be. I am suggesting that you accept things and people as they are and then work with others in a way that is patient, loving, and kind as you work together to close the gap between what is and what could be.

Accept that everyone is doing the best they can. Like golf, accept that you (and others around you) need to practice and develop skills to improve and close the gaps wherever they exist. The gap is an opportunity to learn, improve, and embrace things as they are and not what we wish they were. Acceptance is clarity about what is real.

What is the alternative when you see the gap? Denial, resistance, and rejection? Am I going to give up golf because I don't hit the ball as far as I used to? Am I going to resist and reject the reality that I am older, less flexible, slower, and fighting back and hip issues? No. The best course of action is to accept it and make the most of what I can do. I can work on my flexibility and strength and do some exercises that help my back and hips. And I can hit the 8-iron where I used to hit pitching wedge. The scorecard asks the score, not the club used.

The same holds true for issues off the course. I can work to improve my effort, my attitude, and my skills in working with others. And, hopefully, they will do the same. I can see people and situations as they are and accept them as such, instead of holding on to a perception of how I wish they were.

The gap is a gift. The gap shows you where you need to grow. The gap reveals where there is tension between what you want and expect versus what is real. Acceptance is a huge part of the answer. Accept. It is better than denial, resistance, and rejection. Accept people and circumstances as they are and then choose to act accordingly.

CONTROL VS SURRENDER

Golf teaches us that we cannot control the wind, the bounce, or the lie. We can only control our response. Surrender is not weakness, it is wisdom. It allows us to flow with reality rather than fight it.

Surrender is a close cousin of acceptance. As much as I dislike hitting my clubs a shorter distance than I did a few years ago, I must surrender to that reality. I have tried swinging harder. I have tried taking a bigger turn with my body. I bought a new driver. Guess what? My yardages are still ten percent shorter. Sometimes I still hit my pitching wedge when I now need an 8-iron, and then I climb into the sand for my next shot because I was stubborn and came up well short of the green.

I have had to accept reality. I have had to surrender to father time. In doing this, I have discovered something very interesting —there is freedom in accepting and surrendering. I am no longer struggling to regain the past, and I am scoring better. I am enjoying the game more and building confidence in my shot making ability. I am no longer fighting myself or the ghosts of days gone by. Rather than fighting against myself and reality, I am hitting more club—and I am getting closer to the hole in the process.

There is strength in surrendering. It is not weakness. Surrendering to what is real takes strength. Surrender is not giving up;

it is giving in. Surrender is laying down the desire to struggle and fight and scratch and claw for something that is neither realistic nor worth the energy and emotion. Surrender is a loving choice that says, "I am no longer willing to fight because the costs far exceed the gains. I am going to embrace reality, not illusion."

To surrender is to acknowledge that I cannot control the outcome and all the elements that affect the process. All I can do is control my attitude and my effort. I cannot control the result. And I sure as heck can't control other people—that is a fool's effort.

There is one last thing about the concepts of acceptance and surrender, and that is the opposing concept of resistance. There are appropriate times to resist (like peer pressure, etc.) and hold true to personal boundaries. But in general, I agree with the concept that what you resist owns you, that what you resist, you magnify and give power to.

Think about it: if you resist something, it becomes an obstacle that remains in your way indefinitely. If you are in a room and you resist going near a particular chair, you have made your room smaller. That chair now has power over you. And your focus on that chair creates a barrier for you. In fact, you may focus so much on resisting the chair that you miss out on the best aspects of the room.

If you resist telling the truth, that lie or that withholding of truth will create trouble for you. We have all experienced the fallout of lying or not being transparent when we should have been. We have all experienced situations where we made our world smaller because we did not go to a party for fear we might run into someone we were not comfortable seeing. We have all experienced cases where we resisted admitting mistakes or apologizing when we should have, and this resistance has cost us in our relationships. What you resist owns you.

When you have weeds in your garden, what do you do? Do you deal with the weeds and help your garden grow, or do you resist dealing with the weeds and watch your garden die out? Whatever you resist owns you. What you resist, you give power to and magnify.

Resistance is futile. Accept. Surrender. Swim with the current. Set your sails to make the best use of the wind. Don't fight it. Work with, not against. Claim your power and your freedom. Use your energy to move forward instead of being drained by resistance. Accept. Surrender. You'll be glad you did.

Swing Thought:

Takeaway: What you resist owns you. What you resist you magnify and give power to.

Contact: Acceptance gives you the freedom to grow and move forward.

Follow Through: Surrender (giving in) is an act of love that gives you power over what you can't control.

Inspirational Quote: What you resist not only persists but will grow in size. – Carl Jung

Scripture: Accept one another, then, just as Christ accepted you, in order to bring praise to God. – Romans 15:7

Zen: The bamboo that bends is stronger than the oak that resists and breaks.

Golf Anecdote: Tom Watson once said that accepting bad breaks with grace was key to his longevity in the game.

NO JUDGMENT AND NO EGO

Judgment impedes clarity. Ego demands perfection. Acceptance clears the mind and opens the heart. In golf, letting go of ego allows us to play freely and authentically.

Let me ask you, what is your definition of a "good putt?" Many people define a good putt as one that goes in the hole, and any putt that doesn't fall is a bad putt. I disagree.

Have you ever hit a putt that was right online, and then it hit a small unseen rock or a footprint or a leaf or caught a gust of wind causing the ball to veer off course and miss the hole? Have you ever hit a putt just the way you wanted, only to watch it roll past the hole because you misread the break? Have you ever hit a putt that caught a big portion of the hole but lipped out or went 360 degrees around the hole but did not fall? And how well do your putts fall when you play on greens that are freshly covered with sand and aeration holes?

I am asking that you consider an alternate definition of what constitutes a "good putt." To me, a good putt is one you hit on the line and with the speed you desire. In essence, I define a good putt as one that is hit just as I planned. If I hit my putt where I want and with the speed I want, then I've hit a good putt.

All I can control is the line and the speed of the putt. I can't control whether or not it falls. My putt can be thrown off by any number of things along the way. And, if I hit a putt with the line and speed I intend and it doesn't fall, I will walk away with the confidence of knowing I hit a good putt.

My confidence is not determined by a result which I cannot control. I can control the process, but I can't control the result. Make a good stroke. The rest is up to gravity and good fortune.

I find this approach to be helpful away from the golf course as well. There is so very little I can truly control when it comes to results. But I can control my process—my effort and my attitude. And, when my effort and attitude are good, then good results usually follow. When I accept and surrender to what I cannot control, good results usually follow, and my stress level is greatly reduced.

The truth is, I live with a very low stress level. Why? Because I believe in acceptance and surrender—those concepts are the antidote for the stressors of judgment and ego.

Webster defines judgment as the ability to form opinions, make decisions, or reach conclusions based on careful thought, discernment, or consideration. For this discussion, I am talking about judging others and being judged by others.

Judging others is a fool's game, a folly in which we are often wrong. We see or hear something and quickly form an opinion. We judge a person as good or bad based on this opinion. We assign motivations to their actions or inactions. And when we are in the other chair of this dynamic, we are judged by others based on their impressions or opinions of us.

But how complete are these impressions and opinions? How much do we really know when judgments are made? The imagery of an iceberg is useful here. My 66 years of experience tells me that most opinions are formed based on a small amount of information above the water line. And those opinions are missing the great majority, the large berg beneath the surface.

I have been so very wrong about others, and others have been so very wrong about me, that I find no value in trying to judge or be judged. Judging others is a game of illusion. If you want to know who or what or why, then ask. Be curious. Connect. Go deeper. Accept and surrender to the fact that you don't know what you don't know, particularly when it comes to other people and the motivations for why they do what they do. Accept and surrender to the fact that they are people who deserve respect and the benefit of the doubt. Don't judge—be curious. And accept people as they are.

What about other people's opinions of you? Don't get hung up on what others think of you. They don't know you. They don't know your intentions and motivations. Their judgments are wrong. Take them with a grain of salt. Judging others is a disservice to you and them. Judgment is problematic.

The same is true of ego. Webster defines ego as the self, the "I" as contrasted with others in the world, including pride, confidence, or self-importance—sometimes healthy, sometimes inflated.

Ryan Holiday has a great book on this subject, *Ego is the Enemy*. Holiday writes, "It has wrecked the careers of promising young geniuses. It has evaporated great fortunes and run companies into the ground. It has made adversity unbearable and turned struggle into shame. Its name? Ego. And it is the enemy—of ambition, of success, of resilience. It is the internal opponent warned against by every great philosopher, in our most lasting stories and countless works of art, in every culture, in every age. In the pages of this book, we fight to destroy it, before it destroys us."

While our ego can be helpful, it can also be our worst enemy. Have you ever known anyone you would describe as "being their own worst enemy"? I have. I have been that person. And I have played golf with a few people who fit that mold.

Rather than accepting their shots, rather than accepting their limitations, ego driven people fight with themselves and their results. It isn't pretty. The first step in growing is accepting where we are and our need for growth. Accept. Surrender. The only person you are fooling is yourself.

I want to be as clear as I can here: if you want to live a low-stress life filled with happiness, it all starts with acceptance and surrender. Accept who you are as you are and accept others as they are. Then you can work on improvement. Accept that you are doing the best you can do, and so are the people around you. Then you can work on being better.

I love Maya Angelou's thought here, "be the best you can be. And, when you can be better, then be better." No judgment, no ego. Accept. Surrender. Be.

Inspirational Quote: Don't judge each day by the harvest you reap but by the seeds that you plant. – Robert Louis Stevenson

Scripture: Do not judge, or you too will be judged. – Matthew 7:1

Zen: When I let go of what I am, I become what I might be. – Lao Tzu

Golf Anecdote: Annika Sörenstam focused on process over perfection, allowing her to stay grounded and consistent.

SUMMARY

Acceptance is a quiet strength. It frees us from the illusion of control, dissolves judgment, and opens us to grace. Surrender is also a quiet strength. When we surrender, we quit fighting and resisting, choosing instead to work in cooperation with reality. On the course and in life, acceptance and surrender are on the path to peace and presence.

HOLE RESULT: 345-YARD PAR 4

The concepts of acceptance and surrender dictate that we play the hole as it is designed. A solid drive down the right side of the fairway leaves us 125 yards to the front right pin. A cut right 8-iron finds the green eight feet left of the hole. We make a good stroke and start the ball half cup left of the hole with perfect speed. Gravity carries the ball down the slope and into the left corner of the cup. Birdie! Using Next (Hole 7) and Acceptance gets a stroke back. Score: 1 over through 8.

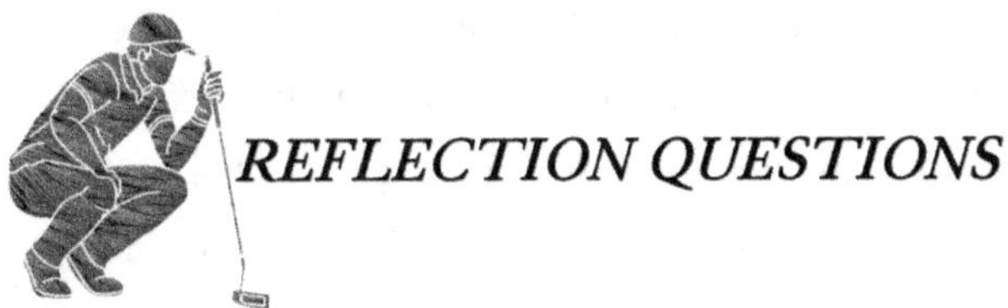

REFLECTION QUESTIONS

1. What are you resisting where acceptance can help you?
2. What areas of your life are you trying to control that might benefit from surrender?
3. How does judgment affect your ability to be present and compassionate?
4. Where are you experiencing ego as your enemy?

BOOK RECOMMENDATION: *THE LET THEM THEORY* BY MEL ROBBINS

Mel Robbins's book, *The Let Them Theory* speaks to acceptance by encouraging us to stop trying to control others and to surrender by releasing the illusion that we can dictate their choices. It's about reclaiming peace by letting people be who they are, even when their actions don't align with our expectations.

Acceptance in The Let Them Theory:

- Acceptance does not equal agreement: Robbins emphasizes that acceptance means acknowledging reality without resistance, not condoning or approving of it.

- Letting people be themselves: The theory teaches that when you stop trying to change or manage others, you gain clarity about who they truly are.
- Boundaries and detachment: Acceptance here is about recognizing where your control ends and theirs begins. It's a boundary-setting practice that reduces anxiety and frees emotional energy.
- Practical example: If someone consistently shows they don't prioritize your relationship, Robbins suggests believing their actions instead of making excuses. Acceptance allows you to redirect your energy toward people who genuinely care.

In short, Mel Robbins' *Let Them Theory* reframes acceptance as acknowledging reality without resistance, while surrender is releasing control over others' choices. Both practices lead to freedom, clarity, and inner peace.

SONG: "WHAT A WONDERFUL WORLD" BY LOUIS ARMSTRONG

Louis Armstrong's classic hit, "What a Wonderful World" encourages acceptance by inviting listeners to acknowledge the beauty of life even amid hardship, choosing gratitude and wonder over resistance or despair. It's a musical embodiment of accepting reality as it is—both its pain and its joy—while focusing on curiosity and what remains good.

The 1967 song uses simple wonders as anchors by cataloging everyday images—green trees, red roses, babies crying—as the song models acceptance of life's ordinary gifts, reminding us that peace can be found in what is, not in what we wish were different.

MOVIE TO WATCH: *SHREK* (2001)

Shrek features acceptance by showing that true happiness comes from embracing who you are and allowing others to love you for your authentic self. Both Shrek and Fiona learn to accept their identities, flaws, and differences rather than conforming to societal expectations.

Acceptance of Others:

- Breaking stereotypes: *Shrek* flips fairy-tale conventions. The "ugly ogre" becomes the hero, the princess embraces imperfection, and the sidekick is a talkative donkey. This challenges viewers to accept others beyond appearances and labels.
- Love beyond expectations: The romance between Shrek and Fiona shows that acceptance of each other's true selves is stronger than societal ideals of beauty or status.
- Friendship as acceptance: Shrek and Donkey's bond demonstrates that accepting quirks and differences is what makes relationships meaningful.

In short, Shrek is a masterclass in acceptance—of self, of others, and of life's imperfections. Its enduring message is that authenticity, not conformity, leads to love, belonging, and peace.

9 HOLE #9: CONFIDENCE & TRUST

175-YARD PAR 3

This hole, called "Confidence and Trust," is a challenging par 3. The difficult tee shot plays 165 yards over water to a slightly elevated green. If you miss right, you will be in a deep sand trap. Short left is another deep sand trap, and if you carry the sand left, your ball will likely bound down and left out of bounds. Over the green leaves a blind chip shot back up the hill. In short, there is no bail-out area here. You must hit the green or you are likely to make a big number on this hole.

CONFIDENCE AND TRUST

Trust is the foundation of confidence and clarity. In golf, trusting your swing, your club, and your decision is often more important than choosing the perfect strategy. This chapter explores the tension between trust and doubt, and how decisiveness—even with the wrong club—can lead to better outcomes than hesitation with the right one.

Golf is the only sport where your opponent is grass, wind, and yourself. And the greatest opponent, by far, is yourself. The linkage of mind and body is essential for success in golf. And the weak link for most golfers is the mind.

Bobby Jones, perhaps the greatest to ever play the game, was quoted as saying, "The toughest four inches to conquer on the golf course is the four inches between your ears." Jones is so very right.

The golfer's mind, uncontrolled, can be a place of great suffering and turmoil. The game can be so very humbling and frustrating that the mind of the golfer can be a hotbed for seeds of doubt.

Doubt is a silent saboteur. It creeps in just before the swing, often just before contact. Confidence and trust, on the other hand, empower action. In golf, trusting your ability, preparation, and instincts leads to solid execution.

My good friend Ron Nahser has an interesting habit when he plays a water hole. When he is preparing to play over a pond, Ron will change balls. He puts his good ball in his pocket and drops a scruffy junk ball to attempt his next shot. What does the act of changing balls tell you about Ron's mindset?

When Ron changes to a water ball, one he doesn't mind losing, he has already admitted defeat. This is not only doubt, it's defeat. Ron has already lost that ball before he hits it. And what do you expect his success rate is when hitting over water? If you said, "almost zero," you would be correct.

I finally got after Ron for this routine when we played last. I told him, "Just trust your swing. Don't change balls, change your thinking. This shot is just like when you were on the range. If you hit your 7-iron right, that water is not even close to being in play!" I was so happy for Ron when he hit his good ball over the water and onto the left edge of the green. Confidence and trust are good things!

You see, the problem with doubt is that it makes a remote possibility seem so real that it creates near certainty. Fear makes us focus on the possible negative outcome, and it shakes our confidence and trust. The key is to focus not on doubt and fear, but to focus on trust and success. Focus on the positive outcome and trust your ability—do not fill your mind with your fear.

I have played this hole hundreds of times. And yes, I've hit my ball into the sand left and right. Yes, I've hit my ball over the green only to face a very difficult blind chip shot. I've hit balls into the water and out of bounds. I've made some big scores on this hole.

I have also made several birdies here, and I've nearly made a hole in one a few times. Typically, I make par on this hole. Why? Because I trust my swing. I have confidence in my ability. I know this tee shot is dangerous, but I focus on the center of the green. And just before I start my swing, I tell myself, "You've got this, Scott. It's just like hitting balls on the range. Good tempo. Solid contact. Trust is a must." And I trust my swing. Usually, the results are good. Trust is a must!

How do the concepts of Confidence and Trust help us off the course? The processes are the same. It doesn't matter where you are or what you're doing. Your confidence and trust in yourself and your ability must be greater than your doubts and fears. Your focus must be on where you want to be. It's fine to be aware of danger, just don't focus on it. Do not get fixated on the negatives. Have confidence and trust yourself.

Psychologists speak of "the self-fulfilling prophecy." The self-fulfilling prophecy is a process in which we create in reality (through our own actions) what we first expect to happen in our thoughts. This is the foundation of the saying, "Whether you believe you can, or you can't, you're right." It is the same concept upon which Napoleon Hill built a legacy with his emphasis on visualization in his book *Think and Grow Rich*.

What we create in our minds, we create in reality. This is why your trust in your own ability must be greater than your doubts, and your confidence must be greater than your fears. Carry these formulas with you always: Trust > doubt. Confidence > fear.

Inspirational Quote: Trust yourself. You know more than you think you do. – Benjamin Spock

Scripture: Trust in the Lord with all your heart and lean not on your own understanding. – Proverbs 3:5

Zen: The mind that trusts itself is light and free.

Golf Anecdote: Dustin Johnson, known for his calm demeanor, often attributes his success to trusting his swing and not overthinking.

DECISIVENESS OVER PERFECTION

Golf teaches us that a committed swing with the wrong club often yields better results than a hesitant swing with the right one. Decisiveness breeds confidence, while indecision breeds doubt and error.

One of the greatest challenges a golfer faces is the "in-between yardage." Even the best players in the world have great difficulty when indecision creeps into their process. "Is this an easy 6-iron or a hard 7-iron? Do I want to hit a draw or a cut shot into the pin?"

Indecision creates doubt, and doubt creates bad swings and bad results. When you doubt, you weaken commitment, and you unsettle confidence and trust. Sports psychologist Bob Rotella talks about this in his book *Golf is not a Game of Perfect*.

Rotella's experience produces this wisdom: "The wrong club hit with commitment is better than the right club struck with indecision."

If you watch televised PGA Tour golf, you will notice the most frequent statement a caddie gives his professional golfer is "Commit to the shot." This is another way to say, "Trust your swing." Do not let indecision create doubt. Rather, let commitment fuel trust.

Inspirational Quote: Indecision is the thief of opportunity. – Jim Rohn

Scripture: Let your yes be yes, and your no, no. – Matthew 5:37

Zen: When you walk, walk. When you sit, sit. But don't wobble.

Golf Anecdote: Brooks Koepka once said he'd rather commit to a decision and be wrong than hesitate and lose focus.

BUILDING CONFIDENCE AND TRUST THROUGH REPETITION

Confidence and trust are built through repetition and experience. The more you practice, the more you trust your instincts. In golf this means trusting your swing because you've honed it over time. You are confident because you have prepared yourself for this moment.

One of the most important lessons I've learned is "Success breeds success." This is the seed of confidence and trust. Confidence and trust in your own abilities is reinforced by success. And what is the seed that yields trust and success? Practice and repetition. As Tony Robbins says, "Repetition is the mother of skill."

There is no secret here. Trust and success are the result of practicing the right things right. Muscle memory is developed through repetition. Game time performance is sharpened through practice. If you want to improve your putting, spend time in practice.

If you want to be a better chipper, practice chipping. If you want to drive the ball better, practice with the driver. Repetition is the mother of skill. Confidence and trust are built through practice and successful preparation.

One word of encouragement here: if you want to get better at something, ask for help from someone who has great skill where you are seeking to improve. There is no shame in learning from the best. In fact, seeking help is a great strategy for improvement. Find someone who is highly skilled at what you want to do and ask them to help you learn what they are doing. Success leaves trails. If you do what successful people do, you will likely be successful too. When you realize that you don't know what you don't know, why not choose to learn from the best?

Get help. Acquire knowledge. Do the work. As Tiger Woods says, "In golf, you have to earn it in the dirt. Practice. And keep practicing until it is routine." Repetition builds skill. Practice builds confidence and trust in your own abilities. Doubt is eliminated when you stand over a shot knowing you have hit this same shot successfully hundreds of times before. Trust > doubt. Confidence > fear.

This same concept applies off the course too. Whether you are learning guitar, making a presentation, or cooking a meal, the key is to practice. Rehearse. Build confidence, trust, and skill through practice and repetition. Every musician started out as a beginner at some point. Every presenter was a beginner too. Everyone who is good at what they do has been a beginner and then learned and sharpened their skills through practice. They may be gifted, but they honored their gifts through the hard work of practice and preparation.

Eric Clapton was once a beginner. Every chef started out imperfectly. And every accomplished presenter has worked through nerves and learned to trust their abilities through practice and repetition. Toastmasters International is a renowned organization that has one primary focus—to help people develop public speaking skills through practice and repetition.

Inspirational Quote: Practice does not make perfect. Practice makes permanent. – Vince Lombardi

Scripture: Whatever you have learned or received or heard from me or seen in me—put it into practice. – Philippians 4:9

Zen: The way to do is to be. – Lao Tzu

Golf Anecdote: Gary Player tells the story of a spectator calling him "lucky" after he holed several bunker shots in one tournament. Player's response was, "Well, the harder I practice, the luckier I get."

SUMMARY

Confidence and Trust are choices and practices. They overcome doubt, empower decisiveness, and grow through repetition. On the course and in life, confidence and trust lead to clarity, success, and peace.

HOLE RESULT: 175-YARD PAR 3

The pin is located on the back left portion of the green. This is a sucker pin, one which we do not need to aim at. There is no rule in golf that says you must aim at every pin. Left is dead here. I grab my 5-wood and focus on the center of the green. As I get ready to swing, I remind myself that I have hit this green over one hundred times before. I just need to make good contact—this shot does not have to be perfect, just good. A solid swing leads to a good shot finding the right center of the green. A two-putt from 30 feet results in an easy par 3 on a demanding hole. Trust > doubt. Confidence > fear. Score on the front 9: 1 over par 37.

REFLECTION QUESTIONS

1. Where in your life do you struggle with doubt and/or fear?
2. How can you practice decisiveness in your daily choices?
3. What habits can you build to strengthen your confidence and trust in yourself and others?
4. Where have you grown confidence and trust in your life through practice and repetition?

BOOK RECOMMENDATION: *ATOMIC HABITS* BY JAMES CLEAR

The NY Times bestseller *Atomic Habits* by James Clear was first published in 2018. *Atomic Habits* focuses on the power of small, consistent actions—tiny habits that compound into remarkable results over time.

Clear's core idea centers on the fact that habits shape identity. Clear argues that habits aren't just actions; they're votes for the type of person you believe yourself to be. Each repetition of a habit reinforces identity: "I am the kind of person who prepares," rather than "I hope I'll be ready."

There's a natural parallel here: Clear's emphasis on small, repeatable actions mirrors the discipline of golf and the building of confidence and self-trust through practice and preparation:

- Preparation creates evidence. When you've put in the work—whether it's practice swings, journaling, or rehearsing—you accumulate proof that you can rely on yourself.
- Confidence and trust are built through consistency. Just as Clear emphasizes tiny, repeated actions, preparation is about showing up daily, even when the stakes feel low. Over time, this builds confidence and trust that you'll show up when the stakes are high.
- Preparation reduces uncertainty. In golf, standing over a shot with the memory of countless hours of practice creates calm. In life, preparation gives you the same anchor—your body and mind know you've already rehearsed success.

SONG: "A MATTER OF TRUST" BY BILLY JOEL

Billy Joel's hit "A Matter of Trust" is a song that emphasizes that trust isn't automatic—it's earned and reinforced over time. Joel sings about the fragility of trust, how it can be broken, and how it must be rebuilt through consistent action. The refrain, "It's a matter of trust," underscores that trust is the foundation of resilience and connection.

MOVIE TO WATCH: *THE KARATE KID* (1984)

The Karate Kid is a masterful work showing practice disguised as repetition. Mr. Miyagi has Daniel perform seemingly mundane tasks—waxing cars, painting fences, and sanding floors. These repetitive motions build muscle memory and discipline, even though Daniel doesn't see it at first.

Daniel's confidence and self-trust are built through preparation. When Daniel finally realizes those motions translate into defensive techniques, he learns that practice has quietly built his confidence. He can trust himself because he's already rehearsed the movements thousands of times.

Identity shift: much like James Clear's idea of habits as "votes for identity," Daniel transforms from an insecure teenager into someone who trusts in his own capability—because practice has proven it.

Self-trust is not about bravado—it's about knowing you've already done the work. Like Daniel LaRusso sanding floors, golfers often wonder if the repetition matters. But every swing, every drill, every routine is a quiet rehearsal of trust. Both on and off the course, when the test comes, you don't have to hope. You know, because practice and preparation have already written the answer.

10 HOLE #10: PERSONAL RESPONSIBILITY & ACCOUNTABILITY

537-YARD PAR 5

We start the back nine facing a hole named "Personal Responsibility." This is a wonderful par 5, well trapped and cut through trees while having out of bounds on both sides. The tee shot requires 130 yards of carry over water and tall grass. Sand traps are reachable both left and right from the tee. The second shot angles slightly right with a sand trap on the right edge of the fairway. A good layup will leave you 75 yards to a green that slopes from back left to right front. A small pond and thick heather guard the right side of the hole from 60 yards out and running up to the green. Danger lurks, but this is a chance for birdie.

PERSONAL RESPONSIBILITY AND ACCOUNTABILITY

Personal responsibility is ownership. Accountability is integrity. In golf and in life, we play our own ball, and we keep our own scorecard. This chapter explores the power of personal responsibility, the courage to own our actions, and the grace of being accountable to others.

Golf is a "gentleman's game" with rich traditions based on honesty and personal responsibility. There are no referees or umpires. Each golfer is called to the highest standards of fair play. We hit our own shots, keep our own score, and we apply the rules and call penalties on ourselves. That is what gentlemen do. Gentlemen take responsibility for their own actions, and they do this with honesty above all else.

Webster's Dictionary defines personal responsibility as "The quality or state of being responsible, accountable, or answerable." In essence, it means individuals are expected to take ownership of their actions, decisions, and the consequences that follow.

In golf, I am responsible for my shots, the results of my play, and the actions that form my character. I am answerable to both myself and the other players in my group. I am called to play within and to apply the rules of the game. No cheating. No lying. No questions asked or inferred by my actions and choices. Honesty should be clear and evident for all to see.

The golf ball goes where I hit it. There is no one to blame for my results. When I find my ball in the trees it is because I hit it there. When my ball sails out of bounds or gets baptized in a pond, I hit it there. Yes, I can be distracted by other players or wind or birds, but I cannot blame them for my bad results. Similarly, when results are good it is a function of my good swings. In golf, there is no hiding, and there is no one else to blame.

Most importantly, golf teaches that I am responsible for my own thinking, my own choices, and my own attitude. No one else is responsible for my mindset. No one else is responsible for my behavior. Whether I behave well or act like a bad sport, it is up to me. Whether the sun shines or the weather is gloomy, it is up to me to play with a sunny disposition. Responsibility begins with acknowledging our own role in every outcome.

The question is: Do you accept responsibility for your attitude and behavior, or do you give this power to circumstances? Do you control your attitude, approach, and results, or do you let results dictate your attitude and approach? Are your enjoyment of the game and its results your responsibility, or do you find a way to blame others for your experience?

Life is like golf in this respect. There is only one person responsible for your thoughts, your attitude, your temperament, your execution, and results—and that is you. Whether an outcome is good or bad is up to you. Results and perspective are a matter of your own personal choices. Do you accept responsibility for this? Do you claim your power and claim your responsibility, or do you cede your power to someone else via blame?

Who is responsible for your mood? Who is responsible for you having a good day or a bad day? Who is responsible for what you say and do or what you don't do? Yes, we are and will be influenced by the environment around us. But we are each ultimately responsible regardless of what influences us.

Can you make me mad? Can you make me happy? Can you make me do something or not do something? Yes, you can influence me. Yes, I can react involuntarily (laughter for example). But your influence and stimulus are something I am responsible for responding to. Notice the subtle but powerful difference between reacting and responding. Reacting is a powerless action. Responding is a powerful and responsible intentional action.

Inspirational Quote: The price of greatness is responsibility. – Winston Churchill

Scripture: Each of you should carry your own load. – Galatians 6:5

Zen: You are the sky. Everything else—it's just the weather.

Golf Anecdote: Jack Nicklaus once called a penalty on himself that no one else saw. That moment defined his character as much as any championship.

ACCOUNTABILITY TO SELF AND OTHERS

Accountability is not about guilt—it's about growth. It's the willingness to be answerable, to learn, and to improve. In golf, we keep our own score, but we also play the game with others. Integrity builds trust, both on the course and in relationships.

In golf, we are accountable. We are not only responsible for our score, but we are also accountable for our score. By saying accountable, I mean we are answerable for our score. We must answer to ourselves, our playing partners, and all who play the game. That can be a tall order. It can be hard to claim a 9 on a hole for the scorecard. It can be difficult to finish the round and admit your score was near the national debt. It is no fun to struggle for four hours and have both you and your friends leave the course knowing you recorded an embarrassing score.

That is accountability. We have a duty to account for our play —good or bad. Golf makes accountability easier to live with. How is that? The game requires everyone to be accountable. It is part of the fabric of the game. And that fabric has ensnared every golfer at some point. We have all had to claim bad days and bad holes.

Do you know who recorded the all-time highest (worst) score on a single hole on the PGA Tour? The person accountable for that worst score is three-time major winner Tommy Armour. In fact, less than one week after winning the 1927 U.S. Open, Armour recorded a 23 on the 17th hole during the Shawnee Open while hitting 10 balls out of bounds.

Other high scores on a single hole as recorded by the best players in the world include a 19 by John Daly (2025 Sanford International) and a 16 by Kevin Na (2011 Valero Texas Open). The interesting thing about Na's 16 is that he was 4 under par on the other 17 holes of that round. Na went on to win his first PGA Tour title six months later. That is golf. That is accountability, good and not.

Like golf, life brings us both good and bad. Like golf, life is designed as a linear path played in a very crooked reality. And as with golf, in life we are accountable.

We are, first and foremost, accountable to ourselves. It takes great character to be honest with ourselves and to be accountable to ourselves. I will admit that I have not always had this character. I've had to learn it. I've had to look in the mirror and commit to being better. The interesting thing is that this gets easier with age and experience.

When you let go of perfection and face your errors and limitations honestly, it gets easier to accept yourself as you are and commit to learning and improvement. Accountability is actually an empowering act. Accountability is a freeing choice. When you no longer need to keep up an image, a façade, it is easy to be accountable. It is necessary to be accountable. To refuse to be accountable to yourself is to be delusional. Do you want to be real and grow, or would you rather choose to be delusional and stagnate?

Accountability is a critical step toward improving self-esteem. When you can be honest with yourself about your failings, you can also be real about your intentions and your successes. A good self-image is built on accountability. In fact, you cannot have a good self-image without accountability. You can be faux or you can be real. Be real.

Accountability extends beyond ourselves. We are also

accountable to others, to those around us and to those we don't even know. We have duties to family, friends, co-workers and employers, and to our community and our world. This is called our legacy.

What is your legacy? What do you want your legacy to be? Think about it. Are you "accountable to the dash?" The dash? That is the space on your tombstone between your date of birth and the day you die. The dash is what you did with that time. The dash is how you used the gift of your life—all your choices and actions and impact in this world. The dash is the accountability of your time on earth.

Inspirational Quote: Accountability breeds response-ability. – Stephen Covey

Scripture: So then, each of us will give an account of ourselves to God. – Romans 14:12

Zen: What the superior man seeks is in himself; what the small man seeks is in others. - Confucius

Golf Anecdote: Jordan Spieth's candid post-round interviews often reflect his accountability—he owns both his triumphs and his mistakes.

COURAGE AND GRACE

Taking responsibility requires courage. Offering accountability requires grace. Golf teaches us to face the consequences of our choices with humility and to support others in doing the same.

I have four tattoos on my arms; my right inside forearm hosts a Celtic Trinity symbol and a Japanese Kanji symbol for Truth. My left inside forearm holds a Siddhartha (Buddha) and a Kanji symbol for Courage. These are on the insides of my forearms so I can see them easily. I want to see them and be conscious of what I am about. As you can tell from this book and its design and messages, I am a Zen Christian who wants to live in Truth and Courage.

These tattoos are outward signs of internal responsibility and accountability. I am branded with what I want to be about and known for. The tattoos are signs of my thoughts and commitments. One of the reasons I chose these tattoos came from the desire to be accountable and responsible for living in harmony with these symbols.

I want my dash to reflect these beliefs and characteristics. It is my hope that my thoughts, words, and actions speak so loudly that you can clearly see the courageous Zen Christian living truth in all I do. I am responsible for living this out, and I am accountable to myself and to my friends and family for living this out. This is not easy. In fact, it is very difficult.

Owning my character is challenging. Living in alignment with ideals is difficult. Taking responsibility and being accountable for 100% of my words and deeds is a tall order. It is so much easier to avoid, to blame others, to give up my power. But, at the end of the day, I am responsible and accountable to me. I know what my intentions and my actions are about.

The courageous thing to do, the right thing to do, is to look in the mirror and be honest and open with myself. What have I done well? Where do I need to be better? Where do I need to forgive and heal myself and help to heal others because I have done damage?

This courage is needed on the golf course with every round. This courage is needed off the course with every day. The good news? The reward of this courage is strength, learning, and growth. The best thing about knowing you need to be better is that it leads you to grow and be better! It is not easy, but nothing worthwhile is. Courage implies hard work and going forward when it is difficult. This is when and where you grow. This is grace.

Being responsible and accountable is the act of taking the sculptor's hammer and chisel and chipping away all that is not you. That is how Michelangelo said he made his famous statue of David—he took the stone and chipped away all that was not David. What a wonderful metaphor for building character.

Be courageous. Own your thoughts, words, and actions. Take hold of the hammer and chisel and chip away all that is not you! That is responsibility. That is accountability.

Inspirational Quote: You must take personal responsibility. You cannot change the circumstances, the seasons, or the wind, but you can change yourself. – Jim Rohn

Scripture: Whoever conceals their sins does not prosper, but the one who confesses and renounces them finds mercy. – Proverbs 28:13

Zen: Nothing ever goes away until it has taught us what we need to know. — Pema Chödrön

Golf Anecdote: Lee Trevino once said, "You don't know what pressure is until you play for five dollars with only two in your pocket." Responsibility is showing up anyway.

SUMMARY

Responsibility is the foundation of character. Accountability is the bridge to trust. The two are related ideas, but they operate at different levels of selfhood and relationship.

Personal responsibility is internal, individual, and self-governed. It's about who you choose to be and how you conduct yourself regardless of who is watching. Accountability is what happens when your behavior intersects with other people, commitments, or systems. Accountability is relational, observable, and socially governed.

In golf and in life, owning our actions and being answerable to others leads to growth, connection, and integrity.

HOLE RESULT: 537-YARD PAR 5

A solid drive down the left side of the fairway sets up a good angle to finish this hole. The three wood second shot starts a bit right and bounces toward the pond and cat tails down the right side. After a short search, the ball is found in the thick grass along the hazard line. Is it in the hazard? Yes, just barely. Can the ball be hit? Not as it lies. You decide to take a penalty drop and hit your fourth shot from within two club lengths of the spot where the ball was found in the hazard.

After knocking a wedge to 18 feet, a two-putt resulted in a disappointing bogey 6. That is personal responsibility and accountability. Score through 10 holes: 2 over par.

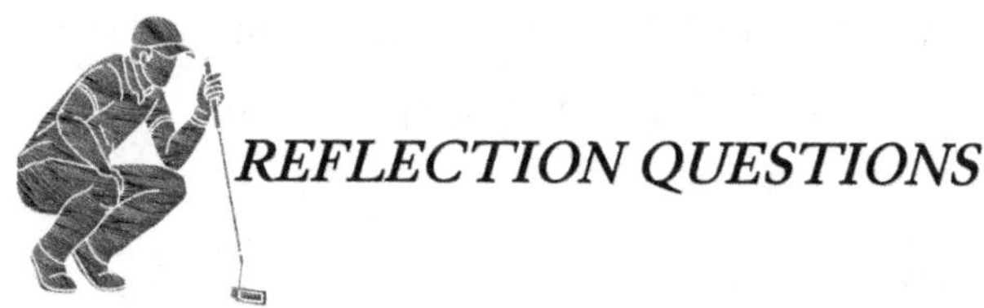

REFLECTION QUESTIONS

1. Where in your life are you avoiding responsibility, and what might change if you embraced it?
2. How does accountability strengthen your relationship with yourself and others?
3. What daily practices help you stay honest with yourself and others?
4. What do you want to chip away in your character?

BOOK RECOMMENDATION: *THE 7 DECISIONS* BY ANDY ANDREWS

In Andy Andrews' book *The 7 Decisions*, personal responsibility and accountability are the foundation of every principle. Andrews frames success as a matter of conscious choices rather than circumstances. The very first of the seven decisions is explicitly about taking responsibility for your life. The other six decisions build on that mindset by requiring accountability in attitude, action, learning, and perseverance.

Why This Matters:

- Responsibility is empowerment: Andrews reframes responsibility not as a burden but as the key to freedom.
- Accountability drives transformation: Each decision requires you to hold yourself accountable daily, not just in theory.

SONG: "MAN IN THE MIRROR" BY MICHAEL JACKSON

Michael Jackson's "Man in the Mirror" is essentially an anthem of personal responsibility and accountability, expressed through music. The song insists that change begins with the individual: "If you wanna make the world a better place, take a look at yourself and make a change."

This lyric is a direct call to accountability—before pointing fingers outward, you must first examine your own actions, choices, and mindset. The "Man in the Mirror" symbolizes the inner confrontation we all must have. Responsibility starts with honest self-assessment.

Instead of blaming society, politics, or others, the song emphasizes that transformation is a personal duty. By holding yourself accountable, you influence the world around you. Responsibility is not isolated, it radiates outward.

"Man in the Mirror" stresses that growth and change are not external gifts but internal commitments, and it stresses that courage is required for accountability to work.

MOVIE TO WATCH: *DEAD POETS SOCIETY* (1989)

Dead Poets Society is a challenging and thought-provoking film that depicts the importance of personal responsibility and accountability by showing how individuals must choose whether to conform or take ownership of their lives, voices, and passions.

Key Themes of Responsibility & Accountability:

- Carpe Diem ("Seize the Day")

Mr. Keating's famous mantra is a call to personal responsibility. It challenges students to stop waiting for permission and instead hold themselves accountable for making their lives extraordinary.

- Individual Choice vs. Conformity

Welton Academy represents rigid tradition and external control. Keating urges students to think for themselves, highlighting that accountability means owning your choices rather than blindly following authority.

- Neil Perry's Story

Neil's passion for acting collides with his father's expectations. His tragic arc underscores the consequences of failing to reconcile personal responsibility with external accountability. It's a reminder that true responsibility involves courage to live authentically, even under pressure.

- Todd Anderson's Growth

Todd begins shy and hesitant, but through Keating's encouragement, he learns to take responsibility for his voice. His final stand, "O Captain, my Captain," is an act of accountability, owning his beliefs despite institutional punishment.

This film resonates because it displays responsibility as empowerment: the film reframes responsibility not as obedience but as the freedom to choose. The movie also reveals accountability in action: each student must decide whether to conform or to act on their passions, and those decisions carry consequences.

11 HOLE #11: ACTION, EFFORT, AND SHOWING UP

403-YARD PAR 4

Our 11th hole is called "Taking Action." This is a challenging par 4, well trapped with the fairway cut through trees leading to a difficult two-tiered green. The tee shot requires placement between a large sand trap on the right and a narrow trap covering the left center of the fairway at 225 yards. The second shot angles slightly right with a sand trap fronting the right side of the green. The back and front halves of the green are separated by a three-foot ridge which challenges chipping and putting. Par is a great score here, particularly when the pin is back on the upper ridge.

ACTION AND EFFORT

Action is the movement that propels the shot. Effort is the bridge between intention and impact. In golf and in life, it's not enough to dream—we must swing. This chapter explores the importance of taking action, the value of showing up, and the quiet power of persistence.

Dreams remain dreams until they are acted upon. In golf, as in life, it is not enough to visualize the perfect swing or imagine success—you must step onto the tee, take the club in hand, and execute the shot. Action transforms intention into reality.

One of the great, and most challenging, qualities of golf is its combination of the mental and physical aspects of the game. Success in golf requires you to both think well and to flawlessly execute your shot. As the great wordsmith Yogi Berra would say, "Golf is 90% mental. The other half is physical."

Every golfer, regardless of skill level, has experienced that heavenly moment, that rare shot, where the plan and the picture of the shot in your mind are produced physically by your body and your swing. I truly enjoy the shot from the trees that requires a perfectly controlled trajectory through a small gap and curved hard right or left to find the target that cannot be seen from where you are. I love playing the most challenging shots-the high cut, the low draw, and the knock down shot, flighted perfectly into the wind.

I don't know with certainty what heaven is like. I hope it is a place where every shot you hit matches the picture you have for that shot before you swing the club. To be successful in golf, you must control your emotions and thinking, and you must control your golf ball. For me, flawlessly executing that pictured shot is heaven on earth. There is no better experience than being "in the flow / in the zone" where you are controlling both your emotions and your golf ball, when you see the shot in your mind and then you make it happen with flawless execution.

Execution is the process and result of the action and effort of your swing. You can't think your ball off the tee—you must act and hit the ball for it to move. This is where golf gets tough. I can picture a perfect shot, but nothing happens until I employ action and effort to produce the shot. The mind and body must work together and be in sync for anything good to happen. And it's easy to get out of sync.

I can't think a putt into the hole—I must use action and effort to produce the stroke that sends the ball into the cup. I love putting. This is where the scoring is really done. And I enjoy the process of putting: choose the line, choose the speed, pick the target, relax, trust your ability, make a good stroke. The putt starts with the picture, and it ends with the action and effort of the stroke. The results will be good if the execution matches the thinking.

That's how life is, right? You plan, you envision, and then you execute with action and effort. If you want to go on a trip, what do you do? You choose a destination, determine when you are going, how you will get there, and buy tickets if needed. You figure out your lodging needs and make reservations. You make arrangements with friends you might visit. You pack and you choose some sights to see as you plan your agenda. Then, the time comes to fly and check into your hotel, eat at the restaurants, and visit the sites and friends you wanted to see. You plan, and then you act.

In my accounting management career with State Farm Insurance, I became a big believer in the Quality Management process of Edwards Deming. In short, Deming espoused a continuous improvement process of four steps; Plan, Do, Check, and Adjust. I've found this to be a useful model in all facets of my life. No matter what I am doing, I find it helpful to plan, do, check, and adjust. This is what learning and improvement in life are all about.

What happens if you don't act? What is the result if you do not invest the effort? Your plans are wasted. Your dreams are unfulfilled. Your wishes remain wishes and your goals are unmet. Your mental energy produces nothing. It is like placing your golf ball on a tee and never swinging the club. You, and your ball, go nowhere. You are stuck. The world moves on around and without you. There is no movement, no progress, no learning.

That is the importance and value of action and effort—they are the difference between wishes and results. They're the difference between thinking and doing, between growing and moving forward or being stuck right where you are. All the best thinking in the world produces nothing without effort. Yes, everything begins in the mind. But action and effort are required to go from the mind to manifestation in the real world.

Bills don't pay themselves. Your refrigerator does not fill itself. Your laundry does not wash itself. All of these needs require action. There are things we simply must do. Educational degrees don't earn themselves. Vacations don't plan themselves. Books don't write themselves. Fulfilling dreams requires action and effort. And that action and effort is so worthwhile when you are fulfilling your dreams.

I have a confession to make. This book has been something I've thought about writing for years, beginning in 2013. I've kept notes and articles, and I've read stories and books written by others. I started the outline and jotted down rough notes on a sheet of paper 12 years ago. But I did not take significant action to write this book until two months ago.

Why did I wait? Fear and laziness—the enemies of action and effort.

I thought about writing for years. I talked about this book for years. But I gave it little action and effort. I dabbled. I thought. I gathered. I considered. I wondered. I worried. Do I have enough to say? Are my thoughts important? Are they relevant? What will people think? How much time will this take? How will I write the book? What format should I use? How will I get it published? The questions and doubts were numerous and I was stuck in mental paralysis.

What changed? Why write the book now? Why go forward in the face of all these questions and doubts? How did I move beyond fear and laziness? The answer: inspiration—coupled with action and effort. The first step is the hardest. I finally took the first step.

The inspiration came from three places. First, I was inspired by my brother, Mark, who completed his first album at age 72 after years of song writing and recording. Second, I was struck by a Mel Robbins podcast in which guest Emma Grede encouraged listeners to "get out of their heads and take responsibility for starting toward their goals and dreams." These two things ramped up my motivation and my desire to get under way. My fears were overcome by desire.

The third, and perhaps the most important inspiration, came from my wife. Carol encouraged me to use artificial intelligence to help me get started. I had zero involvement with AI. I had no idea how to use it or what it could do. The thought of trying AI was both unfamiliar and uncomfortable.

I was both astonished and encouraged when my one page of 19 topics on life lessons from golf became 40 pages of outlines and writing prompts. Suddenly, the doubts were gone. The first step, the hardest step, was completed. The overwhelming task was now under way and manageable. Yes, it is still challenging. But the action and effort are so very engaging and rewarding. The process of writing is both grounding and enjoyable. And it is energizing. I look forward to each new chapter. Action begets action, effort creates new effort.

The writing of this book is a validation of a lifetime of thought, action, and effort. It is also a validation, the embodiment of, Newton's first Law of Motion—the Law of Inertia which states that "An object at rest stays at rest, and an object in motion stays in motion at constant speed and direction unless acted upon by an external force." It is good to be in motion and taking action.

Let me acknowledge and address the importance of taking the hardest first steps, where life is extremely difficult, and the stakes are high. It is difficult to take the hardest action of leaving a marriage, of changing careers, of wrestling with the question of whether I should stay or should I go? It is hard to stay in an abusive relationship or a toxic work environment. It is difficult to choose the unknown even when the known is undesirable.

Only you can know the depths of despair you are wrestling with. All I can say is, be true to yourself. Take the actions and put in the best effort you can in the way you believe is best. Talk to others. Get help. Find a good counselor or life coach. Take comfort in knowing that even Tiger Woods, the best athlete on the planet, has a swing coach and a team of helpers. You do not have to deal with it alone. Know that you are loved by many people.

Seek help but make up your own mind for your own reasons. Trust your gut. Listen to your inner guide. Take action. Don't stay stuck in a miserable situation. It may be a hard decision, but the situation only changes with action and effort—whatever form that takes.

No matter what we are undertaking, the first step is the hardest. The first action is the toughest. Like waking up and going to the gym in the morning, the first step is crucial. If you stop and think about it, you may well justify skipping the workout. It is easy to be lazy and fearful. It is easy to skip a workout or a practice session or round of golf. Don't be lazy. Trust > fear. Take the first step. Show up. Follow the Nike theme—Just do it! Make progress.

Whatever you need to do, whatever you want to do, whatever you dream of doing, the key is to take the first step. Get out of your head and put action and effort to work. Show up. Give it your best. Move forward and let Newton's Law help you! Taking action is claiming your power. Giving effort is a freeing investment. Let go of whatever is holding you back and take action toward the life that is calling you! Perhaps you will write your own book in six months after years of delaying action.

Action and effort are vital in golf and life. Consider these quotes on action and effort:

An ounce of action is worth a ton of theory. – Ralph Waldo Emerson

Success seems to be connected with action. Successful men keep moving. They make mistakes, but they don't quit. – Conrad Hilton

Effort only fully releases its reward after a person refuses to quit. – Napoleon Hill

For every disciplined effort there is a multiple reward. – Jim Rohn

All the so-called 'secrets of success' will not work unless you do. – Anonymous

Determine never to be idle. No person will have occasion to complain of the want of time who never loses any. – Thomas Jefferson

Energy and persistence conquer all things. – Benjamin Franklin

Do not let what you cannot do interfere with what you can do. – John Wooden

The only place where success comes before work is in the dictionary. – Vidal Sassoon

Ideas don't work for people unwilling to do the work. – Robin Sharma

Success is the sum of small efforts, repeated day in and day out. – Robert Collier

Constant effort and frequent mistakes are the stepping stones to genius. – Elbert Hubbard

You don't have to be great to start, but you have to start to be great. – Zig Ziglar

The journey of a thousand miles begins with a single step. – Lao Tzu

A jug fills drop by drop. - Anonymous

Do, or do not. - Yoda

Thought + Action = Success – Emma Grede

Ideas inspire, but only action creates change. Progress is born not from thought alone, but from the courage to act. True growth comes when belief is paired with effort. Wisdom without movement is incomplete. The path opens only when steps are taken. Why? Because action is the antidote to stagnation. Effort is not glamorous, it's gritty. It's the early mornings, the grind and preparation, the slow progress. But over time, effort compounds. Golf teaches us that mastery is not given, it is earned through action and effort - that is true no matter what you are trying to accomplish.

Scripture: Be doers of the word, and not hearers only, deceiving yourselves. – James 1:22

Scripture: Whatever you do, work at it with all your heart, as working for the Lord. – Colossians 3:23

Zen: Knowing is not enough; we must apply. Willing is not enough; we must do. – Goethe

Golf Anecdote: Ben Hogan famously said, "The secret is in the dirt," referring to the hours of practice —action and effort— that built his legendary swing. His book, *Ben Hogan's Five Lessons: The Modern Fundamentals of Golf*, is the quintessential instruction manual on the action and effort needed to execute the golf swing.

SUMMARY

Action and effort are the engines of growth. In golf and in life, showing up, practicing, and persisting lead us toward mastery and meaning. Action and effort make good things happen!

HOLE RESULT: 396-YARD PAR 4

A solid drive down the right center of the fairway avoids the traps and sets up a good look at the green. The demanding second shot calls for a 175-yard carry over the green-side trap. The pin is back right on the upper tier of the green. This is a really tough pin to find. The shot calls for a cut three wood. The swing is good, and the ball starts perfectly toward the center of the green, and drifting right, finds the upper tier 8 feet from the stick. This may be the best shot of the day. The birdie putt is struck beautifully, with perfect speed, and it gradually breaks 6 inches from left to right, finding the center of the cup. Three perfect shots lead to a rare birdie on a very tough hole. This must be what heaven is like! Score through 11 holes: 1 over par.

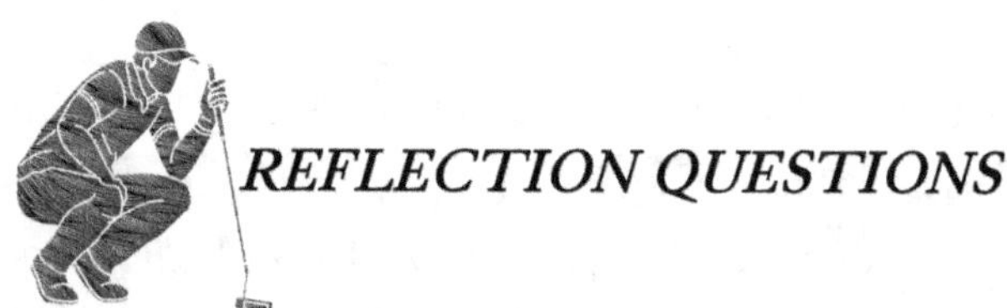

REFLECTION QUESTIONS

1. Where do you need to get out of your head and take action in life?

2. What areas of your life need more consistent effort?
3. Where do you find the barriers of fear and laziness holding you back?
4. Where do you need to take the first step toward your dreams and goals?

RECOMMENDED BOOK: *THE 7 HABITS OF HIGHLY EFFECTIVE PEOPLE* - STEVEN COVEY

Stephen Covey's *The 7 Habits of Highly Effective People* connects deeply to action and effort as each habit is essentially a call to intentional action, backed by consistent effort. Covey emphasizes that effectiveness isn't about quick fixes or personality tricks—it's about disciplined choices and sustained effort that align with principles. How the 7 Habits incorporate action & effort:

1. Be Proactive

Action: Take initiative rather than waiting for circumstances to dictate your life.
Effort: Requires constant awareness to choose responses instead of reacting automatically.

2. Begin with the End in Mind

Action: Define a clear vision or mission before starting tasks.
Effort: Sustained planning ensures that daily actions align with long-term goals.

3. Put First Things First

Action: Prioritize important tasks over urgent distractions.
Effort: Demands consistent discipline to focus on what truly matters, even when it's harder.

4. Think Win-Win

Action: Approach relationships with mutual benefit in mind.
Effort: Balance assertiveness with empathy, avoiding shortcuts like manipulation.

5. Seek First to Understand, Then to Be Understood

Action: Listen actively before speaking. Listen to understand not to respond.
Effort: Genuine listening takes patience and energy but builds stronger connections.

6. Synergize

Action: Collaborate to create outcomes greater than the sum of the parts.
Effort: Effort is needed to value differences and work through conflict productively.

7. Sharpen the Saw

Action: Invest in renewal—physical, mental, emotional, spiritual.
Effort: Requires consistent practice of self-care and growth, not just occasional bursts.

SONG: "UNSTOPPABLE" BY RASCAL FLATTS

Rascal Flatts' song "Unstoppable" presents action and effort as an anthem about action, resilience, persistence, and moving forward despite mistakes or setbacks. The lyrics emphasize that progress comes from effort, and that determination makes you "Unstoppable" in both love and life.

Originally tied to the Olympics, the song was adapted to highlight not just romantic love but also the unstoppable drive of athletes—showing how effort and action create triumph.

MOVIE TO WATCH: *THE SECRET LIFE OF WALTER MITTY* (2013)

The Secret Life of Walter Mitty is a beautiful and poignant portrayal of how stepping out of daydreams and into real experiences transforms a passive life into one of courage, growth, and fulfillment. Walter's journey, portrayed by Ben Stiller, is a vivid reminder that action and effort—not fantasy—creates change.

Key Themes Connecting to Action & Effort

- From fantasy to reality: Walter begins as a man who escapes into heroic daydreams but avoids real challenges. His transformation comes when he acts, leaving his comfort zone to chase a missing photo negative across the world.
- Effort as growth: Each step requires effort —climbing mountains, skateboarding down Icelandic roads,

facing danger. These actions build confidence and reshape his identity.

- Courage through doing: The film emphasizes that courage isn't found in imagining bravery, but in doing brave things. Action and effort are the bridge between intention and transformation.
- Breaking monotony: Walter's effort to pursue adventure breaks the cycle of routine and shows how meaningful life results from deliberate action, not passive dreaming.

This movie is a real treat of cinematic beauty, romantic comedy, and the wonder of the human spirit in action. It is a show that reveals the importance of action and effort in fulfilling dreams. This movie also exemplifies the role of action in manifesting in joyful reality those things we might otherwise hold as empty fantasy. Watch and enjoy—you'll be glad you did.

12 HOLE #12: EMOTIONAL MASTERY
137-YARD PAR 3

The 12th hole is called "Emotional Mastery." This is a fun but dangerous par 3. The green is small, well trapped, and bisected by a four-foot ridge. The tee shot requires placement on the proper section of the green. Long is dead, so it's best to miss short here. The front pin gives a scoring opportunity as the ridge acts like a backstop, funneling the ball back toward the cup. Birdie and double bogey are both in play, depending on the quality of your tee shot.

EMOTIONAL MASTERY AND EMOTIONAL INTELLIGENCE

Emotions are both important and powerful, but they can be overly powerful and not always wise. Logic is steady, but it can lack heart and passion. In golf and in life, we must train the mind to guide emotion or risk being ruled by reaction. This chapter explores the tension between feeling and thinking, and the discipline of emotional mastery.

TRAINING THE MIND

Golf is a mental game. A missed shot can spiral into a bad round if emotions take over. Conversely, a great shot can provide an adrenaline rush that leads to quicker tempo and a few holes of poor results. The best players learn to pause, breathe, and reset. Training the mind means choosing response over reaction.

Arnold Palmer's quote captures the very essence of the emotional roller coaster that is golf. "Golf is deceptively simple and endlessly complicated; it satisfies the soul and frustrates the intellect. It is at the same time rewarding and maddening—and it is without a doubt the greatest game mankind has ever invented."

This is so true, and it is both the allure and beauty of the game. Every golfer has experienced "the thrill of victory and the agony of defeat" in this game. We have all found joyous stretches of a few holes when the game seems easy. Our mind is clear, and the execution is flawless. For a brief time, everything clicks into place, and we get a taste of what we are capable of. Then, in the blink of an eye, the game can be terribly aggravating, and it suddenly seems impossible. Nothing works well—our driver is awful, we can't hit an iron to save our lives, and we hit putts with horrible speed and terrible direction.

The emotional swings can take us from celebration to filling the swear jar in a heartbeat. The mind starts racing, the heart is pounding, and the sweat is rolling. Take a moment and think about how your body reacts when you're excited. Now think about what is happening in your body when you're frightened or angry.

In these scenarios, your mental state is drastically different, yet your body reacts the same way—mind racing, pulse pounding, and sweat flowing. Golf challenges us in moderating these physical and emotional swings.

Golf teaches us, if we are willing to learn, the importance of training our minds when our emotions increase, and the body reacts. Golf teaches us to control our thoughts, breathing, and pace of play to then control our body's reaction to the influx of emotions. We learn to embrace opposites. We learn to respond in paradox to our emotional stimuli and bodily reaction.

When the golfer's mind is racing, we should learn to seek calming thoughts—perhaps laughter, peaceful music, or thoughts of serene and quiet places we enjoy. We should intentionally choose to slow the mind down when our heart rate quickens.

When the heart is pumping and the sweat is flowing, the best golfers in the world learn to slow their pace of walking, moving, and thinking. Excitement and fear are conquered by calming and peaceful thoughts, decisions, and actions. Tour players learn to "slow the game down" by taking more time and slowing their process and breathing. When emotions and stakes rise, professional golfers slow the pace of decision making and movement. They choose to slowly and methodically think and breathe.

This is a learned process. Training the mind is often learned through adversity and bad experiences. Tour pros call this "learning to win." So often, you see a professional close to winning, yet they just can't seem to control their thinking, and thus they can't control their emotions, their bodies, and their performance enough to finish on top. I watched Payne Stewart go through this in the early 1980s. In 2025 Tommy Fleetwood struggled in the same way. Both learned to train their minds, and they learned to win—in a big way.

"Learning to win" on the PGA Tour refers to the process by which golfers develop the mental, emotional, and strategic skills needed to close out tournaments under pressure. It's not just about hitting great shots—it's about handling nerves, managing mistakes, and building the confidence to perform when victory and disaster are both on the line.

Mindset is key: coaches describe winning as an art, requiring composure, patience, and belief. Coaches? Yes. Most professional golfers, and many professional athletes, have coaches who specialize in sports psychology. These coaches help their athletes to improve performance and find more joy in their work by helping them train their minds. Why?

Because everything starts in the mind (Sound familiar?). Sports psychologists help athletes focus on thoughts and breathing techniques that best help them manage their thinking, their emotions, and their performance. They focus on managing the process of playing golf. It is all about process.

When I play golf, the stakes are generally small. There is little pressure. I might play for a beer, a trophy, or position in a golf league. Usually, I play simply for fun, and what little pressure I feel is self-imposed. I'm not playing golf for a living. My family's well-being is not dependent on my results. Frankly, no one is going to remember my score a year from now, including me.

That doesn't mean I don't care. That doesn't mean I don't experience emotions on the course. Trust me, I can enjoy the game immensely, and I can battle frustration with every shot. That's the beauty of the game. You get instant feedback. That means you have instant emotional stimulus. The question is, what are you going to do with that stimulus?

Are you going to control your emotions, or are your emotions going to control you? To be fair, your emotions are valid whatever they are. The proper question is are you going to be an adult and choose how to respond to those emotions, or are you going to be a child and simply react? There's a huge difference.

To me, controlling my mind and emotions starts with finding the approach in golf that best serves me—the point of equilibrium in Aristotle's concept of the Golden Mean between excess and deficiency—where I live in the paradox of "try, but don't try." Trying too hard is excess, not trying is deficiency, and neither approach works well. So, I try, but don't try. My good friend, Ron Nahser, tells me that in Tai Chi the concept is described as push, no push. In a similar way, I care, but don't care. Balance good, golf good!

Think of this as a matter of perspective. My results matter, but they don't matter. Seriously, in the long run of life, my golf score on any given Thursday is rather insignificant. The same is true for any single drive or putt. Hence, there should be little pressure and little cause to get caught up in emotions, particularly negative ones, on the course.

I know a few grown-ups who act like eight-year-olds on the course. They throw clubs. They kick bags. They yell and curse. Why? They haven't trained their minds, so they don't behave appropriately. They act like spoiled kids throwing tantrums. They are totally reactive and out of control. I have seen high level corporate executives break clubs and gouge their putters into the green. Don't be that guy. My guess is they behave the same way in the office. Who wants to work with that? Keep things in perspective. Maintain control.

The other trick I use, beyond keeping things in perspective with try, not try, is to be mindful of my process. What am I thinking? What am I feeling? I try to be aware of what is going on inside my head. And to be honest, I am at my best when I am not really thinking about or feeling anything. I play best when I am empty and unattached to results. Don't think, just play.

Think before the shot—choose your club, plan your play. Once over the ball, just do it.

When I am "in the zone" it is almost an out of body experience. There is no tension. No forcing anything. I am aware. I am alert and present. There is a peacefulness and connection of mind and body. My thoughts are light and positive.

My pace is easy and relaxed. I notice little things like birds and animals. I am not pre-occupied or anxious. I believe in my ability and trust my swing. I do not judge my shots—I merely accept the results and go play the next shot the best I can. No anxiety. No doubts. I am just playing.

What about those times when I'm not in the zone, those times when the game is hard? The main thing I try is to empty my mind and emotions. I seek opposites. If I feel rushed, I slow down. If I feel doubt, I recall good shots. If I feel like I'm forcing things, I relax and embrace patience. Accept. Enjoy. Let go of trying so hard. Let it be simple. Be patient and let it come to you.

If I'm fighting my swing, I focus on tempo and go 80% or imagine swinging in slow motion. If I'm feeling frustrated, I focus on gratitude and think about how lucky I am to be playing a great game with great friends. I think about the process, not results. I control what I can control—my attitude and my effort. I'm not going to let a few poor golf shots ruin my outlook on life.

All these efforts are an attempt to train my mind-to be aware of my process and then seek an antidote to the enemy within. They are efforts to get out of my own way, to control my thoughts and feelings versus having my thoughts and feelings run me. This is a matter of claiming my power instead of giving the reins to my eight-year-old inner self. Remember, golf is about controlling your emotions and controlling your golf ball.

The most important part of the course is the four inches between your ears.

Emotional mastery is the ability to recognize, understand, and manage our own emotions while also being attuned to the emotions of others. In golf, this means staying composed under pressure and showing empathy and sportsmanship toward fellow players. It's about having fun and enjoying the experience, regardless of the results. It's about trying but not trying, keeping things in perspective.

Isn't that one of life's great lessons—keeping things in perspective? No matter where we are and what we're doing, aren't we called to master our emotions and make the most of opportunities? Shouldn't we choose how to respond versus simply reacting to whatever stimulus we experience? In essence, should we go through life like an eight-year-old or should we claim our power and approach our emotions and results as an adult?

I know, there are people and situations that trigger the worst in us. There are situations when it's damn hard to be our best selves. I get that. I've been there and I've said and done things that are far from my best. I have told myself "They made me..." and that is just plain denial. No one can make you say or do anything. Claim your power. Activate the switch and put a pause between stimulus and response.

We are not Pavlov's dogs. We are not B.F. Skinner's rats. We have the ability to choose our responses and not just succumb to reaction. We can learn. Children become adults. We can stand back and look objectively and give ourselves time and permission to choose the best way to respond. Golf teaches us to do just that. Life teaches us to do just that. Claim your power. Be patient. Respond smartly. Choose wisely. Master your emotions in all things.

Inspirational Quote: You will either control your mind, or your mind will control you. – Napoleon Hill

Scripture: Be transformed by the renewing of your mind. – Romans 12:2

Zen: Rule your mind or it will rule you.

Golf Anecdote: Tiger Woods was known for his ability to compartmentalize—staying focused despite distractions, setbacks, or pressure. He trained his mind so he could play his best when it mattered most. Tiger had a process of remembering and building on good shots and results, while at the same time forgetting bad shots and results. Tiger's strength was his mind and his ability to focus on positives. He let the bad results and thoughts go, and he chose to dwell only on the positives in every situation. Tiger mastered his emotions, and the results are undeniable.

EMOTIONAL INTELLIGENCE

Emotions are not the enemy, they are signals. But when left unchecked, they can sabotage performance. Golf teaches us to feel without being overwhelmed, to acknowledge without being consumed.

Emotional intelligence is the ability to recognize, understand, and manage our own emotions while also being attuned to the emotions of others. In golf, this means staying composed under pressure and showing empathy and sportsmanship toward fellow players. In life, it means staying composed in relationships and showing empathy toward your spouse, your children, your parents and siblings, and your co-workers and friends.

The concept of emotional intelligence is a relatively new one. Psychologist and journalist Daniel Goleman published his best-selling book *Emotional Intelligence* in 1995. That book is broadly credited with bringing the concept into mainstream business, education, and leadership culture—only 30 years ago.

Emotional intelligence resonated because it gave language to something people intuitively felt—that success isn't just about intellect, it's about self-awareness, empathy, and managing relationships. It also aligned with the growing interest in leadership psychology and personal development of the time.

Emotional intelligence is the ability to perceive, understand, use, and manage emotions—both your own and other people's. It's about recognizing what you feel, recognizing what others feel, and then using that awareness to guide your thinking, decisions, and behavior.

It is not about denying your emotions. We aren't like my childhood hero Mr. Spock from the Star Trek series. Our emotions are valid. They may not always be an accurate reflection of what is happening in the world around us, but our emotions are a sign of how we interpret that world.

My good friend Ron Nahser explores the idea that we each have "filters" that shape how we interpret the world in his book, *Learning to Read the Signs: Reclaiming Pragmatism in Business*. Ron argues that these filters have deep historical roots and shape how people in business (and life) interpret situations, make decisions, and understand their purpose.

Ron says we each interpret the world through our filters—inherited assumptions, cultural narratives, personal histories, and philosophical lenses. These filters shape what we notice, what we ignore, what we assume, and how we make meaning.

Emotional intelligence, meanwhile, is about perceiving, understanding, and managing emotions—in yourself and others. When you put the two together, you get a deeper insight: emotional intelligence is the skill that helps you recognize your filters and choose how much power to give them.

Without emotional intelligence, filters operate unconsciously. With emotional intelligence, filters become visible—and therefore adjustable. In essence, your filter is the story you are using, and emotional intelligence is awareness that you are using a story at all.

On the course, a golfer's "filters" might include "I'm bad with my driver," "I always choke under pressure," or "fast greens ruin my putting." This negative self-talk often compounds bad results through a self-fulfilling prophecy – bad thinking creates bad results.

In life, our filters might include "my wife doesn't love me," "my kid is always screwing up," or "my boss is a horrible manager." Since we tend to experience what we focus on, these filtered thoughts can exaggerate the negatives in our relationships. To a hammer, the world is full of nails.

Emotional intelligence is the ability to notice the filter, understand the emotion behind it, regulate the reaction, and choose a more constructive interpretation. That is the difference between spiraling and recovering.

Do you ever think about your filters—the lenses through which you interpret everything around you? Do you ever consider that perhaps you might be wrong? That there may be, and likely are, alternative ways to interpret what you see and experience? Is it possible you are seeing only a small part of what is happening—the tip of the iceberg—and the truth includes so much more beneath the surface? Are you willing to consider that the motives of others are quite different than the motives you have assigned to their actions?

Emotional intelligence is about embracing a process of awareness and curiosity around your emotions and filters. Why do you feel as you do? What is underneath your emotions? What filters are you bringing in interpreting the events before you? The key is to question and understand your perspective and to do the same with others. Accept. Be curious. Don't judge, inquire. Gather perspective. Learn. Understand, then respond.

Consider the story of the blindfolded (or blind) men and the elephant. This parable tells of a group of blind men who encounter an elephant for the first time. Each man touches only one part—a different part—of the animal and forms a conclusion based solely on that limited experience.

Their descriptions differ wildly. The man touching the trunk says the elephant is like a snake. The one touching the ear says it's like a fan. The one touching the leg says it's like a tree trunk. The one touching the side says it's like a wall. The one touching the tusk says it's like a spear. The one touching the tail says it's like a rope.

In some versions of the story, the men argue, accuse each other of dishonesty, or even come to blows because each believes his interpretation is the whole truth. They each have an incomplete picture of reality, and yet each man is convinced his own perspective is the truth. The emotions run strongly. The filters guide their thinking and actions. Without emotional intelligence, there is no understanding of what is really before them.

Seek emotional intelligence. When emotions arise, seek to become aware not only of their existence, but also the underlying filters behind them. The stronger the emotions, the more important it is to question them and seek to understand the emotions and perspectives of other people as well. Steven Covey's 5th Habit of Highly Effective People is "seek first to understand, then to be understood." That is emotional intelligence.

Inspirational Quote: Feelings are much like waves, we can't stop them from coming but we can choose which ones to surf. – Jonatan Mårtensson

Scripture: The one who has no rule over his spirit is like a city broken down, without walls. – Proverbs 25:28

Zen: Let your thoughts pass by like clouds in the sky.

Golf Anecdote: One of the most feared shots on the PGA Tour is the 137-yard tee shot at the 17th hole at the TPC at Sawgrass. The small island green is very elusive and many times the tournament is lost on this frightening par 3. In the first round of The Players Championship in 1999, Fred Couples watched his first shot splash into the pond short of the island green.

Couples chose to take his penalty stroke and re-tee from the same spot. He also chose to use the same club when attempting his next shot. Undaunted, he swung his pitching wedge and sent his third shot toward the green. Amazingly, his ball flew straight into the cup, recoding a "hole-in-three." Freddie's ability to accept the bad first shot and respond with emotional intelligence resulted in one of the most memorable holes ever played in golf.

SUMMARY

Emotions and logical thinking are both essential. In golf and in life, mastering the mind means honoring our emotions while choosing thoughtful action. It is the path to clarity, resilience, and grace under pressure. Emotional mastery is not a destination; it is a life-long journey that accompanies us on the roller coaster of life both on and off the golf course.

HOLE RESULT: 137-YARD PAR 3

With the pin on the right front portion of the green just below the bisecting ridge, a 125-yard 9 iron is the perfect club. A well struck shot lands at the top of the ridge, just beyond the pin. After a brief moment, the ball starts to drift down the slope toward the cup. It trickles down and left, then disappears—it's in the hole for a hole-in-one! Unbelievable! Score through 12 holes: 1 under par.

So, full disclosure here—this is a recreation of my only ace. This happened on the 16th hole at Hickory Hills Country Club in Springfield, Missouri, the home course of Payne Stewart. As a big Payne Stewart fan, this stands as my single favorite moment in a lifetime of unforgettable moments on the course. I was fortunate to share this with my brother Mark Dotson, cousin Steve Stufflebam, and great friend Matt Lacey almost one year after Payne's tragic death. Very emotional and meaningful, even as I write about it almost 25 years later. That is the joy of golf!

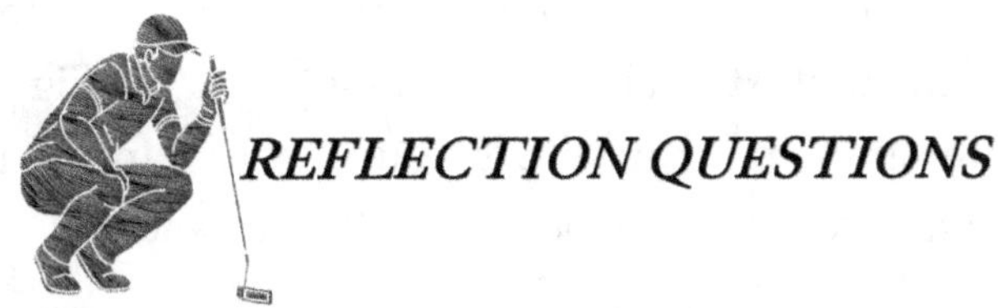

REFLECTION QUESTIONS

1. When do emotions tend to override your mind, and what helps you regain balance?
2. What is your process when you are triggered and flooded with emotions?
3. What "filters" do you bring to the table, and how do you overcome them?
4. On a scale of 1 to 10, where are you with emotional intelligence? Curiosity? Empathy?

RECOMMENDED BOOK: *MASTER YOUR EMOTIONS* – THIBAUT MEURISSE

The book *Master Your Emotions* by Thibaut Meurisse is about internal emotional management (emotional mastery). Meurisse's book focuses on:

- identifying emotional triggers
- understanding the stories behind emotions
- breaking automatic patterns
- choosing intentional responses
- building habits that stabilize your emotional life

This is essentially about emotional mastery—the internal discipline of noticing, naming, and navigating your emotional landscape. When you combine the inner work of emotional mastery with the external work of emotional intelligence, the result is an approach that allows you to thrive in the moment between stimulus and response—both on and off the golf course.

SONG: "I CAN SEE CLEARLY NOW" BY JOHNNY NASH (COVERED BY JIMMY CLIFF)

"I Can See Clearly Now" is more than a catchy melody-it is a framework for emotional mastery. Emotional mastery begins with clearing the internal weather. The song is fundamentally about a shift in inner perception:

- Obstacles ("obstacles in my way")
- Emotional fog ("the dark clouds")
- Internal resistance ("the pain")

These aren't external events, they're internal states. Emotional mastery is the ability to recognize when your inner weather is stormy so you can consciously shift it. The song captures that moment when the storm breaks and clarity returns. Emotional mastery isn't about suppressing emotions; it's about seeing your emotions and then seeing through them.

The song isn't passive. It's not "I hope things get better." It's "I can see clearly now." That's agency. That's ownership. That's the essence of emotional mastery. You don't wait for the world to change—you see it and change your relationship to it.

MOVIE TO WATCH: *INSIDE OUT* (2015)

Inside Out is practically a masterclass in emotional mastery disguised as an animated film. It's one of the clearest cinematic illustrations of how emotions work, why they matter, and what happens when we try to control or suppress them.

The film teaches "the value of all emotions—from Joy to Sadness—and their vital roles in personal growth". Emotional mastery isn't about eliminating emotions; it's about understanding their function.

- Joy reminds us of what matters
- Sadness signals loss and invites connection
- Anger protects values
- Fear keeps us safe
- Disgust maintains boundaries

This mirrors the core of emotional intelligence: perceiving, understanding, and using emotions wisely. One of the strongest themes in the movie is "Joy learns the importance of Sadness in

Riley's emotional balance". That's emotional mastery in a nutshell.

Joy's initial strategy—control, override, suppress—fails. Only when she allows Sadness to participate does our heroine regain equilibrium. Mastery isn't dominance—it's integration.

A quote from the movie states, "Memories look different when you let more than one emotion touch them." This is profound.

Emotional mastery means allowing complexity. A memory can be bittersweet. A victory can carry relief. A mistake can carry pride. When we allow emotional layering, we gain wisdom instead of reactivity. The key is to be aware of our emotions and filters, then choose curiosity in order to learn and respond—that is emotional mastery.

13 HOLE #13: COURAGE AND FEAR

416-YARD PAR 4

We come to the 13th hole named "Courage and Fear." This is a super demanding par 4, to the point of being a frightening hole. Trees and out of bounds line both sides of this hole, and a fairway trap crosses 220 yards from the tee. A solid drive carries the trap, leaving a long second shot into a very small green just beyond water. The green is well trapped, sloping severely from right to left. The green complex falls off left to the out of bounds markers only 10 yards from the pin. This hole is tougher than a two-dollar steak, and par is a great score here.

Fear is natural—but it need not be final. Courage is not the absence of fear, but the decision to move forward anyway. In golf and in life, we face hazards, unknowns, and pressure. This chapter explores how courage transforms fear into fuel and how boldness leads to breakthroughs.

FACING FEAR WITH BOLDNESS

Courage is a mindset. It's stepping up to the tee with confidence, even after a bad hole. It's choosing the aggressive line when the moment calls for it. Boldness is not bravado—it's belief in your preparation. It's choosing courage over fear.

Every round of golf presents challenges—water, bunkers, tight lies, out of bounds. Fear whispers "play it safe," but courage says, "trust your swing." Facing hazards is not reckless, it's choosing intentional risk with preparation. In golf, and in life, it is a requirement to face shots and challenges that test your mettle. The greatest rewards come when you conquer the greatest tests. Character is not built from easy wins; character is built from facing and overcoming difficulty.

Let's be honest, some shots in golf are downright scary. The game will often place you in a position where you must be at your best to succeed, where less than your best is disastrous. That is the story of Roy McAvoy in the movie *Tin Cup*. That is the story played out weekly on the PGA Tour. The one who can execute the demanding shot under intense pressure, with enormous consequences, becomes a worthy hero. Those who fail in critical moments are scrutinized.

That is the essence of courage and fear—facing the outcome defined as success or failure. That is one of the wonderful aspects of golf. Every round, we get to stand over each and every golf shot and face our inner nature, our fears and our character, for four plus hours. Not only that, but this Shakespearean drama is played out in front of our closest friends. Will this next shot be glorious or humiliating. Can I conquer the demons within?

It is easy to be fearful over the golf ball. The ball can literally go anywhere! We may even swing and miss. Perhaps that is why

Winston Churchill described golf as "a game whose aim is to hit a very small ball into an even smaller hole, with weapons singularly ill-designed for the purpose." My son, Joel, would joke that my drives would best be predicted by a hurricane prediction cone—they could go anywhere within a very broad and general path.

Joel and I once played with a friend who hit his first tee shot out of bounds and over a house way left of the course. Our friend re-teed and hit his next shot out of bounds and over a house way right. Those two shots created great laughter and great fear. It took incredible courage for our friend to tee up his third ball and pull the trigger, but he did it. He even found the fairway with ball number three using that same driver. Courage won out.

My go to shot that induces fear is the "shank." That is a shot where the ball is struck by the hosel of the club, sending it almost straight right. I would not wish the shanks on my worst enemy. I believe the hardest shot in golf is the next one after a shank. The shanks are contagious, and they tend to come in bunches. The shanks are debilitating, and the mere mention of the word strikes fear in the heart of almost every golfer.

It takes great courage to swing the club after a shank. Fear is real at that stage, and the experience of having hit one shakes me to the core. At that stage, I am extremely aware that the ball could go literally anywhere. Point and hope is a bad way to play golf. But I have been there many times. Fortunately, I have experienced the shanks enough to find courage and discover a solution.

Building on the lesson of the last hole (emotional mastery), I start by reminding myself that I have overcome the shanks before. If I slow my swing down and focus on closing the toe of the club at impact, my next shot will be better. Also, while standing over the next shot, I choose courage. I tell myself it's ok to go forward, that I can and have conquered this before. In essence, I accept the bad shot, focus on process, and choose to go forward even though I know there is a very real possibility that the next shot may go straight right again. That is courage—going forward when uncertainty and failure are ever-present.

I watched my brother Mark fight this on one of our trips to Hot Springs Village. On one hole, Mark was right in front of the green, about 10 yards short. He proceeded to shank four chips in a row. He literally drew a box around the green without ever hitting it. On the next hole, Mark left his approach in front of the green, again about 10 yards short. He looked at me and said, "Oh good, I get to hit another pretty little chip." We died laughing. Then, he courageously knocked his chip up next to the pin. I love Mark—he is hilarious and courageous, just what you would want from an older brother. He faces fear with humor, and that is a great way to disarm the demons within.

I have been to Austin, Texas, many times to visit Brother Mark, and he has taken me to play his home course Blue Bonnet Hill lots of times. There is an interesting story of fear and courage there.

For many years, there was a young man who I would see practicing every time Mark and I played at Blue Bonnet. I would see him on the range, at the chipping green, and also putting. He was very systematic about his practice. I figured he was a pretty good player. Eventually, I asked Mark if he ever played with him. I was shocked when Mark responded, "No, I have asked him to join us several times, but he won't go out on the course. He doesn't think he's good enough to play."

Wow. That's what fear can do to us. Fear of failure, rejection, inadequacy. Fear of losing control. Fear of aging, illness, or death. Fear of pain or uncertainty. Even fear of success. Fear locks us up and limits our world. It can be paralyzing. Fear can be debilitating.

Fear is at the heart of most dysfunction and addiction. It is at the heart of most failure to grow and move forward. Fear is at the heart of most relationship issues and most anxieties and mental illnesses. Fear fuels racism and hatred of those who are different from us.

I've seen fear paralyze my son's growth. I've seen fear cost me my first marriage. I've seen fear in business circles and work dynamics, and I've seen it at work in friendships and sporting events. There are few things in life more powerful than fear.

What is the antidote to fear? Safety. Safety from within (internal safety), safety from within relationships (relational safety), and safety from outside (external safety). In golf, safety is provided by a repeatable swing (internal), the advice of a caddie (relational), and our understanding of the course (external). In marriage, safety comes from our understanding of ourselves, the reassurance of our spouse, and the support of family, community, and faith.

So, how does courage come into play with fear? Courage is the bridge between fear and safety. Courage is the hard first step that leads from fear to safety. Courage is the choice to move forward, to be vulnerable, and to risk failure. Courage faces the worst of our fears while taking the action needed to build safety and seek what matters most. Courage is what we must embrace and live by to face our fears and achieve safety on higher ground.

Fear tells us we may crash and burn, so we're better off not trying. Courage is choosing to go forward, to risk that we may crash and burn, knowing we want to live in the safety of success beyond that fearful place. This is the essence of the saying, "It is better to have tried and failed than to have never tried at all."

This same sentiment is found in, "It is better to have loved and lost than to never have loved at all." These are statements claiming the power of courage over fear.

This is the reason for my courage kanji tattoo previously mentioned on hole 10. This is the essence of courage > fear. Can you have safety and joy and happiness without courage? Perhaps. The turtle is safe in its shell. But, if you want to thrive and flourish and grow, then you must embrace and live in courage. Turtles bask in the sun on a log only when they climb out of their shell and leave the safety of the pond. Be Master Oogway (Youtube him)!

Inspirational Quote: Courage is resistance to fear, mastery of fear—not absence of fear. – Mark Twain

Scripture: Be strong and courageous. Do not be afraid; do not be discouraged. – Joshua 1:9

Zen: Don't fight fear, don't run from it—befriend it. Invite your fears to tea. - Buddhist saying

Golf Anecdote: Seve Ballesteros was known for his fearless creativity, taking bold shots others wouldn't dare, and often pulling them off with flair.

TRANSFORMING FEAR INTO FUEL

Fear can paralyze or it can energize. When acknowledged and redirected, fear becomes a source of focus and intensity. Golf teaches us to breathe and play through fear, to swing through doubt, and to trust our ability in the moment.

Golf's toughest holes and most difficult shots practically force us to make a choice. Are we going to shrink in the face of fear, or are we going to rise up and overcome fear with courage? Are we going to cower in the face of challenges, or are we going to bring our best when it is needed most?

Maybe that's why we love underdogs so much. Is it the display of courage and the rising above fear that is so captivating? I must admit that most of my favorite movies are based on courage winning out—*Rocky, Remember the Titans, Rudy, Miracle, Invincible, The Outlaw Josey Wales, The Sting, Top Gun, Finding Forrester, It's a Wonderful Life, Forrest Gump, Shrek, Finding Nemo,* and many more.

I think people draw inspiration from the witness of courage. We tend to believe, as presented in the movie *The Edge*, "What one man can do, another can do." Consider the "Impossible Barrier" of the four-minute mile.

In 1886, it was scientifically determined that a human being could not run a mile in less than 4 minutes. In 1945, the mile record was set at an "impossible to break" 4:01.3. The barrier was established. No man could run a faster mile. And that was true—until May 6, 1954, when Roger Bannister ran a mile in 3:59.4. Human limits had been rewritten.

Bannister's record lasted only 46 days. In fact, in the next 5 years, 11 other runners broke the 4-minute barrier. Bannister proved the barrier was only psychological. Once he did it, others believed they could do it as well, and they did. Bannister is widely quoted as saying, "Just because they say it's impossible doesn't mean you can't do it." He used the challenge as fuel. He used courage to fuel his training. Bannister went from fear to courage to safety in his accomplishment. He did not see the barrier. Bannister saw beyond it. That is courage.

Inspirational Quote: Everything you've ever wanted is on the other side of fear. – George Addair

Scripture: When I am afraid, I put my trust in you. – Psalm 56:3

Zen: Only when we are no longer afraid do we begin to live. – Dorothy Thompson

Golf Anecdote: Jack Nicklaus credited his ability to win under pressure, in part, to embracing the possibility that he might lose. "When you accept that you might lose, it takes the fear out of it, and that then helps you perform your best when it matters most. The players who fear losing are the ones who struggle the most with winning."

Compare that perspective to Michael Jordan, one of the winningest basketball players of all time. Jordan hated losing. Jordan said it was his hatred of losing, not his love of winning, that fueled his career. Both men, perhaps the best ever in their respective sports, understood the power of fear, and the power of using courage to overcome it.

SUMMARY

Courage is the quiet strength to face fear and move forward. In golf and in life, it's the difference between hesitation and break-through. When we choose boldness, we unlock growth, joy, and freedom. Courage leads us to overcome fear, and it allows us to thrive and flourish beyond self-imposed limits.

HOLE RESULT: 416-YARD PAR 4

Coming off a hole-in-one, the adrenaline is flowing. And now we face perhaps the most difficult hole on the course. The tee shot is slightly pulled and not quite flush, landing in the left corner of the fairway trap. We are now facing a 185-yard second shot from the sand with 175 yards to carry the water. This is a scary shot. The lie is good, and a 5-wood should clear the lip of the trap and reach the downwind green. This is what we play for—the challenging shot that makes or breaks a round. The courageous choice is rewarded, and a fantastic shot finds the front of the green. A fist pump and two putts later make par. Score through 13 holes: 1 under par.

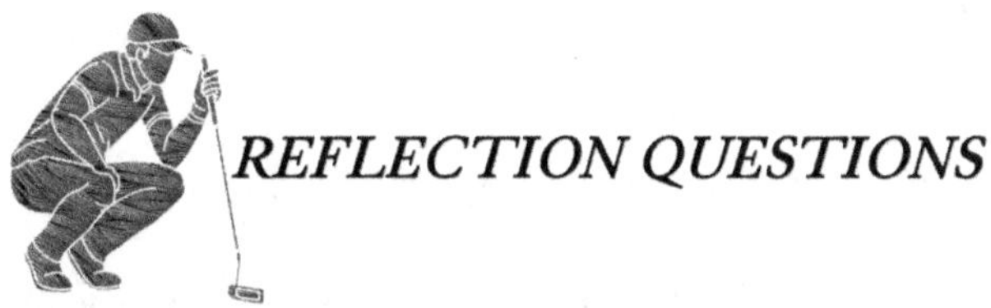

REFLECTION QUESTIONS

1. What are some of your biggest fears?
2. How do you respond when faced with risk or uncertainty?
3. What practices help you cultivate courage in your daily life?
4. What is the best example you have personally experienced where you chose courage over fear? Would you choose the same again?

BOOK RECOMMENDATION: *BRAVING THE WILDERNESS* BY BRENÉ BROWN

Brené Brown's book, *Braving the Wilderness*, is fundamentally about courage in the face of fear, especially the fear of disconnection, rejection, and standing alone. Brown argues that true belonging requires the courage to stand alone, even when it feels risky, uncertain, or emotionally exposed. The "wilderness" is her metaphor for that place of fear, vulnerability, and uncertainty.

Brown's BRAVING acronym (Boundaries, Reliability, Accountability, Vault, Integrity, Non-judgment, Generosity) is a courage practice—a set of behaviors that help you move through fear rather than collapse under it.

True belonging, in Brown's definition, is belonging to yourself and showing up authentically, staying connected to humanity even when you stand alone versus betraying yourself to fit in. This is the power of courage that leads to safety and dissolves fear.

SONG: "LAY IT ON THE LINE" BY TRIUMPH (1979)

"Lay It on the Line" (Triumph, 1979) is essentially an anthem about choosing courage over the fears that keep people stuck, silent, or half-committed. In the song, the narrator is calling out someone who keeps hesitating, avoiding clarity, and hiding behind excuses. Underneath that behavior is fear: fear of rejection, fear of commitment, fear of vulnerability and fear of disappointing someone.

The heart of the song is a demand for honesty—not perfection, not guarantees, just truth. To "lay it on the line" means to stop hiding, stop hedging, stop protecting yourself with ambiguity and to say what is real. That is courage. It is the emotional equivalent of stepping into the wilderness.

The narrator is tired of mixed signals and emotional half-measures. They want clarity, even if it's uncomfortable. This is courage in relational form—courage to ask for what you need, courage to risk hearing the truth, courage to stop tolerating uncertainty, and courage to stop betraying yourself to keep the peace. It's the same principle Brené Brown teaches. You cannot belong to others if you abandon yourself.

The song makes it clear that fear has consequences. In fear, you lose time, you lose trust, you lose connection, and you lose yourself. Fear keeps you stuck. Courage moves you forward.

"Lay it on the line" is the moment of courage—the moment someone finally says, "Enough hiding. Let's be real." Courage is the bridge between the fear of being honest and the safety that comes from clarity. Courage > fear. Lay it on the Line.

MOVIE TO WATCH: *SAVING PRIVATE RYAN* (1998)

Saving Private Ryan is one of the most powerful cinematic explorations of what courage looks like in the presence of overwhelming fear. The opening Omaha Beach sequence presents a vivid portrayal of the brutal nature of war—pain, death, anguish. And it shows the courage of those who marched in toward the hailstorm of bullets despite their fears.

The squad's mission of risking many to save one recognizes that every soldier is afraid, but they each choose the courage needed to march forward anyway. The movie also depicts the use of fear as a bonding agent with the soldiers. They are one in their knowledge of the dangers of war, and they care for each other in that knowledge. In this way, courage becomes relational, collective, and something you choose for the good of the person next to you.

The film shows that courage is not the opposite of fear—it's the response to it. The battlefield presents terror and futility, yet the characters repeatedly choose duty, sacrifice, leadership, and integrity. This is courage as a behavioral response, not an emotional state.

It's not a movie about being fearless. It's a movie about being human and choosing courage anyway.

14 HOLE #14: COMMITMENT AND INTEGRITY

315-YARD PAR 4

The 14th hole is named "Commitment and Integrity." This short par 4 offers a scoring opportunity with a good drive. A solid tee shot carries the pond and trap left. The hole's defense is a deep sand trap in the center of the fairway, 225 yards from the tee. Also, the pin is protected by a deep trap covering the center of the green. The fairway has plenty of room to the right, but the angle into the pin is not as appealing from that side. Commit to a target and par or birdie should result.

Commitment is the promise we make to ourselves. Integrity is keeping that promise. In golf and in life, success is built not just on talent, but on consistency, character, and follow-through. This chapter explores the power of persistence and the strength of living in alignment with our values.

COMMITMENT

Merriam Webster defines commitment as "an agreement or pledge to do something in the future." This includes promises, vows, or obligations—anything you formally or informally bind yourself to. Cambridge adds that it's "a promise or firm decision to do something" and "willingness to give your time and energy to something you believe in."

Commitment is the deliberate, ongoing choice to align your actions with your stated values, promises, and agreements, especially when it's inconvenient. It's not just a feeling or intention; it's a pledge (what you say you will do), a pattern (what you consistently do), and a posture (the attitude of showing up with reliability, loyalty, and follow through).

Commitment is about showing up, investing your time and energy, and establishing a reputation for reliability. It is about choosing to do and support what you have said you would, even when you have an inner voice telling you to quit or avoid going forward.

In golf, it means keeping your tee time. It is shown by staying on the course when conditions aren't perfect or when your game is just awful. It means grinding and going on when your ego is deflated and your energy is low. It means participation when you are less than 100% and you don't have your A, B, or even your C game.

Charles Dicken's must have been a golfer because golf is truly "the best of times and the worst of times." Commitment is playing through the worst of times—cold, rain, wind, heat, humidity, and days when the ball just seems to taunt you and the inner demons have the volume turned up loud.

We are now on Hole 14, and I can start to feel the effects of walking 4 miles so far in this round. My legs are beginning to feel a bit heavy. My back is starting to ache and my hips are tightening. Walking becomes labor. This is when I must grind a bit and pay attention to my pace and breathing. I tell myself I only need ten more good swings, and we are done.

I can tell that my playing partners are also starting to feel the effects of walking for three hours in the hot sun. The pace is slower, and the swings are more erratic than a few holes before. This is the part of the round where scores tend to rise, when fatigue starts to show up on the scorecard. It's time to dig deep and call on our commitment to finish strong.

That is commitment—staying the course when it is easy to fold and quit. Commitment is hanging in there when it is uncomfortable, sometimes even distasteful. Why do we do this? Character. Responsibility. Compassion. Relationships. Challenge. We stay the course because we owe it to ourselves and our playing partners to finish what we started and to do what we said we would do—no matter how hard that is. Trust Jimmy Valvano. "Don't give up, don't ever give up."

Commitment is at the heart of self-esteem and character. Commitment is at the heart of relationships. Hall of Fame football coach Lou Holtz has a great Youtube video, "Trust, Commitment, Love," in which he details the philosophies that helped him be so successful in life. Watch it. It is the best 7 minutes you'll use today.

Holtz believed we all—every one of us—have three unasked questions we use to navigate relationships; Can I trust you? Do you care about me? Are you committed?

Think about that for a moment. Do you agree with Holtz? I do.

No matter who you are with, no matter what the relationship, doesn't it all revolve around trust, love, and commitment? And, if one of those is missing, what kind of relationship do you have? No relationship—no marriage, no friendship, no family, no workplace—can work without trust, love, and commitment.

One of my best friends says that if I accidentally killed someone, I could count on him to bring the shovel. That is commitment. I can think of a few friends who would loan me an emergency $10,000 with no questions asked. That is commitment. Think of the people in your life who you know, without a doubt, you can count on—that is commitment. And they know they can count on you and your commitment in return.

It takes no character and no talent to quit and give up. Commitment is showing up, even when it's extremely difficult. Commitment is showing up with no guarantees. In fact, commitment is investing all your heart and soul, knowing failure is possible, perhaps even likely. Commitment is courage on steroids. Be known for your commitment.

Inspirational Quote: Commitment is what transforms a promise into reality. – Abraham Lincoln

Scripture: Let your yes be yes, and your no, no. – Matthew 5:37

Zen: The way is in the practice.

Golf Anecdote: Commitment in golf isn't measured by the size of your dreams but by the consistency of your habits. Tiger Woods didn't become Tiger Woods because he was gifted. He became Tiger because he made a decision and then honored it every day. From age two, he practiced with a level of devotion that outlasted boredom, fatigue, injury, and pressure. His story reminds us that greatness isn't a moment; it's a pattern. Commitment is the quiet, daily choice to keep showing up, especially when no one is watching.

LIVING WITH INTEGRITY

Integrity is doing what you say you'll do—even when no one is watching. In golf, it's calling a penalty on yourself, playing by the rules, and respecting the game. Integrity builds trust and self-respect. Integrity is the alignment between your values, your words, and your actions—consistently, even under pressure.

At Q-School in 2025, where a single stroke can change a career, Ben Kohles stood over a ball nestled in leaves. When it moved as he brushed debris away, no one else saw it—but he did. Calling the penalty cost him the lead, his momentum, and ultimately his PGA Tour card. In a world obsessed with winning, Kohles chose something rarer: integrity. He walked off the course without the card he wanted, but with the character he refused to lose.

That is integrity—doing the right thing regardless of the cost or outcome. Lou Holtz tells us, "There is never a right time to do the wrong thing, and there is never a wrong time to do the right thing." Integrity is about your moral compass and your choice to follow or ignore it. Integrity is about your character and the thousands, actually millions, of choices you make in your lifetime that are either good and true, or not.

Integrity is also about the degree to which your actions align with your words. Are you known for saying one thing but doing another? Or are your words and your actions in full alignment?

We all know people who say one thing, but their behavior says another. We know we can't really accept their words and rely on them. People who say, "I'll call you," but the phone never rings. People who claim, "I'll see you on Sunday," but they don't show up. People who have a bagful of excuses for why they did not do what they said they would.

Whether you use a zero-tolerance policy or a three-strike rule, there are people who just write themselves out of your life because they lack integrity. Their behavior answers Lou Holtz's three questions. No, I can't trust you. No, I don't believe you care about me. No, you are not committed. You say one thing, but your actions say something different. Behavior is a language, and behavior speaks much louder than words.

I know lots of people who say they want to do something, but then they never seem to do it. Why is that? Why do people say they want to travel and never go anywhere? Why do people say they want to take better care of themselves, but their eating habits and lack of exercise tell the opposite story? Why are churches filled with people who are often unkind and unforgiving? Why do marriages so often end in divorce?

What is the opposite of integrity? Hypocrisy—behavior that contradicts what one claims to believe or feel. The truth is, we are all hypocrites to some degree. We all have moments when our behavior does not align with who we claim to be. That is part of the human condition. That is part of being imperfect, as we all are.

But we can learn to live with greater integrity. We can become more aware of our hypocrisy. We can learn to better align our behavior with our claims of who we want to be and what we want to be about. And, as we do so, our self-esteem improves. Our relationships improve. We model integrity and inspire others to do the same. We build a reputation for being true to our word and true to ourselves. People see our actions, and they know what we are about without ever having to ask.

One day this past summer, I was meeting a young golf professional, Cole Benson, at his apartment to take him to lunch. Cole is 21, just starting his journey to be a professional, and hoping someday to be a head pro at a golf club. I told him I would pick him up at 2:15 pm.

I pulled into his driveway at 2:14. Cole ran out to the car, pulling a shirt on over his head. "I knew you would be here at 2:15," he said, "I admire how you do what you say you'll do."

I learned this early in life—the product of good parenting. Do what you say you'll do. Be on time. If you are going to be late, call and let them know you value their time and that you want them to know you are on the way. Nothing is worse than a no-show or being late without notice. Live with integrity. Be respectful. Show others you are worthy of their trust, that you care about them, and that you are committed to their well-being.

Let your character and your behavior match your words. Behavior is a powerful language.

Inspirational Quote: Integrity is choosing courage over comfort; choosing what is right over what is fun, fast, or easy. – Brené Brown

Scripture: The integrity of the upright guides them. – Proverbs 11:3

Zen: When you walk, just walk. When you sit, just sit.

Golf Anecdote: Bobby Jones once lost a major by calling a penalty on himself that no one else saw. When praised for his honesty, he replied, "You might as well praise a man for not robbing a bank."

SUMMARY

Commitment is the fuel that sustains progress. Integrity is the compass for direction. In golf and in life, these virtues shape who we become and how we impact the world around us. Show up. Say what you mean and do what you say. Let your behavior speak loudly about who you are—your behavior is a powerful language that shows who you are and what your true character is about.

HOLE RESULT: 315-YARD PAR 4

With fatigue settling in, once again, the tee shot is slightly pulled and not quite flush, landing in the tall grass near the edge of the water. I hit a provisional tee shot that settles perfectly in the fairway. My good friend Regan Heitz would say, "Junior is always good." After a short search in the tall grass, I find my ball nestled down just a couple of inches out of bounds. I could play it and no one would know, but golf is a gentlemen's game. Integrity matters. I take the penalty, make a disappointing double-bogey and head to the next hole. Score through 14 holes: 1 over par.

REFLECTION QUESTIONS

1. What commitments have you made that need renewed attention?
2. How do you practice integrity in your daily decisions?
3. On a scale of 1 to 10, how hypocritical are you?
4. Where does your behavior need to change to better align with your words and values?

BOOK RECOMMENDATION: *INTEGRITY, THE COURAGE TO MEET THE DEMANDS OF REALITY* BY HENRY CLOUD

Henry Cloud's central thesis is that integrity is not just honesty, it's the capacity and character structure allowing a person to meet reality head-on and create trust.

Cloud defines integrity as "the courage to meet the demands of reality." This is more than moral uprightness; it's the ability to face difficult truths, make hard decisions, take responsibility, and follow through even when it's uncomfortable.

Commitment is meaningless without the character to stay engaged when reality pushes back.

Cloud emphasizes that people with integrity "create and maintain trust." Trust is built when words match actions, promises are kept, people show up consistently, and they don't "screw it up" with character gaps. Commitment is essentially a promise over time. Integrity is what makes that promise believable.

Cloud lists "finishing well" as one of the traits of integrity. Finishing well requires perseverance, consistency, ownership, emotional regulation, and staying connected to others even under pressure. This is commitment in action—not just starting but staying the course.

Cloud's "wake" metaphor says every person leaves behind two trails: results and relationships. The committed person leaves a wake of completed tasks: honored agreements, people who trust them, and relationships strengthened by consistency. Integrity is the alignment that ensures your wake is clean, not chaotic.

SONG: "I WON'T BACK DOWN" BY TOM PETTY

Tom Petty's "I Won't Back Down" is practically a blueprint for the psychology of commitment and integrity. It's one of those rare songs where the emotional posture is the message: steady, grounded, unshakeable. And when you look at it through the lens we often work with—character structure, secure functioning, and the courage to meet reality—it becomes even richer.

The entire song is a declaration of inner alignment. Petty isn't posturing; he's naming a boundary: "You can stand me up at the gates of hell..." "...but I won't back down." This is integrity in its purest form: I know who I am. I know what I stand for. And I'm not trading that for comfort, approval, or fear.

"I Won't Back Down" is a musical embodiment of:

- Integrity: staying whole under pressure
- Commitment: choosing a direction and holding it
- Courage: facing reality without collapsing
- Self-respect: refusing to betray your own values

It's the anthem of a person who has decided who they are and is willing to live it.

MOVIE TO WATCH: *THE WIZARD OF OZ* (1939)

The Wizard of Oz is a classic movie with a story about how integrity is formed and how commitment is sustained through courage, mutual support, self-efficacy, and the willingness to face reality with an integrated self.

Dorothy's commitment, and the commitment of the Scarecrow, the Tin Man, and the Lion, leads the group to travel long distances together in support of each other while pursuing the things they most want and need. They stay the course and stay together in the most frightening of times, including the task of retrieving the witch's broomstick.

At its core, Oz is not a children's tale. It's a psychological map—a journey of character formation, courage, and the willingness to face reality with an integrated self. It's Henry Cloud's definition of integrity brought to life: the courage to meet the demands of reality.

Dorothy doesn't choose her storm, but she chooses her response. She sets a clear intention—to get home—and commits to the path in front of her. That commitment is not a feeling. It's a series of actions. She keeps walking, keeps adjusting, keeps learning. She doesn't collapse when the world becomes unfamiliar. She doesn't outsource her responsibility to the Wizard, even when she desperately wants someone else to fix it. She stays in the round.

Her companions—the Scarecrow, the Tin Woodman, and the Lion—represent the internal capacities required for integrity: wisdom (clear thinking and discernment), heart (emotional presence and compassion), and courage (action in the presence of fear).

Integrity is the integration of these three. Commitment is the behavior that flows from that integration.

The Yellow Brick Road is the course. It winds, it confuses, it tests. But it also reveals. Each step exposes where Dorothy is strong and where she is still developing. Each challenge forces her to meet reality rather than fantasize about an easier path. And each companion mirrors a part of her she must reclaim.

Even the Wizard plays a role. He is the embodiment of pseudo-integrity—the illusion that someone else has the answers, the shortcut, the magic fix. His unmasking is the moment Dorothy realizes what everyone eventually learns: no one is coming to save you. You must know and take care of yourself. You are responsible for you.

Commitment is not blind devotion. It's not self-abandonment or heroic sacrifice. It's the steady, grounded choice to keep moving toward what matters, guided by an internal structure that holds under pressure. Dorothy's journey is a reminder that integrity is not perfection — it's alignment. It's the willingness to face the truth, stay connected to others, and act with integrity from values rather than fear.

15 HOLE #15: RESILIENCY
423-YARD PAR 4

The 15th hole is a challenging par 4 called "Resiliency." This lengthy hole calls for a good drive and a well-executed second shot to a well-guarded green. A solid tee shot parallels a creek along the right side from tee to green. The second shot angles slightly left and calls for a long entry into the putting surface. Also, the pin is protected by deep traps on both sides of the green. Anything right of the green will be wet, so you must miss left here. Par is a great score on this difficult hole.

Resiliency is the ability to recover, to persist, and to grow through adversity. In golf and in life, setbacks are inevitable, but how we respond defines our journey. This chapter explores the power of resiliency and how golf teaches us to bounce back with grace and grit.

BOUNCING BACK FROM SETBACKS

Every golfer knows the sting of a bad shot or a missed opportunity. But golf also teaches us that one hole doesn't define the round. Resiliency is about learning, adjusting, and moving forward.

The PGA Tour keeps a statistic called "Bounce Back" which measures the resiliency of all the Tour players. Bounce Back measures how often a player makes birdie or better immediately after making a bogey or worse. It's essentially a resilience metric —how quickly a golfer recovers from a mistake.

Who led this statistic in 2025? Who is the most resilient player in the world? The man who best recovers from adversity is the number one ranked player in the world – Scottie Scheffler.

Scheffler has openly said that Bounce Back is one of the stats he takes the most pride in. He attributes his success to accepting mistakes, maintaining emotional composure, and treating each error as a refocusing opportunity. He also emphasizes that controlling his golf ball and limiting mistakes helps him stay steady after setbacks.

This is akin to the concept of Next, previously covered on Hole 7. Compare Scheffler's comments to the process of Next: embracing the result, learning, letting go, and then focusing on the next shot, hole, or opportunity. If this works for the best player in the world, maybe we should incorporate that process into our game and our lives as well.

Inspirational Quote: It's not whether you get knocked down, it's whether you get up. – Anonymous

Scripture: Though he may stumble, he will not fall, for the Lord upholds him with his hand. – Psalm 37:24

Zen: If you are irritated by every rub, how will you get polished?

Golf Anecdote: After a tough start at the 2012 Masters, Bubba Watson rallied with resilience to win the tournament, showing the power of mental recovery. Watson struggled to hold onto his lead as he finished the final round, needing a sudden-death playoff to secure the win. On the second playoff hole, Watson's tee shot was deep in the woods. From the pine straw and with no clear line to the hole, Watson hit a pitching wedge from 164 yards out, hooking 40 yards, and finishing 10 feet from the hole. He won the Masters on that very hole.

GROWTH THROUGH ADVERSITY

Challenges are not roadblocks; they are stepping stones. Golf teaches us that adversity reveals character and builds strength. Resiliency is forged in the fire of difficulty.

I've experienced many good rounds on the golf course, and I've had lots of days that challenged my desire to play again. Every golfer has those days. We all have bad rounds where nothing clicks. Sometimes we go through a stretch of tough rounds. Those days teach us who we are and reveal our character. Those difficulties teach us our shortcomings and the places we need to build mental muscle and better skills.

I've also experienced the same highs and lows as a young athlete, as a father, as a husband, as a manager in my accounting career, and as a business owner when I was an agent for State Farm Insurance. The truth is, no matter what you do and what role you play, you will experience good days and you will experience very difficult days.

One of my best takeaways from M. Scott Peck's book, *The Road Less Travelled*, is what he calls one of the great truths in life. "Life is difficult. But, once we truly understand and accept that life is difficult, then that makes life a bit easier."

Why is that? Why does accepting that life is difficult make life easier? One reason is a truth shared by my good friend Alan McKimmy. "Expectation is a sure road to disappointment." That is so true. When you expect, you make a future desire real in this moment. And, if your expectation relies on another fallible human being, it's a matter of time before you're let down. Anyone in a long-term relationship knows that your biggest hurts and disappointments come from the people you love and those who love you the most.

If you expect life to be easy, you will live a life of great frustration. Life is not easy. Even those who make it look easy will admit that nothing is easy.

Netflix has a great mini-series called *Stutz*. Dr. Phil Stutz is the therapist for actor Jonah Hill. Dr. Stutz has a unique approach to therapy and psychiatry in which he claims our ability to function effectively in life is directly related to our acceptance of the fact that reality includes pain, uncertainty, and constant work. Wow. I thought life was supposed to be easy.

In my first management role as a first line accounting supervisor for State Farm, I was ill-prepared for the reality of what management involved. My college classes were pretty simple. Managers organize work and make sure employees know what to do. It seemed pretty simple. No problem.

The reality is that management was mostly problems. Employees had issues. People moved on. Equipment broke down. Data systems malfunctioned. Stress was high and my enjoyment of this reality was very low. After almost a year, I told my boss the job was not for me. The truth is I wasn't right for the job.

I went home that night, looked at myself, and found resolve and the resilience I needed in me. "I don't fail like this. I achieve. I'm capable, but I need to approach this differently." I decided to embrace problems as teachers and opportunities. I decided I would become the best supervisor on the staff. That's what I do —I figure out how to be successful and be the best.

The job was not the problem. My attitude and expectations were the problems. The job didn't change; I did. At the point when I was about to give up, I chose resiliency. I went to work the next day and told my boss I was going to change my attitude and approach, and I was going to do all the things it took to be the best on his staff. No one was going to work harder, and I was going to work smarter.

I went on to have a very good career at State Farm because of that one day, that one choice to change and to use challenges and the crucible of difficulties to build skills and character. I started reading books and dedicated myself to learning. Problems became opportunities to learn and build confidence. My life changed because, without knowing the term, I chose resilience.

Dr. Stutz emphasizes that pain is inevitable, but suffering is optional. Uncertainty is not a threat, it is the condition for possibility which includes creativity, courage, and connection. He also emphasizes that there is no finish line—the work is the path. These teachings are about growth and personal improvement. They are about accepting and working within reality to be the best you can be versus resisting reality. Remember, what you resist owns you! I chose in 1984 what I saw in his Netflix series in 2019—I just didn't know it at the time.

Inspirational Quote: Out of difficulties grow miracles. – Jean de La Bruyère

Scripture: We also glory in our sufferings, because we know that suffering produces perseverance; perseverance, character; and character, hope. – Romans 5:3-4

Zen: Nothing ever goes away until it has taught us what we need to know. — Pema Chödrön

Golf Anecdote: Stacy Lewis overcame scoliosis and multiple surgeries to become a top-ranked golfer—her story is one of resilience and triumph.

THE MENTAL GAME OF RESILIENCE

The Oxford Dictionary defines resilience as the psychological capacity to adapt, recover, and continue functioning in the face of adversity, stress, trauma, or significant challenges. It's not a fixed trait—it's a dynamic process shaped by mindset, skills, and environment.

Resiliency is as much mental as it is physical. Golf demands emotional control, focus, and the ability to reset after mistakes. The resilient golfer trains the mind to stay present and to stay positive. Next. Bounce back. Never give up. Stay the course and overcome. The bad hole is over. Make the next hole your best hole.

This is one of the great beauties and mysteries of the game. You can struggle all day and suddenly hit your best shot in weeks. You can have a bad hole and follow it with a great one. I once started a round in a golf league 7, 2, 7, 2. My first four holes went triple bogey, eagle, double bogey, birdie. My opponent said, "Scott, I can't tell if you are really good or if you suck at golf." We laughed hard. I parred in and shot 38 for that nine-hole round.

That is golf. That is life. Always in transition. Flowing from the top to the bottom and back again. It is a journey that tests our mettle and our mental fortitude. Along the way, we build character, learn, and grow. We find flashes of the indomitable spirit within us and within the people we love and admire. We go on and we move forward because we can.

Inspirational Quote: Strength doesn't come from what you can do. It comes from overcoming the things you once thought you couldn't. – Rikki Rogers

Scripture: Do not be anxious about anything, but in every situation, by prayer and petition, with thanksgiving, present your requests to God. – Philippians 4:6

Zen: Get the inside right and the outside will fall into place. – Eckhart Tolle

Golf Anecdote: Chip Beck's streak of 46 consecutive missed cuts becomes a vivid golf parable for resiliency because it shows what it looks like when a player keeps showing up long after the applause has stopped, and the narrative has turned against him.

During the late 1990s, Chip Beck—once a Ryder Cup star and the man who famously shot 59—fell into one of the deepest slumps in PGA Tour history. Week after week he packed his suitcase, traveled to the next event, and missed another cut. Forty-six times in a row. The streak became a running joke in the press, a statistic that overshadowed everything he had accomplished. Most players would have withdrawn, reinvented themselves, or quietly disappeared.

But Beck didn't. He kept teeing it up. He kept greeting volunteers with kindness. He kept signing autographs. He kept believing that the game hadn't seen the last of him.

Beck's streak teaches us resilience isn't glamorous. It's not the 59; it's the willingness to return after shooting 78. Identity matters more than outcome. Beck refused to let a slump define his character. Consistency under pressure reveals who we are. His optimism didn't waver even as the results did. Showing up is its own form of courage. Every Thursday morning, he chose to begin again.

Chip Beck's streak is remembered not as humiliation but as a testament to emotional steadiness. He didn't lash out, blame others, or retreat into bitterness. He carried himself with the same warmth and humility he had during his best years.

When he eventually found success again on the Champions Tour, the comeback felt less like redemption and more like confirmation of who he had always been. Beck's game came and went, but his character never wavered. Resiliency wins out.

SUMMARY

Resiliency is the quiet strength that carries us through life's challenges. In golf and in life, it's not about perfection—it's about persistence. Resilient hearts rise, recover, and keep swinging and playing.

HOLE RESULT: 423-YARD PAR 4

After making double bogey on the 14th hole, we now face this very challenging par 4. Resiliency is about bouncing back from the last hole and rising to the challenge here. "Okay, Scott, we're only 1 over. Let's relax and reset. Next."

A solid drive finds the left third of the fairway, leaving a three wood to the green. I pull the second shot slightly left, finding the green-side trap. The sand shot needs to carry 10 yards and then release downhill another few feet to the pin. My 54-degree sand wedge splashes the sand perfectly and the ball lands right where I was looking. As the ball releases toward the pin, I can see this has a chance to go in. Five feet. Two feet. Six inches. It drops. Birdie! Score after 15 holes: Even par.

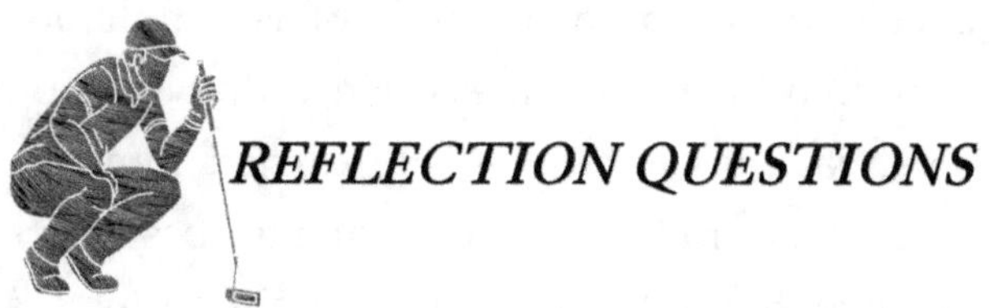

1. How do you generally respond to setbacks in your life?
2. What is your best personal example of showing resiliency?
3. What practices help you stay mentally strong?

BOOK RECOMMENDATION: MAN'S SEARCH FOR MEANING BY VICTOR FRANKL

Viktor Frankl's *Man's Search for Meaning* is one of the most influential works ever written on human resilience. His central claim, that meaning gives people the strength to endure suffering, directly explains how people survive, adapt, and grow through extreme adversity.

Frankl observed in the concentration camps that those who survived were not the strongest physically—they were the ones who had a reason to live. He famously wrote: "Those who have a why to live can bear almost any how." This idea is the backbone of resilience.

Frankl emphasizes that even in the camps—where nearly all external control was removed—people retained one freedom: the freedom to choose their attitude. This is a foundational resilience principle.

Frankl's book is essentially a masterclass in resilience. It teaches that suffering is unavoidable, meaning is essential, attitude is a choice, purpose fuels endurance, and humans can grow through hardship, not just survive it. This book is a must read!

SONG: "WHATEVER IT TAKES" BY IMAGINE DRAGONS (2017)

"Whatever it Takes" frames adversity as fuel for growth. The song opens with imagery of danger, pressure, and vulnerability —"falling too fast," "tripping," "everybody circling"—which mirrors the real emotional landscape of hardship. Instead of collapsing under it, the narrator uses it as motivation. This is resilience: stress becomes a catalyst, not a cage.

The repeated mantra, "Whatever it takes," is described as a symbol of unwavering commitment to push through difficulty and pursue growth. Resilience research calls this persistence despite adversity—the ability to stay engaged even when the path is steep.

"Whatever It Takes" is a resilience anthem because it transforms fear into fuel, pressure into purpose, and adversity into identity. It mirrors the psychological definition of resilience: adapting, persisting, and growing through challenge.

MOVIE TO WATCH: *ROCKY* (1976)

Rocky is one of the clearest cinematic expressions of resilience ever made. Rocky is not the most talented fighter. He's not the fastest, strongest, or most promising. He's a small-time boxer who's been overlooked, dismissed, and underestimated.

Resilience is defined as the ability to adapt, persist, and continue functioning despite adversity—and Rocky does exactly that. He doesn't quit when the world tells him he's average. He doesn't collapse under the weight of his circumstances. He keeps showing up.

Rocky's breakthrough moment comes when he realizes, "All I wanna do is go the distance." This is pure resilience psychology. He shifts from outcome to process. From external validation to internal meaning. From "I must win" to "I must not give up on myself."

Rocky shows that resilience is not talent, perfection, winning, or ease. Resilience is showing up, taking the hit, getting back up, staying in the fight, finding meaning in the struggle, and becoming someone you respect.

Rocky is the cinematic embodiment of the resilient human spirit refusing to be broken.

16 HOLE #16: RESPECT & BEHAVIORAL ACCOUNTABILITY

162-YARD PAR 3

The 16th hole is called "Respect and Behavioral Mastery." This par 3 requires precision, patience, and discipline. It punishes carelessness and rewards intentionality. The green is small and slightly angled from back left to front right and it is protected by water left and sand traps both long and right center. The downhill tee shot requires accuracy with the only bail out area short right. This is a good hole to take par and move on—and bogey is better than the double bogey that is in play here with water fifteen feet left of the stick.

RESPECT AND BEHAVIORAL ACCOUNTABILITY

Respect is not a feeling; it's a behavior. Just as golf demands respect for the course, the rules, the pace of play, and the other golfers, life demands respect expressed through consistent, observable actions. Respect is expressed through attention—listening fully, noticing impact, slowing down before reacting.

Respect is revealed in the small things: tone, timing, follow-through, honesty, and self-control.

Golf is a gentlemen's game rooted in long-standing traditions. Golf etiquette is the unwritten code of conduct that keeps the game safe, smooth, respectful, and enjoyable for everyone on the course. Think of it as the emotional intelligence of golf: the habits that show awareness of others, the environment, and the rhythm of the game.

Those habits show respect for safety. Don't swing when someone is too close. Don't walk ahead of your playing partners. Don't hit until the group ahead is clearly out of range. Yell "Fore!" if a shot might hit someone.

Golf etiquette is also built upon a respect for the pace of play. Be ready when it's your turn. Take only one or two practice swings. Keep up with the group ahead, not just ahead of the group behind, and if you're falling behind, let faster groups play through.

Good golf habits include respect for the course. Replace or fill divots. Repair ball marks on greens. Rake bunkers after use. Avoid damaging the cup when removing your ball.

The game also is built on respect for other players. Stay still and quiet during someone's swing. Don't stand in their line of sight or shadow. Don't walk on someone's putting line. Celebrate, but don't gloat—win and lose with class and dignity. You see, golf is a game of respect. Dress appropriately and behave well. Have fun and be respectful. Be kind and show others that you respect yourself, them, and the game. Unfortunately, golf events can be the best of times and the worst of times when it comes to fan behavior as evidenced by The Masters and The Ryder Cup.

The fan behavior at The Masters is exemplary. Masters fan conduct is famously polite and supportive. Augusta National expects "patrons" to behave with quiet respect, move calmly, avoid distractions, and honor the traditions of the tournament. The rules are enforced more tightly than at any other event on tour, and violations can lead to ejection or permanent loss of ticket privileges—and those ticket privileges are the most sacred in golf.

At The Masters, there are no electronic devices allowed—no cell phones, no smart watches, no tablets, and no cameras. There is no running allowed as spectators are required to walk at all times. All patrons must wear collared shirts, maintain quiet during shots, avoid blocking the views of others, and respect the marshals and volunteers. The Masters emphasizes—actually requires—tradition, courtesy, and calm. The result is a viewing experience unlike any other: serene, orderly, and deeply respectful of the game.

In contrast, The Ryder Cup matches have become an event known for disrespectful, and frankly, vulgar behavior. The combination of intense rivalry and alcohol has produced some of the rudest behavior imaginable—not only toward players, but also toward players' wives and children. The matches in New York in September of 2025 were held amidst a new low of fan behavior. As an American, I was embarrassed for our players and our country in witnessing the horrendous fan behavior at these matches.

There was no excuse for fans to yell "F* you Rory," as Rory McIlroy stood over his ball throughout the weekend matches. This happened not once, but frequently, to Rory. Even the first tee announcer led a group cheer of "F* you Rory," leading to her termination. What was she thinking? Sad. Several of the visiting Team Europe players were verbally abused like this. That kind of behavior is well outside the traditions of golf, and I hope the Ryder Cup organizers require a return to the roots of golf tradition—respect and good sportsmanship—for all matches going forward. The players, and the game, deserve it!

Unfortunately, it seems as though behavior in our society these days is much more like Ryder Cup behavior than Masters behavior. It starts at the top with our president—he seems to have a third-grade nickname for everyone who opposes him: former President "Sleepy Joe" Biden, "Little Marco" Rubio (our Secretary of State—4th in line of presidential succession) and others. Presidents should act presidential, not like third graders.

We live in a time where "road rage," "trash talking," "social media shaming," and dominance are king. Family therapist Terry Real says our dominance based patriarchal society is destroying our culture, our relationships, and our world. The loss of respect as a virtue in our world is extremely costly.

The answer, according to Real, is a return to a respect-based model for relationships where compassion and integrity are cherished and people are treated as different, but equal. People are not better or worse; we are each different and equal. I miss the world in which we can disagree and still be friends who respect each other and each other's rights to our own opinions. When did we forget how to disagree respectfully?

Fortunately, there are pockets of society where respect is still a virtue. I see it in small acts of kindness in everyday life: people holding doors for others, people sharing generously with others in need, people showing patience in the Starbucks line, a man picking up a plastic bag blowing in the wind in the grocery store parking lot, friends attending funerals for the family members of their neighbors, and countless other acts of respect, showing that the well-being of others still matters.

In our own homes, we honor and respect each other when we actively listen to understand, when we support the learning and growth of our family members, when we help a neighbor with a problem, and when we allow space for others to rest, recover, and manage emotions. We cook for each other, clean dishes, give our time, and share the best of ourselves emotionally, intellectually, spiritually, financially, and physically.

Respect is about honoring others, their needs, desires, and their personal preferences. Respect is about listening and sharing equally. Respect is about each person seizing their personal power without imposing that power on the people they love. Respect is about living in a way which shows that I matter, and so do you! Every life matters. Everyone deserves our respect. Everyone is worthy.

Inspirational Quote: Respect is earned by actions, not granted by titles.

Scripture: Show proper respect to everyone. – 1 Peter 2:17

Zen: Gossip dies when it hits a wise person's ears. – Buddha

Golf Anecdote: Jack Nicklaus's concession at the 1969 Ryder Cup is one of the most iconic acts of respect in golf, arguably the defining example of sportsmanship in the sport.

The Ryder Cup was tied 15½–15½. Everything came down to the final match: Jack Nicklaus (USA) vs. Tony Jacklin (Great Britain). On the 18th green at Royal Birkdale, Jacklin had a 2½-foot putt to tie the match. If he missed, the U.S. would win outright. If he made it, the Ryder Cup would end in a tie for the first time ever.

Before Jacklin could putt, Nicklaus picked up Jacklin's marker, conceding the putt. This meant the match was halved, the Ryder Cup was tied, and no winner was declared. Nicklaus later said, "I didn't think it was right for him to have a chance to miss it." This was an extraordinary act of sportsmanship and respect. Nicklaus wasn't being generous—he was being principled. He believed that no Ryder Cup should be decided by a short putt under crushing pressure. This is respect personified.

THE IMPORTANCE OF BEHAVIORAL ACCOUNTABILITY

Behavioral accountability is the natural companion to respect: If I respect you, you can see it in how I behave. Behavioral accountability is the practice of taking responsibility for your actions, their impact, and the commitments you've made—consistently, transparently, and without defensiveness. It's the opposite of avoidance, blame-shifting, or emotional excuses.

Accountability is not punishment, it's alignment. It's the bridge between intention and impact. It's how relationships stay safe, predictable, and trustworthy.

Behavioral accountability is keeping commitments, owning mistakes, repairing harm, and speaking truth with humility. Behavioral accountability is acting with respect, and it is revealed when it costs you something. By showing respect, behavioral accountability strengthens connections rather than threatening them.

Golf requires respect for the rules, imposing behavioral accountability through penalty strokes. If you hit your ball out of bounds, the penalty is stroke and distance, meaning you drop another ball at the same spot, add two strokes to your score, and play on. If you lose your ball (can't find it after a three-minute search), the penalty is similar to an out of bounds ball—return to the spot where you first hit the lost ball, drop another ball, add two strokes and play on. If you hit your ball in the water, drop another ball, add one stroke, and play on. If your ball moves because you are clearing the area around it, add a stroke and play on. If you tee off in front of the tee markers, re-tee behind the markers and add two strokes—you are now hitting shot three. In match play, the penalty is loss of the hole.

Behavioral accountability on the course includes acting in

accordance with and in the spirit of the rules and etiquette of the game. It involves behaving with respect for others and for the game itself.

The difference between the fan behavior at The Masters and the Ryder Cup comes down to behavioral accountability. At The Masters, fans behave appropriately because they respect the traditions of Augusta National and The Masters. Fans also behave extraordinarily well there because the tournament organizers hold fans accountable for their behavior with a zero-tolerance policy. I don't think it's a coincidence that the hardest ticket to get in sports is the same event that has the best fan behavior and the highest degree of behavioral accountability—yes, that is The Masters at Augusta National Golf Club.

If there is one moment that defines respect and behavioral accountability in golf, it is captured in a photo taken by CBS cameraman Erik Leidal at the conclusion of the 2021 Masters. Japan's Hideki Matsuyama won the Masters that year, and his caddie, Shota Hiyafuji, returned to the 18th green after all the players, spectators and press had already left the grounds.

Appearing alone on Augusta's 18th green, Hayafuji carried a furled yellow flag in one hand and a flagstick in the other. Tradition says the Masters winner takes the 18th flag home with him. It's the caddie's job to secure it. Returning the unadorned flagstick to the cup, Hayafuji checked that task off the list. Then it happened.

Pausing, spontaneously, in what he thought was a private moment, Hayafuji took one step back, turned to the course before him, removed his hat, and bowed. In Japanese culture, the meaning of a bow can take on many forms. A bow says hello or goodbye. It is a sign of respect. A bow can be an apology, or it may be an acknowledgment of status.

Hiyafuji's act was one of reverence and gratitude – a sign of respect when he believed no one else was looking. His was a nod to the sacred grounds of Augusta National, and it became a viral sign of respect from a humble and deeply appreciative man. Meditate on this photo for a moment. Be with him as he shows respect and gratitude for the experience of a lifetime. Let this moment sink into your being and take its lesson with you wherever you go. This is respect and behavioral accountability.

Unfortunately, there seems to be a glaring lack of behavioral accountability at the Ryder Cup matches. Fan behavior shows that many fans are not holding themselves accountable for respectful behavior at these matches. And it is unfortunate that the event organizers do not seem to be holding fans sufficiently accountable for their behavior either.

The result is abhorrent behavior from many people that taints the image of the event. The competition and caliber of play at the Ryder Cup matches is fantastic. The fan behavior is embarrassing at best. Why? It is all about the lack of behavioral accountability.

How does this concept play out in our lives off of the course? Let's start with self-respect. Self-respect is the root of behavioral accountability. Respecting yourself means telling yourself the truth. Be honest with yourself. The last person you should deceive is you. Hold yourself to high standards of behavior. Be the best you that you can be.

Meister Eckhart, one of the most influential Christian mystics in Western history, best known for his teachings on the "ground of the soul," once said, "A human being has so many skins inside, covering the depths of the heart … thirty or forty skins or hides, as thick and hard as an ox's or bear's, cover the soul. Go into your own ground and learn to know yourself there."

Plato was known to teach on the importance of "knowing thyself." Later in life, Plato shifted his teachings to "know your soul." This is the starting point for personal behavioral accountability.

Behavioral accountability is similar to emotional intelligence. The difference is that behavioral accountability is about actions and behavior versus understanding emotions. Remember, behavior is a language. Behavior speaks louder than words. This makes it vitally important that you are accountable first to yourself, and to others, for the behaviors and actions you choose to undertake. No one can make you do something—you are the master of your own ship and your own behavior.

How do we show behavioral accountability? We own our choices without making excuses. We understand and we claim our power to choose, to act, to speak, to do. We do not blame others, rather we accept responsibility for what we do and what we fail to do. We hold ourselves to high standards of behavior. We admit and own our mistakes. We are honest and transparent. We apologize when we do damage. We repair relationships. We respect the needs of ourselves and others for space, for individuality, for opportunities to learn and grow. We recognize that our behavior is our responsibility and nobody else's.

Does this mean our speech and behavior are perfect? No. We are not perfect. We are all flawed. But we can learn and grow and improve as we strive for perfection. This is another paradox in golf and in life—we are not perfect, but we should strive for perfection. Joy and grace exist in the process of seeking improvement.

Let's look at a case study for behavioral accountability. Suppose my wife and I are having a disagreement, and she feels triggered and needs time to decompress. If I am emotionally unregulated and pursue her through a closed door, my behavior shows that I am not being accountable for my actions.

First, I am out of control—my emotions are controlling me. Also, by ignoring the closed door, I am disrespecting my wife's need for time, space, and safety. I am dominating the agenda and forcing my will to meet my needs on her when she needs safety. I am not building trust and connection; I am damaging both with dominance.

Behavioral accountability would be reflected by respecting her needs and wishes for time, space, and safety. If I were behaving properly and accountable for my behavior, I would be open to my wife's needs as much as I was focused on my own. I would be in control of my emotions and my actions. I would be acting in ways that build trust and connection instead of eroding them. I would be calm in the storm, not creating the storm.

The simple truth is, life is built on relationships, and relationships are built on behavioral accountability—consistent, respectful, trustworthy, compassionate behavioral accountability. Trust and connection are built on dependable behavior, and relationships and repairs are dependent on behavioral ownership, awareness, and kindness.

No relationship can survive when one of the members is unwilling to be honest about their behavior, when they are unwilling to accept responsibility for their words and deeds, and when they are unwilling or unable to admit their mistakes and apologize and learn from them. Good relationships require us to act with authenticity, respect, and accountability.

Inspirational Quote: Integrity is choosing courage over comfort; choosing what is right over what is fun, fast, or easy." – Brené Brown

Scripture: Be doers of the word, and not hearers only, deceiving yourselves. James 1:22

Zen: You are perfect as you are, and you could use a little improvement. - Shunryu Suzuki

Golf Anecdote: The Brian Davis Self-Penalty (RBC Heritage, 2010)

One of the most striking modern examples of behavioral accountability in golf happened during the 2010 RBC Heritage at Harbour Town. Brian Davis, an English golfer, was in a sudden-death playoff against Jim Furyk—his best chance ever to win a PGA Tour event.

On his first playoff hole, Davis hit his approach into a hazard area near the green. As he prepared to play his next shot, his club brushed a loose reed during his backswing. No one saw it. Not the cameras. Not the officials. Not his opponent. But Davis felt it.

Davis immediately called over a rules official and said, "I think I moved something. Slow-motion replay confirmed it: his club had indeed touched a loose impediment in the hazard. Penalty: two strokes. Outcome: he lost the tournament.

Jim Furyk was stunned. Spectators were stunned. Commentators called it one of the most honorable moments in modern golf. Davis later said, "I play by the rules. That's the game." That is behavioral accountability.

SUMMARY

Respect and behavioral accountability sit at the heart of both golf and a well-lived life. Golf makes this visible in a uniquely uncompromising way: there's no referee, no hiding, no short-cuts. Players call penalties on themselves, protect the integrity of the course, and honor their competitors because the game only works when everyone chooses honesty over advantage.

That same ethic translates powerfully into everyday life. Respect creates trust, safety, and connection, while accountability builds reliability and character. Together, they form a quiet contract: your actions matter, and they affect the people around you. Whether on the fairway or in relationships, these two qualities shape environments where people can grow, collaborate, and show up as their best selves.

HOLE RESULT: 162-YARD PAR 3

This hole has a red-light pin with the cup center left and only 15 feet from the edge of the lake. A solid six iron should reach the front of the green. Avoiding the water, I hit a slight push, missing the green right. Only 5 feet from the putting surface, a little 9 iron chip runs up the slope, stopping 3 feet short of the hole. Par is secured with a solid tap in putt. Score through 16 holes: Even Par

REFLECTION QUESTIONS

1. How do you show respect through your actions?
2. Where in your life do you avoid accountability and what does that cost you?

3. How does your behavioral accountability need to improve when you are triggered?

4. What is one area where you want and need to raise your behavioral standards? Why?

BOOK RECOMMENDATION: *DARING GREATLY* BY BRENÉ BROWN

Daring Greatly speaks to respect and behavioral mastery in a surprisingly direct way: Brown argues that vulnerability is the gateway to courage, integrity, and aligned action—the very ingredients of both respect and accountable behavior. Her framework shows that you cannot practice real respect for others (or yourself) without the willingness to be seen, to own your choices, and to close the gap between your aspirational values and your practiced values.

Brown's concept of "minding the gap"—holding your lived behavior up against your stated values—is essentially a blueprint for behavioral accountability. She argues that courage requires aligning action with principle, even when it's uncomfortable. Behavioral mastery in her framework includes owning your choices instead of hiding behind defenses or excuses.

It also includes recognizing your armor (perfectionism, numbing, cynicism) and choosing more courageous behaviors, addressing shame so it doesn't drive reactive, disrespectful, or avoidant patterns, and repairing ruptures rather than pretending they didn't happen.

This is the same muscle required in relationships, leadership, and even golf: the discipline to act with integrity when no one is watching.

SONG: "FATHER AND SON" BY CAT STEVENS (1970)

Cat Stevens' "Father and Son" is one of those rare songs that quietly teaches respect and emotional accountability without ever using the language of psychology. When you look at it through the lens of respect and behavioral mastery, it becomes a powerful study in how two people can completely miss each other—not because they don't care, but because they don't yet have the skills to bridge the emotional gap.

The father's voice is full of care, but it's also full of certainty. He believes he knows what's best, and he speaks from a place of authority rather than curiosity. He wants to protect his son. He wants to guide him. But he doesn't actually hear him.

The son, meanwhile, respects his father deeply—you can feel the ache in his voice—but he feels unseen, unheard, and misunderstood. He's not trying to rebel. He's trying to express his inner world. He wants space to become who he is, not who he's told to be.

The tragedy is that both love each other, but neither feels respected in the way they need to be respected. This is the core lesson: respect isn't about intention; it's about impact. You can love someone and still fail to honor their experience.

Respect requires seeing the other person's reality. Behavioral mastery requires managing your own reactions so you can stay present enough to do that.

MOVIE TO WATCH: *REMEMBER THE TITANS* (2000)

Remember the Titans is a wonderful film in which respect and behavioral accountability transform individuals, relationships, and entire systems. Beneath the football storyline, the film is really about people learning to see each other, own their actions, and choose integrity over comfort—the same actions required for healthy teams, families, and communities.

At the start, the players don't lack intelligence or talent; they lack respect born from understanding. The previously segregated teammates carry inherited narratives, biases, and fears born in racism. They assume they already know who the other person is. They protect themselves with distance, sarcasm, or hostility.

The turning point comes when they're forced into proximity and honest conversation. Gerry and Julius confronting each other is the clearest example: respect emerges only when they drop their armor and speak truthfully about effort, selfishness, and responsibility.

Coach Boone demands respect not as obedience but as recognition of shared humanity and shared purpose. The film shows that respect isn't politeness; it's the willingness to see someone fully and let yourself be seen in return. The Titans don't become a great team because they like each other. They become a great team because they learn to take responsibility for their behavior. In that process, both victory and deep life-long relationships are created and lived out in respect and appreciation.

17 HOLE #17: BELIEF AND THE INNER GAME

434-YARD PAR 4

With two holes to go, we have a chance to post an excellent round of even par. But the 17th hole will require our best if we are to stay even. This long par 4, called "Belief," demands our best drive. Then we need our best fairway wood second shot to a small and well-guarded green. The fairway is a dogleg right cut through trees with traps in reach both right and left. The green is slightly elevated, and the pin is protected by deep traps on both sides of the green. This hole plays like a par 5, so recording par 4 here is a rare achievement.

Belief is the foundation of performance. In golf, as in life, what we believe shapes how we act, how we respond to challenges, and how we grow. This chapter explores the power of belief—the inner game that determines our outer results.

THE POWER OF BELIEF

Belief is more than optimism—it's conviction. It's the quiet voice that says, "You can do this," even when doubt creeps in. Golf teaches us that belief must precede achievement. Before the swing, before the score, there is belief.

In my experience, doubt shows up in your golf swing and in your results. Whether you are on the tee, in the fairway, or on or near the green, any lack of belief in your club choice or your ability will lead to a poorly executed shot. When you doubt your read on the green, the chance of sinking that putt is almost zero.

The gap between good golfers and elite golfers is enormous, and it has surprisingly little to do with raw swing mechanics. The real separator is deeply rooted belief. Belief leads to consistency under pressure, which is built on a foundation of mental skill, emotional regulation, and decision-making discipline.

What separates Tiger Woods and Jack Nicklaus from "Joe Schmoe" on the PGA Tour is the inner game, the deeply rooted belief in their ability when the circumstance demands it most. Every tour player is highly skilled. Every tour player has spent a lifetime honing their craft. Every tour player has the physical skills to win. It is the inner game, the mental game, and belief that elevates the performance of the elite players.

Like confidence, belief is built through preparation, practice, and repetition. Belief goes deeper. Belief is reinforced by habits and behavior. Confidence says, "I can." Belief says, "I have, and I will." Belief conquers doubts. Belief eliminates doubts.

When I play golf, I can tell you there is a huge difference in results when I approach a shot with belief. When I believe, when I truly believe, execution is solid. When I approach a shot with hope, where doubt is present, execution is spotty at best. I rarely pull off a good shot if I don't believe I have that shot and will execute it without any doubt. When I believe I will make the putt, I almost always do. Belief is critical.

Why is belief so critical? Gregory Dickow, an American pastor, author, and broadcaster best known as the founder and senior pastor of Life Changers International Church, speaks to the importance of the inner game and the power of belief in this way:

Your thoughts become your beliefs.

Your beliefs become your behaviors.

Your behavior becomes your habits.

Your habits form your character.

And your character determines your destiny; it determines how high you will go.

Everybody has that opportunity right where they are in life. Make progress in that process. Today!

Dickow is spot on here. I'm not sure that many people consider "the process" of our thinking leading to beliefs, to behaviors, to habits, to character, and to our destiny.

The truth is, our results are a consequence of our thoughts and the process of thoughts becoming habits that produce outcomes. What does this mean? If you want to change your results, you must start by changing your thinking.

Is there another way to change results? Absolutely. James Clear, author of *Atomic Habits*, argues that the first thing to change is your identity—your belief about who you are. How does this work? According to Clear, there is a feedback loop that starts with identity and self-belief. *Atomic Habits* is about focusing on systems of behavior and actions as they form your identity.

Clear says you don't change your life by trying to think differently first. You change your thinking by behaving your way into a new identity. According to Clear, habits are not about goals, they're about identity. Good habits aren't just actions. They are votes for the type of person you believe you are. When you repeat a behavior, your brain updates its self-image: "I practiced my short game today" → "I'm the kind of golfer who prepares."

For Clear, identity follows action, not the other way around. Clear emphasizes that the brain updates its beliefs based on evidence. And the evidence comes from tiny, repeated behaviors. Every action you take is a vote for the person you wish to become. True behavior change is identity change. Choose your identity, and act in ways that reinforce that identity.

This means you don't need a massive breakthrough to think differently. You need small, consistent proof through consistent action.

Systems will change thinking more reliably than motivation according to Clear. His famous line is: "You do not rise to the level of your goals. You fall to the level of your systems of action."

According to Clear, systems—the process of actions and habits you repeat every day—create predictable behaviors. Predictable behaviors create predictable thoughts. Predictable thoughts create a stable identity. Process dictates results and identity.

This is why elite performers—athletes, writers, leaders— don't rely on motivation. They rely on systems (processes) that shape their thinking automatically. They place their belief in managing systems of small behaviors that change identity, thoughts, and the direction of their efforts.

Whether you believe in the thought model presented by Gregory Dickow or the system of *atomic habits* offered by James Clear, what you believe matters.

The atheist behaves differently than the person who believes in God. The person who believes in the Atkins diet behaves differently than the person who believes in the Mediterranean diet. The person who believes in abundance behaves differently than the person who believes in scarcity. The spouse who believes their partner is trustworthy behaves differently than the spouse who believes their partner cannot be trusted.

Let me ask you, what do you believe? Why do you believe these things? Earlier I encouraged you to spend time thinking about what you value (and what you do not value). This is a good time to consider what you believe. Take a sheet of paper and record what you believe. This is a powerful exercise. Why? What you believe matters. Even atheists worship something.

Your thinking, your behavior, your habits, your character, your results, and your destiny are intimately intertwined with your beliefs. Choose your beliefs wisely.

Inspirational Quote: Whether you think you can, or you think you can't—you're right. – Henry Ford

Scripture: Everything is possible for one who believes. – Mark 9:23

Zen: When you realize the truth, you find that you have always believed it. - Zen proverb

Golf Anecdote: Jack Nicklaus—The 1986 Masters: Belief Awakens a Champion

By 1986, Jack Nicklaus was 46 years old. Sportswriters said he was finished. He hadn't won a major in six years. His putting was shaky. His swing looked slower. Even his son Jackie, who was caddying for him, later admitted he didn't expect anything magical. But Jack still believed something quietly, stubbornly, internally: "If I get into contention, I know how to win."

That belief, rooted in decades of proof, was dormant, not dead. Standing on the 15th tee on Sunday, Jack was several shots back. He turned to Jackie and said something that still gives golfers chills: "Let's see if we can make a little noise." That wasn't bravado. That was belief reactivating.

Nicklaus made eagle on 15, birdie on 16, birdie on 17, and par on 18 to post 65. The roars rolled across Augusta like thunder. Players ahead of him felt the pressure. The leaderboard shifted. And Nicklaus won his 18th major.

Why is this story the perfect example of belief? Nicklaus didn't suddenly find a new swing. He didn't magically become younger. He didn't rely on hope. He relied on identity-level belief:

- I know how to win.
- I've done this before.
- If I get close, I trust myself.

His belief didn't create talent; it unlocked it. The deeper lesson? Belief is not positive thinking. Belief is remembered evidence. Nicklaus had decades of proof that he could close. When he chose to believe again, his body responded. Belief is the bridge between preparation and performance. It turns ability into action.

SUMMARY

Belief is the inner compass that guides us through life's fairways and roughs. In golf and in life, belief shapes our actions, fuels our courage, and defines our outcomes. Cultivating belief is not just a mental exercise; it's a spiritual practice.

HOLE RESULT: 434-YARD PAR 4

This hole is as tough a par 4 as you will ever face. A solid drive in the left center of the fairway leaves an uphill shot from 190 yards out. The green is small and kidney—shaped, with traps right and left. There is no good bailout area, and missing right leaves a shot straight up a steep hill through trees.

If I catch a good three wood, I can reach the left corner of the green. I have done it before on this hole. I stand over the ball, "good tempo, Scott. Don't force it, no tension. Relax and make a good swing. You don't have to be great, just good. Just get it in the neighborhood, and you can make 4 with a good chip." The swing and contact are solid, but the ball is just left of the target. Now we face a tough chip shot, a flop shot over the trap. Long is dead and short is in the sand.

Trust is a must. I take a long and slow swing with my 60-degree wedge. The ball carries the trap and lands softly on the fringe, trickling to five feet from the cup. The fast par putt breaks a foot from left to right. I know this from years of playing this hole. "Trust the process, Scott, and make a good stroke. You've got this. You can feel it." The stroke is good and the ball moves steadily down to the cup from left to right, catching the top left of the hole and falling in. That is a well-earned par! Score through 17 holes: Even par.

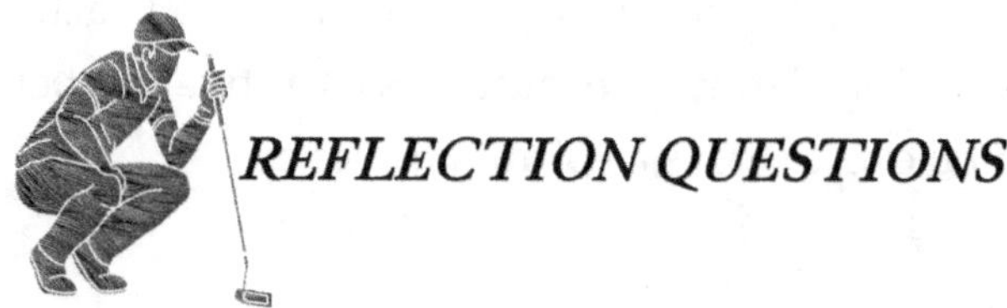

REFLECTION QUESTIONS

1. What beliefs are shaping your current path?

2. How do you strengthen your belief in yourself during difficult times?
3. What practices help you stay grounded in your inner truth?

BOOK RECOMMENDATION: WHAT MATTERS MOST BY JAMES HOLLIS

James Hollis's *What Matters Most* is one of the clearest bridges between belief, identity, and the inner game—not just in golf, but in any domain where performance depends on the mind. Hollis isn't writing about sports, yet his ideas map almost perfectly onto the psychological architecture of elite performance.

Hollis argues that the central task of adulthood is to move from fear-based living to soul-directed living. That shift is fundamentally about belief: belief in your own agency, belief that you can tolerate uncertainty, and belief that you can carry your own life forward.

Hollis teaches that growth requires stepping into discomfort and uncertainty. Belief is the courage to answer that summons. The inner game is the movement from fear to freedom. Hollis says the central question is: Does this choice enlarge me or diminish me?

The inner game asks the same question. Does this thought enlarge my ability to perform? Does this belief free my swing or tighten it? Does this story help me trust myself or undermine me? Belief becomes a performance tool when it is liberating, not constricting. Belief is the soul's permission slip for performance.

SONG: "DON'T STOP BELIEVIN" BY JOURNEY (1981)

"Don't Stop Believin" by Journey is a song about holding onto belief when circumstances don't justify it. The characters in the song are uncertain, searching, lonely, and in transition. Nothing in their external world guarantees success. And yet the refrain insists: keep believing anyway.

This mirrors the inner game perfectly: belief is not a reaction to circumstances. Belief is a stance you take in spite of them. "Don't Stop Believin'" isn't telling you to be cheerful. It's telling you to stay connected to who you are becoming.

In summary, "Don't Stop Believin'" is the anthem of the inner game. It's the reminder that belief is not a feeling—it's a choice to stay aligned with your larger self even when the moment feels small." In fact, belief is the refusal to shrink.

MOVIE TO WATCH: *FIELD OF DREAMS* (1989)

Field of Dreams is one of the most powerful cinematic metaphors for belief—not belief as wishful thinking, but belief as a courageous inner stance that shapes reality.

Belief precedes evidence. Ray Kinsella hears a voice, "If you build it, he will come." There is no proof, no guarantee, no logic, no external validation. And yet he acts. This is the essence of belief: belief is a commitment made before certainty exists.

Belief requires stepping into the unknown. Ray plows under his corn—his livelihood—to build a field no one else understands. This is pure James Hollis: the soul calls you toward expansion, the ego screams for safety, and growth requires stepping into uncertainty. Ray's choice is the same choice every golfer faces over a pressure shot. Will you shrink into fear or expand into trust?

The voice Ray hears is symbolic—it's the inner summons Hollis describes: the call to authenticity, the call to meaning, the call to a larger life. No one else hears it because belief is always personal.

Belief creates connection. The entire film is about reconnection: Ray and his father, Ray and his own courage, Ray and his deeper purpose. Belief opens the door to healing. In performance terms, belief reconnects you with your natural self. When you believe, you stop interfering. You stop controlling. You let your true ability emerge. Belief is contagious. At first, Ray is alone in his conviction. Then Annie believes. Then Terrence Mann believes. Then Moonlight Graham believes. Belief spreads. Belief is a social force.

The entire story is a psychological journey from doubt to trust, from fear to courage, from confusion to clarity, and from inherited stories to chosen identity. Ray's final act—playing catch with his father—is symbolic. Belief brings you back to yourself. That's the inner game in its purest form.

Field of Dreams is a story about belief as a transformative force. Belief that asks you to trust your inner summons, act without guarantees, and step into a larger version of yourself. It's the same belief required to play the inner game of golf and to succeed in any chosen endeavor—marriage, parenthood, friendship, work, whatever you choose.

Belief is the courage to build the field before you see who will come.

18 HOLE #18: HUMILITY AND FLEXIBILITY: BE LIKE WATER

527-YARD PAR 5

The 18th hole is a beautiful par 5 called "Humility and Flexibility: Be Like Water." This par 5 calls us to be like water, but the key to this hole is to avoid the water. The elevated tee shot is challenged by a tree-lined out of bounds left. There is also a series of traps and a creek right, so the tee shot must find the fairway below.

Our second shot angles slightly left, requiring precision to negotiate the out of bounds left and the pond on the right that starts at 125 yards out and leads to the right portion of the green. Long hitters may have a chance to reach this hole in two shots.

My strategy is to play two smart shots and reduce this hole to the shot that matters most—an approach from roughly 90 yards. The pin is protected by deep traps left and front center of the green. Anything right is wet. This hole offers a birdie chance, but big numbers are also in play. Finish well. Three good swings, and we cap off a great round of golf!

HUMILITY AND FLEXIBILITY

Humility and flexibility are quiet strengths. In golf, as in life, the ability to adapt and the willingness to learn are essential and ongoing. This chapter explores how humility opens us to growth and how flexibility allows us to navigate change with grace.

THE STRENGTH OF HUMILITY

Humility is not weakness—it's wisdom. It's the recognition that we don't know everything and that every round, every shot, is an opportunity to learn. Golf teaches us to stay teachable, to accept feedback, and to grow from our mistakes.

Humility is the steady, grounded recognition that you are not the center of the universe. It's the ability to see yourself accurately—your strengths without exaggeration, your limitations without shame—and to stay open to learning, correction, and growth.

Humility is the quality of being grounded, teachable, and free from arrogance, marked by an honest awareness of one's strengths and limitations and a willingness to learn from others. It is not self-deprecation; it's self-accuracy. It's strength without swagger. It's confidence without entitlement. It's the posture that keeps you curious instead of defensive.

Humility is the quiet confidence that requires no stroking of the ego. It is a heavenly virtue that strengthens relationships while creating inner peace and stabilizing power. It doesn't need Facebook likes or to count the number of Instagram followers. Humility says, "There is so much I don't know, but I do know that you matter to me."

Humility is grounded and self-aware without being self-promoting; open, curious, and teachable; honest, connectional, and collaborative; and willing to admit mistakes and value the perspectives of others. Humility is supportive, encouraging, and seeks win-win. It is the opposite of pride. Pride is self-promoting, arrogant, boastful, competitive, closed, defensive, craving validation, hides mistakes, blameful, anchored in ego, and dismissive of others. Pride plays win-lose and seeks power. Pride is dependent and needy.

It's interesting how the paradox of pride and humility plays out; the prideful man claims he is important, and this makes him small, and the humble man is powerful because he makes himself small.

Golf is a very humbling game. The golf course is a place where the ego goes to die—and that is a good thing. The best golfers play with a calmness and patience that rarely exists in the hustle and bustle of our busy lives. Golf offers a simplicity that is cleansing. Play at a steady pace. No agendas beyond getting the ball in the hole. No traffic. No interruptions. No crowded "to do" lists. Golf is just you, a few friends, a good walk, and an occasional opportunity for magic (or disaster) to happen with every swing at the ball.

It is easy to feel our smallness on a golf course, and that itself is humbling. We are immersed in our limitations on the golf course, and that is humbling. We are very aware of what we do not know on the golf course, and that is humbling. And we are keenly aware of how difficult it is to make the ball go where we want it to go and to make that little ball go in that tiny hole, and that is humbling.

Golf also has a way of turning hierarchy upside down. Sons and daughters often hit the ball farther than their fathers and mothers. Education is no advantage on the course. The game doesn't care what your position and salary are at your workplace. Underlings routinely play better than bosses. The ball doesn't care about the expensive car you drive or the square footage in your house.

All of this is to say that golf has a way of cleansing the soul, of reducing ego. Golf has a way of clearing the clutter of everyday life. All that matters for 4 hours is that you enjoy the game and the people around you. Golf connects you to yourself and your best friends. Golf calls you to stay humble and stay grounded!

Inspirational Quote: True humility is not thinking less of yourself; it is thinking of yourself less. – C.S. Lewis

Scripture: Whoever exalts himself will be humbled, and whoever humbles himself will be exalted. – Matthew 23:12

Zen: An unbending tree breaks in the wind. The hard and stiff will be broken; the soft and supple will prevail. — Lao-Tzu, Tao Te Ching

Golf Anecdote: Jordan Spieth's humility in victory and defeat has earned him respect across the golf world. He listens, learns, and leads with grace.

FLEXIBILITY IN THE FACE OF CHANGE

Flexibility is the ability to adjust without losing your center. Golf demands this skill. Weather changes, course conditions vary, and our own mindset shifts. Being flexible means staying grounded while adapting to what is.

A golfer's main strength is his flexibility. There are many ways to get the ball in the hole. The rules of golf allow each player to use a maximum of 14 clubs, each of which usually has a different length shaft and a different loft on each club face. This requires constant adjustment in stance, ball position, and decision making when playing shots. Factor in changes in wind speed, wind direction, temperature, and other factors (including physical energy and flexibility), and the permutations for strategy and results are innumerable.

The best golfers are experts at controlling distance and trajectory. They learn this through practice and spending countless hours "earning it in the dirt." They master full shots, knock downs, three quarter shots, 50% shots, hooks, draws, straight shots, cut shots, and slices. They master flop shots, chip and runs, pitch shots, sand shots, buried lies, and shots from under the lip of the trap. They can handle the ball deep in the rough, "bird's nests," shots from heather, bare lies in dirt, balls in mud and on rocks. This all requires flexibility.

Just looking at all these required shots is humbling. Yet, it is also exciting. My execution of all of these shots is spotty, but I do have most of them in my bag. I may not play them well, but I can play them. That flexibility is empowering. It makes for lots of creativity and fun in trying them. Truth is, my game is better from tough spots than the fairway. Anyone can play from the fairway!

I love creating shots from trouble. I need to—I get lots of experience from trouble spots. This is partly a result of having a clear picture of the required play from inside the tree line. I have more difficulty picturing shots from the wide-open fairway.

One of the great aspects of golf is that it is a game of recovery. And, if you hit the ball like I do, you better learn to recover. I play like Indiana Jones would play golf—always on the edge of disaster. At the end of the round, I am covered in dirt, mud, thistles, and pine needles. Oh, how I love this game! It is exhilarating at times, living on the edge of danger.

The key to recovery is flexibility. Controlling the golf ball—the trajectory, the path, the distance, the curvature—is all about understanding how to control the club face and the golf swing and varying these as the shot requires. Success in golf requires that you adapt what you do and how you do it as the circumstances dictate.

Does life require flexibility? Do circumstances change, requiring your mindset and processes and skills to change? Absolutely! I am fortunate enough to have lived a long life—several lives really—and many of life's greatest lessons have been about the importance of flexibility: learning new processes and skills in different cities, in different jobs, surrounded by different people, during different stages of life.

Life has phases and stages—"seasons" if you will. It seems to me that every 8 years or so, somehow the season of my life has changed. From the young athlete with a broken leg (age 12), to the start of college (18), to the death of my mother and leaving home to start my career (24), to marriage (28), to fatherhood (32), to starting a new career (37), to golf with my wife and son (45), to son in college and back issues (52), to divorce and retirement and marriage again (60), to writing Par for the Soul (66), I feel as though I have lived more lives than a cat.

Along the way, I have morphed and learned and evolved and changed and grown many times over. I am neither the golfer, nor the man I used to be. Seasons change. Circumstances change. Life changes. We change.

I wrote previously that life is always in motion, in transition, and so are we. This is another great paradox that golf has taught me; every round of golf is different, yet the same. And every day of life, I am the same, yet never the same. Are you the same as you were 30, 20, or even 10 years ago? As Brad Pitt, playing

General Manager Billy Bean, said in the movie *Moneyball*, "Adapt or die." Times change, and so do we.

Constantly adjusting and changing, like the golf swing, we are always in motion—in flux. So is the world around us. Life can seem like constant whitewater. It is. And we must be flexible and learn and grow in order to navigate life's eddies and currents, and to learn to be better and push toward the best versions of ourselves in the process.

Inspirational Quote: The measure of intelligence is the ability to change. – Albert Einstein

Scripture: To everything there is a season, and a time to every purpose under heaven. – Ecclesiastes 3:1

Zen: Flow with whatever may happen and let your mind be free. Stay centered by accepting whatever you are doing.

Golf Anecdote: Rory McIlroy's ability to adjust his swing and strategy over time has kept him competitive and resilient.

BE LIKE WATER

Water is both humble and flexible—it flows, adapts, and nourishes. Golf teaches us to be like water: to move with grace, to respond with wisdom, and to remain calm under pressure. This mindset helps us navigate both the fairways and the rough lies of life.

I have always loved fishing for golf balls in ponds on the golf course. In high school, my friend Scott Munro and I would dive the shallow ponds of our local public course in the dark of night. We took home hundreds of golf balls. We would clean them and sort them by condition and brand. We found great joy in this adventure.

I still love to pick golf balls from ponds on the course. It is like Christmas. You may get a pristine Titleist or a muddy range ball. This is not a financially driven habit. It is more about recovery and reuse. It is a treasure hunt, every bit as exhilarating to me as a diver finding a sunken pirate ship. The highlight is the occasional recovery of my own ball.

There is something magical about water. Maybe the attraction is a calling back to our existence in the womb? Perhaps the magic is in water's lessons, the truths that natural order reveals to us. Water is humble. It seeks the lowest place. It does not resist—it accepts. Water is receptive, including the reception of errant golf shots. And, while water is humble and receptive, water is extremely powerful and commands respect.

Bruce Lee, a groundbreaking martial artist, actor, and cultural icon in the 1960s and early 1970s, embraced water as a great teacher. Bruce Lee's "be like water" teaching is one of his most famous philosophical insights, capturing his belief in adaptability, presence, and non-resistance. The full idea comes from a passage he spoke in 1971, emphasizing that water's strength lies in its ability to take any shape and overcome obstacles through flexibility rather than force.

In a TV interview on *The Pierre Berton Show* in December of 1971, Lee taught, "Empty your mind. Be formless, shapeless, like water. You put water into a cup; it becomes the cup. You put water into a bottle; it becomes the bottle. You put it into a teapot; it becomes the teapot. Now water can flow, or it can crash. Be water, my friend."

Lee's philosophy calls us to be like water and be adaptable, to find a way around obstacles, to embrace softness and patience, and to be humble. Water is soft and flexible, yet it is incredibly powerful. Water wears down rock. Water is lowly, yet it commands respect—lakes and oceans are full of ships like the Titanic and the Edmond Fitzgerald. Water reinforces the importance of flexibility. When you are rigid, you break. When you're fluid and flexible, you adapt, learn, and move with life rather than against it.

Water also has a comforting quality. The pitter patter of rain, the babbling brook, the rhythmic crashing of waves on the beach —these have a way of settling the spirit. I often go to sleep at night listening to the sound of rain on my bedside speaker.

When I was young, my mother and I would climb into our Coleman camper during rainstorms, and we would relax and often nap to the sound of raindrops falling on the plastic roof. And there are few things in life that are more enjoyable and comforting than a nice, warm shower or an ice-cold glass of water on a hot summer day.

Take a lesson from water. Be humble. Be flexible. Be open. Be receptive. Embrace softness. Give comfort. Live with a quiet power within. Adapt. Be like water, my friend.

Inspirational Quote: Empty your mind, be formless, shapeless—like water. – Bruce Lee

Scripture: He leads me beside still waters. He restores my soul. – Psalm 23:2-3

Zen: Nothing in the world is as soft and yielding as water. Yet for dissolving the hard and inflexible, nothing can surpass it.

Zen: Be like water making its way through cracks. Do not be assertive, but adjust to the object, and you shall find a way around or through it.

Golf Anecdote: Hideki Matsuyama's calm and fluid approach to the game reflects the essence of being like water— focused, adaptable, and serene. Matsuyama called on these qualities in winning the Masters in 2021.

SUMMARY

Humility and flexibility are vital virtues in golf and in life. They help us grow, adapt, and stay grounded. When we embrace these qualities, like water, we become more resilient, more compassionate, more powerful and more effective in all we do.

HOLE RESULT: 527-YARD PAR 5

This hole is about the third shot. We hit the drive with our 80% swing, finding the center of the fairway. A smooth 5 wood is well placed between the trees left and the water right. The 85-yard third shot is a perfect yardage for a 54-degree sand wedge. The pin is on the back left portion of the green, so our target is 10 feet right of the pin. The contact is good, but the ball starts left of the target, pulled right toward the pin. After a short release, the ball settles six feet short and just left of the cup.

The thought of making birdie and finishing 1 under par briefly flashes in my mind. "Be like water, Scott. Empty your mind," I say to myself. "Just make a good stroke. Slow. Smooth. Trust your line. Focus on the process, and the result will take care of itself."

I hit the putt with good speed and right online. The ball tracks right at the center of the cup, drifts slightly right and falls into the right half of the hole. Thinking of Payne Stewart's 1999 U.S. Open winning putt, I give a fist pump and think, "You beauty!" The birdie here makes the final score a 1 under par 71.

My brother Mark flashes a big smile and gives me a big hug. My mind races through all the people I have played golf with over the years. My cousin Steve shakes my hand, "Way to go Cuz. I love you man." This is my third round of 1 under, my best lifetime score. But this is by far my most enjoyable round.

I am humbled by a lifetime of playing this great game. All the people and relationships, all the beauty, all the laughter and memories, all the opportunities—all the blessings presented by this game, and this life—I am so very fortunate and so grateful and humbled.

With a calm and grateful spirit, we head to the 19th hole to celebrate!

REFLECTION QUESTIONS

1. Where in your life could humility open the door to growth?
2. How do you respond to unexpected changes or challenges?
3. What does it mean to you to 'be like water' in your daily life?

BOOK RECOMMENDATION: *EGO IS THE ENEMY* BY RYAN HOLLIDAY

Ryan Holliday's book, *Ego is the Enemy*, frames ego as the force that blocks growth, while humility and flexibility are the antidotes that keep you learning, adapting, and grounded in reality. Ego says, "look at me." Humility says, "I see you."

Holiday argues that ego convinces you that you already know enough, deserve more, or are above correction. Humility does the opposite. Humility keeps you open to feedback. It allows you to be taught, and it grounds you in reality rather than fantasy. Ego says, "I've arrived." Humility says, "I'm still learning. I don't know what I don't know."

Ego resists change, clings to identity, and fears being wrong. Flexibility—emotional, cognitive, relational—is the opposite. It's the ability to shift, adjust, and respond to what's actually happening. *Ego Is the Enemy* teaches that humility keeps you grounded, and flexibility keeps you adaptable. Together, they neutralize ego's rigidity and open the door to learning, growth, and improvement.

SONG: "HUMBLE AND KIND" BY TIM MCGRAW (2016)

Tim McGraw's song "Humble and Kind" is built on the idea that character matters more than achievement. The song emphasizes staying grounded, remembering your roots, treating others with respect, and not letting success distort your identity. This is humility in action. Stay small enough to keep learning, grateful enough to stay grounded, and aware enough to stay human.

Kindness requires flexibility. Kindness isn't rigid. It asks you to pause, listen, adjust, and respond to what someone else needs. That's flexibility—emotional, relational, and behavioral. Ego is rigid. Kindness is adaptive. When you choose kindness, you're choosing to bend rather than break. You're choosing connection over self-importance.

The song repeatedly emphasizes patience, generosity, forgiveness, and empathy. These require flexibility of mind and heart. You can't be kind if you're rigid. You can't be humble if you're defensive. "Humble and Kind" is the emotional expression of the same principles that humility and flexibility represent philosophically: stay grounded, stay open, stay adaptable, and don't let ego close your heart.

MOVIE TO WATCH: *FORREST GUMP* (1994)

Forrest Gump is a heartwarming study in humility and flexibility —so much so that he becomes a kind of folk-philosopher without ever trying to be one. When you look at him through the lenses of humility as being grounded, and flexibility as adaptability—Forrest Gump becomes a surprisingly rich metaphor.

Forrest embodies humility in a way that's almost radical. He never assumes he knows more than he does. He listens, observes, and responds with sincerity rather than ego. He doesn't posture or pretend. Whether he's meeting presidents, running across America, or shrimping with Bubba's dream in mind, he remains the same grounded, earnest person.

Forrest doesn't cling to status. Medals, fame, wealth—none of it inflates him. He treats the janitor and the general with the same warmth. He lets life be bigger than him. Humility, at its core, is the willingness to be shaped by reality rather than trying to dominate it. Forrest does this instinctively. In psychological terms, Forrest is the opposite of ego-defensiveness. He doesn't need to protect his identity, so he stays open.

Forrest's life is a testament to adaptability. He moves with life rather than resisting it. When football shows up, he runs. When the Army shows up, he serves. When shrimping becomes the next chapter, he learns it. He adjusts without losing himself. His core values of kindness, loyalty, and simplicity stay constant even as his circumstances change wildly.

Forrest doesn't catastrophize or cling. Jenny leaves, and he grieves, but he keeps going. Bubba dies, and Forrest honors him by carrying forward the dream. He responds to the moment rather than the story in his head. That's psychological flexibility in its purest form. Forrest is the embodiment of "non-resistance." Not passivity, but rather responsiveness.

Forrest is the golfer who doesn't overthink his swing. He steps up, trusts his body, and lets the club move. No ego, no tension, no story about what this shot means. Just presence.

Humility = accepting the shot, the life you have.

Flexibility = adjusting to the wind, lie, terrain, and life's circumstances.

Be Like Water = Forrest is the player who does both without drama.

19 THE 19TH HOLE – LIFE IS ABOUT CONNECTION AND RELATIONSHIPS

Golf is more than a game—it's a gathering. The 19th hole represents connection, camaraderie, and the joy of sharing life's journey. This chapter explores how relationships formed on the course reflect deeper truths about community, belonging, and shared purpose.

CONNECTION BEYOND COMPETITION

Golf is often played in silence, but its impact is deeply relational. The shared experience of a round—the highs and lows—creates bonds that last. The 19th hole is where stories are told, laughter is shared, and friendships are deepened.

I have played golf alone, usually just a few holes or maybe nine. The game is still challenging, beautiful, and peaceful as a single. But it is not the same as when you share a round with others. Playing with family and friends is way better than playing alone. The connection, sharing, laughing, and encouraging each other makes the time much more fun and rewarding.

We are made for connection, and golf with others is evidence of that fact.

What is the best gift you can give or receive? I believe it is the gift of time (presence). The most valuable asset we each have is time. We can make more money and increase our treasure. We can learn new skills and improve our talents. But we cannot create more time. Every hour spent is gone forever, and we cannot recapture it or create more of it. Time is finite and valuable. It is the greatest gift we can give to those we love, and it is the best gift we can receive from others. Presence is precious.

I love the people I have connected with on the golf course. My parents gave me a great gift when they introduced me to the game. I started playing with Paul R and Frannie at age 11. I played with friends through grade school, middle school, and high school. I played with co-workers and new friends at six different locations as my career path evolved. I have met strangers who became friends. And I have loved countless rounds with close friends and family for over 55 years.

Golf is a connectional game. In a round of golf where I hit 80 shots over 4+ hours, I figure I spend only 20 minutes actually playing a shot. If I spend 15 seconds over each shot, that is only 20 minutes in 4+ hours. The other 3 hours and 40 minutes plus is spent walking (or riding) and talking with playing partners. That is almost 4 hours of time with and focused on others. Maybe that is why golf is so peaceful and enjoyable—the quiet connection.

While we spend a good bit of time focusing on our own game, when we play golf, we spend the great majority of the time focusing on others. Watching them play their shots, helping each other find lost balls, moving ball markers out of our playing partners' line. When I play golf, I am so outward-focused that I have no concerns or problems in the world.

Think about it. When you focus your energy and attention on others, your cares seem to disappear. There is a lesson here. When you are in your own head or feeling overwhelmed by your own circumstances, try focusing on someone else. Send best wishes or lift prayers for your friends or family in need. Assist a friend or neighbor where they need a hand. Call a friend and take them to coffee. When you are in your own head, focus on others. You will be amazed at the power of focusing on others. And you will feel the joy of giving as well.

Inspirational Quote: The most important shot in golf is the next one—and who you share it with.

Scripture: As iron sharpens iron, so one person sharpens another. – Proverbs 27:17

Zen: When we touch one thing with deep awareness, we touch everything.

Golf Anecdote: Arnold Palmer was known not just for his skill, but for his warmth and connection with fans and fellow players. He made everyone feel part of the game. Perhaps that is why his massive fan base was known as "Arnie's Army."

While covering the 2026 Bay Hill Arnold Palmer Invitational, Golf Channel's Golf Central Pregame revisited Arnold Palmer's final written letter nearly a decade after his passing. The letter was a final act of generosity from a man whose life was defined by connection. The segment highlighted several key elements:

The letter was written to Palmer Lindblad, a young boy whose parents named him after Arnold Palmer following Erin Lindblad's treatment during a life-threatening pregnancy at the Palmer Hospital. The naming wasn't about celebrity—it was about values. They admired Arnold's humility, warmth, and the way he treated people. When Palmer learned about the child who carried his name, he chose to respond personally.

The letter was written shortly before Arnold Palmer's death

in September 2016, making it the last known letter he ever signed. Golf Channel underscored the poignancy of this timing: even as his health declined, Arnold still made time to reach out to a child he had never met.

He welcomed the boy into "Arnie's Army," encouraged him to enjoy the game of golf, and reminded him—gently—that golf is ultimately about character.

The segment placed this letter in the context of Arnold's life-long habit of writing personal notes. He wrote to tournament winners, young players, fans, and friends. His longtime assistant, Doc Giffin, often helped manage the flow, but the words and signatures were Arnold Palmer's.

Golf Channel emphasized that this wasn't a one-off gesture —it was the final expression of a lifelong practice of relational generosity.

CIRCLES OF INFLUENCE

We are shaped by those we spend time with. Golf teaches that who we play with matters. Our partners influence our mindset, our mood, and our growth. The 19th hole reminds us to choose our circles wisely and to invest in relationships which uplift and inspire us.

Motivational speaker Jim Rohn, drawing on concepts from psychology, sociology, and behavioral science, suggests that "you are the average of the five people you spend the most time with." Think about that for a second. Who do you spend the most time with, and how do they influence you?

In his book, *The Seven Decisions*, author Andy Andrews talks about Decision #3—The Active Decision: "I Will Choose My Friends with Care." This "Circle of Influence" decision teaches that your destiny is shaped by the people you consistently allow into your inner world. It emphasizes intentionality: you must consciously choose who gets access to your time, energy, and emotional bandwidth. At its core, the decision says: your associations either elevate you or diminish you—there is no neutral influence.

Sometimes we incorrectly believe we must be independent and handle everything on our own. That is a sure way to fail. Even Tiger Woods, the best player in the world, has a team of people assisting him. There is not one golfer on the PGA Tour who does not have a vital relationship with a caddie, a trainer, travel assistants, and agents. Most have sports psychologists, dietitians, and personal chefs.

Most have families who have helped them from childhood all the way to the tour, and most have spouses and children who share in their lives both professionally and personally.

Who is on your team? Who is in your Circle of Influence? The truth is, we all need a team. We all need friends and family. We all need mentors and people to learn from, people who can help guide us through what we do not know. We all need sounding boards and confidants who want the best for us. We all need others to share experiences with. Life is so much more meaningful, so much richer and deeper, when we share it with others. And we all need people to assist and help us as members of our Circle of Influence.

Inspirational Quote: You are the average of the five people you spend the most time with. – Jim Rohn

Scripture: Let us consider how we may spur one another on toward love and good deeds. – Hebrews 10:24

Zen: A single seed can turn into a forest. A single moment of compassion can change a life.

Golf Anecdote: The Ryder Cup showcases how team spirit and shared purpose elevate performance—players rise together.

The greatest moments in golf are those that are shared with people you love.

LIFE SHARED IS LIFE MULTIPLIED

The joy of golf is amplified when shared. So it is with life. The 19th hole symbolizes celebration—not just of scores, but of connection. It's a reminder that life's greatest moments are those we experience together.

For most golfers, it is traditional to stop in the snack shop or bar at the golf club with their playing partners after the round. This is a time when great shots from the day are discussed and recounted among the group. Sometimes, bad shots or funny moments from the day are enjoyed and recounted as well. This is a place and time when the gift of presence is given gladly. Golf and life are shared over a beer or two.

I mentioned before that I have a tradition of going to Hot Springs Village, Arkansas, to play golf with family and friends. This began with my first visit to see my father in 1985. Brother Mark, Cousin Steve, and I have gathered there almost annually for 40 years now.

We still make the trip and honor Paul R who died in May of 2000, almost a week after our spring visit that year. We started making trips in both May and September in 1995 as we saw dad visibly slowing down. We always considered every trip to be a gift, and we never took the time together for granted. Those trips are full of memories and emotions—some of the most treasured in my lifetime. Some of those special moments are still vividly real today, years and decades later.

These are golf boot camps. Nine rounds of golf in 4 ½ days. Our daily schedule is very simple: wake up, shower, have breakfast, go play 18 holes, have lunch at the course, play 18 more holes, make dinner at our rental house, and end the day with a few drinks and stories. The schedule is the same over four straight days. The only day we don't play two rounds is the day we arrive—when we play an afternoon opening match after flying into Little Rock.

The truth is, I have always considered this revered tradition to be a highlight of every year. Why? The shared time and gift of presence with family and friends. The golf is always fun. But golf is just the activity that brings us together. It is the time and the laughs and the meaningful discussions about life's twists and turns that make these trips so very special. We squeeze a year's worth of fun and love into five days.

One of the first things that gets scheduled following New Year's Day is the spring trip to HSV. I always feel better when time is scheduled to see Brother Mark and Cousin Steve. We determine a fourth player, look at the calendar, and choose a time to go into Hot Springs Village. Those decisions always put a beacon of light on the calendar.

We make tee times, reserve a place to stay, and schedule flights and other aspects of travel 90 days ahead of the visit. Then, we start counting down to arrival. I am lucky—I enjoy a wonderful life. My son Joel and I share a love of golf and the St. Louis Cardinals. I have great friends scattered throughout the country. I love playing golf every Thursday with Ron Nahser, Sid Ross, and Father Kevin Feeney. But, the HSV trips have a special appeal and a history that makes them among the most treasured days of the year.

Life is best when shared. We are made to be in relationship. And the level of joy and flourishing we experience is multiplied by connection. We are not alone in life. We are connected and loved more than we know. We stand on the shoulders of genera-tions of our ancestors. We lean on the shoulders of numerous friends and family members. And those same people lean on our shoulders as well. That is the beauty and joy of life. That is the beauty and joy of golf. Take a moment to marinate in the joy of sharing life with the people you love. It is a blessing that is worth counting every day!

Inspirational Quote: Happiness is only real when shared. – Christopher McCandless

Scripture: Rejoice with those who rejoice; mourn with those who mourn. – Romans 12:15

Zen: The miracle is not to walk on water. The miracle is to walk together on the earth.

Golf Anecdote: After winning a major, players often celebrate with their team, family, and fans—showing that victory is sweeter when shared.

SUMMARY

The 19th hole is a metaphor for life's deeper purpose—connection. In golf and in life, we are meant to walk together, to share stories, and to build community. Life is not a solo round; it's a shared journey.

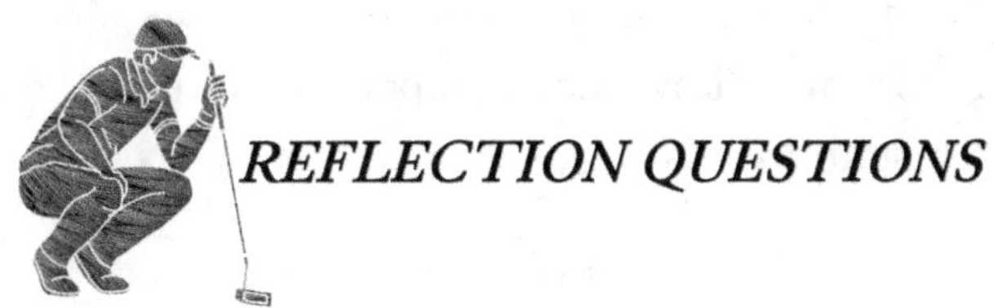

REFLECTION QUESTIONS

1. Who are the people in your Inner Circle, people you share your journey with?
2. How do your relationships influence your growth and mindset?

3. Who do you most enjoy spending time with? Why?

BOOK RECOMMENDATION: SO HELP ME GOLF BY RICK REILLY

Rick Reilly's *So Help Me Golf* is a wonderful collection of stories that speaks to the relationships formed around the game. Through Reilly's trademark humor and storytelling, the book reveals how golf becomes a natural bridge between people—friends, families, mentors, even strangers who become companions over eighteen holes. The course becomes a place where conversations unfold slowly, where vulnerability shows up without being forced, and where shared rituals create a sense of belonging. Reilly's stories highlight how golf deepens bonds, repairs old ones, and gives people a reason to keep showing up for each other.

Beneath the laughs and anecdotes, the book is ultimately about connection. Reilly shows how the rhythms of golf mirror the rhythms of intimacy: patience, presence, accountability, and the willingness to try again after a bad shot. The most memorable chapters revolve around mentorship, family legacy, and the small acts of generosity that define real community. In this way, *So Help Me Golf* becomes more than a sports book; it becomes a portrait of how shared experiences shape the relationships that sustain us.

SONG: "WITH A LITTLE HELP FROM MY FRIENDS" BY JOE COCKER

"With a Little Help from My Friends" is one of those songs that distills the essence of human connection into something simple, honest, and deeply relational. The core message is unmistakable:

we become more ourselves when we are supported by others. The song frames friendship not as a luxury but as a lifeline—something that steadies us, lifts us, and gives meaning to the everyday struggles of being human.

At its heart, the song is about interdependence. It challenges the myth of self-sufficiency by celebrating the courage it takes to lean on others. The repeated emphasis on needing help, getting by, and being understood speaks to the emotional truth that relationships are built on mutual support, vulnerability, and presence. It's a reminder that connection isn't about perfection—it's about showing up for each other in small, consistent ways. In that sense, the song becomes a relational philosophy: life is richer, safer, and more joyful when we allow ourselves to be held by the people who care about us.

MOVIE TO WATCH: MR. HOLLAND'S OPUS (1995)

Mr. Holland's Opus is a powerful movie portraying that the true measure of a life isn't the performance we imagined for ourselves, but the relationships we tended along the way. Glenn Holland begins his career believing his worth will be proven through a grand musical achievement, yet the real "round" he plays is the daily, imperfect, relational work of teaching, parenting, repairing, and showing up for others. The film reveals how connection is built in small, consistent acts—encouraging a struggling student, learning to communicate with his son, choosing presence over ambition. These moments become the quiet strokes that ultimately define the relational scorecard of his life.

When Holland's former students gather to perform his unfinished symphony, the story arrives at its 19th-hole truth: legacy is relational, not technical. The people he invested in return to show him who he became through his connection with them. His opus isn't the music he wrote but the lives he shaped, the repairs he made, and the love he offered even when he felt unseen. In the same way the 19th hole invites honest reflection after the round, this film invites us to ask whether we prioritized connection over performance, presence over productivity, and growth over perfection. It reminds us that the masterpiece of a life is composed through relationships—and that others will one day play back the music we created in them.

CHAPTER 20

The Spiritual Forces: Finding Meaning & Golf in the Garden

How can a game have such an effect on a man's soul? The way I see it, how can it not? You don't choose the game, it chooses you. And when it does, life and golf become forever connected. – Johnny Crawford – 7 Days in Utopia

The round is over, the clubs are put away, and we head home. It was a great day and a memorable round of golf. We played well, and we had fun and a few laughs with good friends. It was a wonderful day on the course. And I ask you to consider—so what?

Previously, I shared that I love golf. I love everything about it. How about you? Do you love golf? If you are still reading, my guess is that you answered yes—you love golf too. Why? Maybe the stories and lessons in the previous 19 holes remind you of your own experiences. Maybe you can relate to some or all of what you read. Perhaps something in these pages resonated with you. So, why do you love golf?

After years of playing, practicing, watching, reading, and talking about it, I know why I love golf. Now, I'll share my answer to why. In doing so, I ask you to join me and share a thought from March 6, 1983—there has to be more to life (and golf) than this. I ask you to consider that yes, indeed, there may be much more to golf and life. Golf is a game. And it is also much more than just a game, particularly when the round is underway and when it comes to an end.

Golf is like life, and they are both like water, in one key respect: they hold meaning on several levels. All three hold meaning and fun and powerful lessons on the surface. And there is much deeper meaning well beyond the surface—deep spiritual meaning.

Consider this quote: Spirituality is not just about finding quiet in a noisy world. It is about finding the sacred in the mundane. - Tara Mohr

Golf is both sacred and mundane. Life is sacred and mundane too. And whether you realize it or not, golf and life can be a path, a journey, of a deeply spiritual nature. In fact, golf is, in philosophical parlance, a journey of "virtuous good."

A virtuous good is something that is good in itself because it expresses or cultivates virtue, meaning it aligns with moral excellence, human flourishing, and the development of character. It's not just pleasant, useful, or advantageous. Golf is good because it forms you and develops your character. Think of golf as a good that strengthens the soul, shapes character toward the good, aligns with what is noble, just, or wise, and is worth choosing even when it costs you something.

Is golf a virtue? It can be—but not in the way we usually talk about virtues like courage or honesty. Golf isn't a virtue by itself, but it cultivates virtues in a way few activities do. Golf is more like a practice ground where virtues are revealed, built, tested, and strengthened. Golf is a virtue-maker.

Golf quietly trains qualities that philosophers have called virtues for centuries:

1. Patience - you can't rush a swing, a round, or your own development. In golf, you live in real time.
2. Humility - the game will hand you brilliance and disaster in the same hour. It teaches you to hold both lightly.
3. Honesty - there's no referee. You call penalties on yourself. That's moral muscle-building.
4. Resilience - every shot is a fresh start. You learn to recover, reset, and respond rather than spiral.
5. Presence - golf punishes distraction and rewards awareness. It is a meditation disguised as sport.
6. Temperance - you learn to regulate emotion, not suppress it. You learn to feel the frustration without letting it swing the club. You learn to respond rather than react.
7. Respect - for the course, for the people you play with, for the game itself. Etiquette becomes character.

In addition, golf acts as a mirror. More than anything, golf reflects back who you are when things don't go your way. Do you rush? Do you blame? Do you tighten? Do you get small? Do you get loud? Do you get curious? Do you lose control? Or do you remain calm and work through the challenges?

Virtues show up in those micro-moments. So, is golf a virtue? Not exactly. But it is a virtue-shaping game—a dojo for the soul, a training ground for character, a place where your inner life becomes visible in the outer world.

THE SPIRITUAL PRACTICES DRIVING THE GAME OF GOLF

Golf is more than a sport. It is a spiritual practice disguised as a game - a landscape where character is revealed, shaped, and strengthened. The course becomes a mirror, the swing a meditation, and each round a pilgrimage through the inner life. These practices form the backbone of golf's deeper wisdom and offer a pathway for personal transformation. Consider the spiritual practices driving the game of golf within you:

1. The Practice of Integrity

Golf is one of the few arenas where you are both player and referee. There is no one to police your score, your drops, or your penalties. Integrity becomes a lived discipline—an alignment between your actions and your inner truth. This practice cultivates honesty, accountability, and self-governance.

2. The Practice of Humility

Golf humbles everyone. A perfect drive can be followed by a disastrous approach. A brilliant round can unravel on a single hole. Humility is not a lesson learned once but a rhythm you learn to move with. This practice cultivates groundedness, perspective, and emotional balance.

3. The Practice of Patience

Nothing in golf rewards rushing. The game moves at the pace of breath, intention, and rhythm. Patience becomes a spiritual discipline—an invitation to slow down and trust the unfolding of the moment. This practice cultivates calm, pacing, and long-view thinking.

4. The Practice of Presence

Every shot demands full attention: wind, lie, slope, feel, intention. Presence is not a performance trick but a way of inhabiting the moment. Golf punishes distraction and rewards awareness. This practice cultivates focus, embodied attention, and clarity.

5. The Practice of Respect

Respect is woven into the fabric of the game—respect for the course, for your partners, for pace of play, for the traditions that have shaped the sport. Golf becomes a training ground for honoring what surrounds you. This practice cultivates courtesy, stewardship, and relational awareness.

6. The Practice of Resilience

Golf is a long conversation with failure and renewal. You will miss. You will recover. You will miss again. Resilience is the ability to begin again without losing heart. This practice cultivates adaptability, emotional recovery, and grit.

7. The Practice of Self-Mastery

The real opponent is never the course or the other players —it is your own impatience, fear, ego, and doubt. Golf becomes a dojo for emotional regulation and inner steadiness. This practice cultivates discipline, emotional intelligence, and self-awareness.

8. The Practice of Curiosity

Golf invites experimentation: new lines, new shots, new approaches. Curiosity keeps the game alive and keeps you growing. It transforms frustration into exploration. This practice cultivates creativity, openness, and a learning mindset.

9. The Practice of Solitude

Even when played with others, golf is deeply personal. It offers rare space to hear your own mind, to reflect, and to meet yourself honestly. This practice cultivates reflection, inner clarity, and self-connection.

10. The Practice of Joy

The pure strike. The walk. The sun. The camaraderie. Joy is the quiet pulse beneath the game—the reason people return to it for decades. This practice cultivates gratitude, lightness, and appreciation.

11. The Practice of Divine Connection

Golf can be a sacred space where the ordinary meets the divine. The vastness of the course, the rhythm of the swing, and the quiet moments between shots invite a sense of awe and reverence. In these moments, golfers often experience a profound connection to something greater than themselves, whether understood as God, Spirit, or the sacred flow of life. The game becomes a prayer in motion, a meditation on grace, patience, and surrender.

This practice cultivates spiritual awareness, humility before creation, and a deepened sense of presence with the divine.

Through golf, we learn to listen—to the whisper of the wind, the call of the earth, and the still small voice within. The challenges on the course mirror life's spiritual tests, inviting trust in a higher power and acceptance of outcomes beyond our control. Golf teaches us to walk gently on the earth, to honor the gifts of the moment, and to find sacredness in the simple act of play.

In this way, golf becomes more than a game; it becomes a path toward God, a practice of sacred presence that draws us closer to the heart of creation itself.

These spiritual practices form the inner architecture of golf. They shape not only how you play the game but how you live your life. Golf becomes a spiritual companion—inviting you into integrity, humility, presence, and joy. Through these practices, the game becomes a teacher, a mirror, and a path toward a more grounded and awakened way of being and living with the divine spirit.

THE COURSE AND THE GARDEN OF EDEN

Early on, I mentioned that I am a seeker—a seeker of meaning, a seeker of capital T Truth. In many ways, my life has been a restless journey. Good, but restless. And golf has always been a distraction from that restlessness. Feeling stressed? Go hit some balls. Feeling out of control? Go practice the short game. Feeling anxious? Go play 18.

The course has always been my sanctuary. The beauty and peacefulness are always calming. It is a place where spirituality thrives. It is where spirit flourishes and the soul finds comfort and rest. And this place of renewal, this sanctuary, is a place where we work on and find the best versions of ourselves. The golf course is a place where we find "our better angels," meaning the nobler, wiser, more virtuous parts of human nature, the inner forces that pull us toward empathy, restraint, integrity, and unity rather than fear, anger, or division.

The work done in this sanctuary, in this game, helps us to move toward and find the best versions of who we are. And this spirit work makes us better individuals, better spouses, better parents, better children, better friends, better co-workers, and better citizens. We live with better energy in our world and the environment around us. Simply stated, whether you realize it or not, golf brings us closer to God, who is love. Golf offers a unique opportunity to connect with God.

Consider the words of my confirmation saint, St. Augustine. "Our hearts are restless until they rest in you Lord." And where was man's heart first formed? In the dirt in the Garden of Eden, in the presence of God. Have you ever considered that the golf course and your love for golf might be driven by a spiritual want and need to rejoin our Creator in the garden? Is it possible that the golf course is your Garden of Eden on earth? It is for me, and it can be for you.

Think about it. Make it a meditation. Do you get a glimpse of heaven and feel the presence of God when you play golf? Is your heart less restless on the course because you are resting in the Lord? Is it possible that you love this game because it is a gift given by God—the gift of play—which you have received without recognizing the spiritual depth of that gift?

St. Augustine would site this as an example of what he called "the virtue God works in us without us." For Augustine, virtue is fundamentally grace, given by God —not merely habit, chosen by man. Both golf and life, bring us to the intersection of virtue, grace, love, and practice in *Par for the Soul*.

Augustine tells us you can practice your swing, you can train your body, and you can study the course. But the inner transformation—humility, patience, love, charity, courage—is not something you "muscle into existence." It's something God initiates, and you learn to cooperate with. It's the difference between trying harder and being changed.

You see, whether you know it or not, when you are playing and working on golf, God is working on you. He is working on your restless heart. He is reaching out for you while you are reaching for your club. He is walking with you as you walk the course. He is helping you find and refine the best version of yourself. He is helping you learn, grow, play, and love. He is calling you to the best version of yourself, to develop your character, to chip away the parts of you that are not virtuous, not loving, for a reason. He is helping you on the path to join him when the round of your life on this earth is over.

Consider this Augustinian meditation: The Virtue God Works in Us Without Us

There is a moment on the course—every golfer knows it—

when the swing stops feeling manufactured and starts feeling given. You don't force it. You don't grind for it. You don't even fully understand how it arrived. It simply settles into you, and you let it happen like something that was waiting for you to be ready.

Augustine says virtue and goodness work the same way. "Virtue is a good quality of the mind, by which we live righteously, of which no one can make bad use, which God works in us, without us."

At first, the words feel strange. We're used to effort. We're used to striving. We're used to believing that the best things in life come from pushing harder. But Augustine invites us into a different posture—one that feels more like receiving than achieving. Sit with that for a moment.

The deepest changes in you have never been the ones you muscled into existence. They were the ones that arrived quietly, like dawn's light slipping through a window you forgot to close.

Patience that surprised you. Compassion that softened you. Courage that rose when fear should have won. Forgiveness that felt larger than your own capacity. These were not accomplishments. They were arrivals. They were God's work in you—before your effort, beneath your effort, beyond your effort.

Your role was simply to say yes. Not to manufacture virtue, but to make room for it. Not to control transformation, but to cooperate with it. Not to perfect yourself, but to stay open to the One who is shaping you from within. Listening. Receiving. Accepting and surrendering to love and goodness while you jettison the patterns of anger, jealousy, and resentment.

This is the quiet miracle Augustine is pointing toward— virtue is not the triumph of willpower. It is the fruit of grace. So today, let this be your meditation:

Breathe. Release the pressure to fix yourself. Let go of the illusion that you must become good by force. Open your hands. Open your heart. Open the small, hidden places where striving has taken root.

And whisper the simplest prayer a soul can offer, "Work in me Lord what I cannot work in myself."

Then step into your day—your relationships, your challenges, your course—with the gentle confidence that God is already doing what you cannot. Virtue is not something you build alone. It is something you receive and build into your character. One swing, one act of will at a time.

And when it comes, it will feel like a swing that finally clicks —effortless, natural, and unforced. Given by the God who loves you.

THE GOLF COURSE AND THE RIVER OF LIFE

There is another aspect of golf, life, and the spirit which I have come to greatly appreciate. In addition to the connection to God and the Garden of Eden, for me, the golf course brings home the lessons that Herman Hesse's Siddhartha learned from the river. This speaks to my Zen Christian beliefs.

Siddhartha is a spiritual story filled with Zen wisdom and Buddhist imagery. Siddhartha, the hero of the story, lives a restless life seeking happiness and meaning. He seeks happiness in asceticism and discipline, then sex and physical pleasure, then money and commercial success, and the rush of gambling—all to no avail. Like St. Augustine, Siddhartha's heart is restless as he seeks and tries and pursues happiness and meaning through the various stages of his life.

Late in life, Siddhartha finds himself working as a ferryman.

One day he is sitting by the river, staring into it. Siddhartha begins to listen to the river and watch it flow. He sees the faces of his father, himself, and his son. Other faces come and go. Thousands of faces. And with each of them, their voices come and go.

Siddhartha begins to understand the energy and flow of life, the transitory nature of life, and the connectedness of all people and all things. He understands the perfection—the OM—of life and life's journey. And he understands that love is at the heart of all of it—at the heart of all life and all things. Siddhartha accepts, he opens his mind and heart, and in doing so, he finds that what he was seeking all of his life—peace and love—was before him the whole time.

In Siddhartha, the river is not just a setting—it is a spiritual mentor, a mirror, and a metaphor for the inner life. It is like the golf course for those of us who love golf. The river teaches Siddhartha what no doctrine, teacher, or ascetic practice could— that wisdom is found in the flow of ordinary life, not apart from it.

Siddhartha learns that the river repeats itself—the currents, eddies, seasons—yet the river is never the same twice. Golf offers the same paradox: the same hole, the same swing, the same club… yet never the same experience. Both teach the soul to pay attention to the subtle shifts within and around us.

One of the great teachings of the river is its non-judgmental acceptance. It holds the quiet and the violent, the clear and the muddy, the beginning and the end. On the course, the golfer is invited into the same posture: to hold a bad shot, a lucky bounce, a perfect drive, or a humiliating shank with the same open-hearted presence. This is the spiritual muscle the golfer is strengthening.

Siddhartha's breakthrough comes when he stops striving and starts listening—truly listening—to the river's voice. Golf has its own version of this: the wind, the lie, the tempo of your breath, the feel of the ground beneath your feet. Both practices insist that wisdom comes not from forcing but from attuning and receiving.

Siddhartha hears the river speak "Om"—the sound of everything belonging. He realizes that life is not a series of separate events but a single, flowing whole. Golf mirrors this insight: every shot is connected to the next, every hole to the round, every round to the season, every season to the story of who you are becoming. The course becomes a river of moments, each one shaping the next. Each one shaping your character.

Siddhartha's enlightenment is not a lightning bolt; it's a slow erosion of ego, like water shaping stone. Golf teaches the same humility. You cannot rush mastery. You cannot bully the game into giving you what you want. You learn to surrender, to trust the process, to let the game shape you.

Like Siddhartha at the river, the golfer discovers that the course is always speaking—not in words, but in the quiet lessons of rhythm, humility, presence, and love.

The river teaches Siddhartha that life is always moving, changing, and renewing itself. No moment is final. No identity is static. This loosens his grip on ego and certainty. In the river's voice, Siddhartha hears joy and sorrow, gain and loss, birth and death—all woven together. He realizes the world is not divided; it is unified. This dissolves his inner conflict. The river becomes his teacher because Siddhartha finally stops trying to achieve enlightenment and instead learns to receive it. Attentiveness becomes his spiritual posture.

Watching the river, Siddhartha sees that past, present, and

future are all connected and present at once—like different currents in the same body of water. This frees him from regret and anxiety. By understanding the unity of all things, Siddhartha becomes capable of deep compassion. He no longer judges others because he sees himself in them. The river shows him that the sacred is not hidden in asceticism or doctrine. It is present in the everyday flow of life—in work, relationships, and simple presence.

Let the golf course be for you what the river was to Siddhartha.

SUMMARY

Golf, like Siddhartha's encounter with the river, becomes a quiet school for the soul. Both settings teach that true transformation happens not through force but through attention. On the course, as by the river, a person learns to slow down, to listen, and to meet each moment without judgment. Virtue emerges not as a moral performance but as a way of being shaped by presence—patience in the rough, humility after a bad swing, courage on a long carry shot, honesty when no one is watching.

Like Siddhartha, the golfer can discover that the sacred is woven into the ordinary flow of life. The golfer discovers the same truth in the rhythm of breath, the feel of the ground, the arc of a good shot. And the golf course can be a taste of heaven, a spiritual return to the Garden of Eden.

God is not found in escape from the world but in deeper, loving participation with it. The river teaches Siddhartha that all things belong; the course teaches the golfer that every shot—good or bad—is part of a larger story of becoming. And what we are becoming is who God wants us to be; the best version of ourselves; someone who gives and receives love joyfully.

In both journeys, spirituality is not an achievement but an awakening: a recognition that grace moves through the mundane, shaping character one quiet moment at a time—one swing, one hole, one round at a time. And, in doing so, we embrace and engage and refine the spirit within us.

PAR FOR THE SOUL: LIFE LESSONS FROM GOLF

THE POWERFUL LIFE LESSONS AND MEANING FOUND THROUGH THE GAME OF GOLF

Understand the importance of mindset; everything begins in the mind.

Harness the critical nature of passion (why) and focus (how).

Take hold of the power of choice and intentionality—master the ship of your own character.

Live a life of love and compassion, caring for and nurturing the souls of others.

Live in the spirit of gratitude and appreciate that every moment is a gift—honor the gift.

Embrace the joy of giving and consciously elevate others in your daily actions.

Learn from mistakes and use them to grow and strengthen your character. Next!

Embrace acceptance and surrender—what you resist owns you. No judgment, no ego.

Build confidence and trust through practice & preparation. Trust > doubt, Confidence > fear.

Strengthen your character by living with responsibility and accountability.

Grasp the power of action and effort and create the life you want. Just do it!

Learn and practice emotional mastery to act and respond wisely, not just emotionally.

Choose to live in courage. Acknowledge your fears but move forward in the face of them.

Live with commitment and integrity. Say what you mean and do what you say—always.

Embody resiliency. Take the shots, recover, and continue going forward. Never give up.

Act with respect and behavioral accountability. They are at the heart of a well-lived life.

Cultivate the importance of belief —it drives your thoughts, habits, character, and destiny.

Let humility and flexibility guide your words and actions. Be like water my friend!

Life is about connection and relationships. Experiences are better when shared.

Appreciate and embrace the spiritual forces in golf and life.

Become the best version of yourself, the person God created you to be, the person who gives and receives love joyfully.

SCORECARD

Hole	Title	Yardage	Par	Score
1	Mindset	395	4	4
2	Passion & Focus	521	5	4
3	Choice & Intentionality	345	4	4
4	Love & Compassion	158	3	3
5	Gratitude	357	4	5
6	Giving	512	5	4
7	Learning From Mistakes	420	4	7
8	Acceptance	345	4	3
9	Confidence & Trust	175	3	3
	Out	3228	36	37
10	Responsibility & Accountability	537	5	6
11	Action & Effort	403	4	3
12	Emotional Mastery	137	3	1
13	Courage	416	4	4
14	Commitment & Integrity	315	4	6
15	Resiliency	423	4	3
16	Respect	162	3	3
17	Belief	434	4	4
18	Humility & Flexibility	527	5	4
	In	3354	36	34
	Total	6582	72	71

RECOMMENDED RESOURCES

Hole	Title	Book	Song	Movie
1	Mindset	The Mental Game	Already Gone	A Beautiful Mind
2	Passion & Focus	Why the Best are the Best	Lose Yourself	Rudy
3	Choice & Intentionality	Choices	Think	Grounghog Day
4	Love & Compassion	The Bible	Power of Love	Finding Forrester
5	Gratitude	Siddhartha	In My Life	It's a Wonderful Life
6	Giving	What You're Made For	Bridge Over Troubled Water	Pay It Forward
7	Learning From Mistakes	Golf is not a Game of Perfect	Brand New Day	7 Days in Utopia
8	Acceptance	Let Them	What a Wonderful World	Shrek
9	Confidence & Trust	Atomic Habits	A Matter of Trust	The Karate Kid
10	Responsibility & Accountability	The Seven Decisions	Man in the Mirror	Dead Poets Society
11	Action & Effort	The 7 Habits of Hughly Effective People	Unstoppable	The Secret Life of Walter Mitty
12	Emotional Mastery	Master Your Emotions	I Can See Clearly Now	Inside Out
13	Courage	Braving the Wilderness	Lay it on the Line	Saving Private Ryan
14	Commitment & Integrity	Integrity, the Courage to Meet the Demands of Reality	Grenade	The Wizard of Oz
15	Resiliency	Man's Search for Meaning	Whatever it Takes	Rocky
16	Respect	Daring Greatly	Father and Son	Remember the Titans
17	Belief	What Matters Most	Don't Stop Believin	Field of Dreams
18	Humility & Flexibility	Ego is the Enemy	Humble and Kind	Forrest Gump

ABOUT R. SCOTT DOTSON

Scott Dotson is a seeker and life-long learner who has studied Success, Sports Psychology and Leadership for over 40 years. His fascination with what makes people the best in their field is coupled with curiosity about the connective tissue between spirituality, practicality, culture, philosophy, psychology and success – particularly in sports and business.

Scott holds a B.A. in Accounting with a minor in Finance from Illinois Wesleyan University. His career with State Farm Insurance encompassed four levels of accounting management in four different locations until he became an agent in Milan, MI. Scott retired at the age of 59 after 40 years with State Farm.

Scott has written one book: Par for the Soul – Finding Meaning and Powerful Life Lessons Through the Game of Golf (2026). Scott is also an excellent speaker offering:

The Golfer's Compass

The Christian Golfer's Compass

The Catholic Golfer's Compass

Presentations can be tailored to your specific desires based on Par for the Soul, specific chapters from Par or other desired topics.

You can contact Scott for speaking interests at: scott.dotson@sbcglobal.net

RECOMMENDATIONS

With warm humor, sublime poignancy, and piercing insights, Scott Dotson leads his readers on an 18-hole pilgrimage through life's challenges and joys. Whether you've never touched a club in your life (though Scott may well inspire you to do so) or you are a devotee of the links, *Par for the Soul* will lead you into deeper self-reflection and discernment of the life choices we all face with our hearts and souls. Packed with practical recommendations from the realms of music, reading, and film, Dotson accompanies his readers as the perfect spiritual caddie. Highly recommended.

Fr. John Kartje, Rector/President, University of Saint Mary of the Lake

As the General Manager (PGA Member) at Barton Creek Country Club in Austin, Texas, where I've watched thousands of golfers for over 40 years—from wide-eyed beginners to seasoned members—chase both better swings and better days, I can say this with confidence: Par for the Soul captures the true joy of the game in a way few books ever have.

Scott Dotson understands what every golfer eventually discovers—that golf is more than a sport. It's a sanctuary, a teacher, and sometimes a mirror. His reflections remind us why we keep coming back: the feel of a well-struck iron, the quiet walk between shots, the small victories that stay with us long after the round is over.

This book doesn't just celebrate golf; it celebrates the spirit of golf. Any player who has ever stepped onto a first tee with hope in their chest will feel at home in these pages.

Dan Budzius, General Manager, Barton Creek Country Club,
Omni Hotels & Resorts

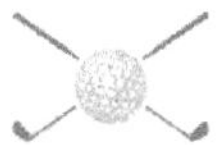

Though I am not a golfer, I thoroughly enjoyed reading Par for the Soul. This book transcends the golf course. The parallels between the golf course and life's daily path make the processes of choosing, owning outcomes, and learning to share from an experience very relatable. The concept of "Next" is a survival tool for the challenging roadmap of life. The format of Par allows the reader to become both reflective and inspired. This is a life-based book for seasoned golfers and those perhaps looking forward to taking up golf one day.

I am already making a list of those in my life who would enjoy Par for the Soul once it is available.

Dr. Cherise Russo D.O., CAQ-PCSM
Primary Care Sports Medicine
Northwestern Medical Group